Digital Diversions:
Youth Culture in the Age of
Multimedia

edited by

Julian Sefton-Green

First published in 1998 by UCL Press

UCL Press Limited
1 Gunpowder Square
London EC4A 3DE
UK

and

1900 Frost Road, Suite 101
Bristol
Pennsylvania 19007-1598
USA

The name of University College London (UCL) is a registered
trade mark used by UCL Press with the consent of the owner.

British Library Cataloguing in Publication Data
A Catalogue Record for this book is available from the British Library.

Library of Congress Cataloging-in-Publication Data are available

ISBNs: 1-85728-856-4 HB
          1-85728-857-2 PB

Typeset in 10/12 pt Times
by Wilmaset Ltd, Birkenhead, Wirral.
Printed and bound by T. J. International, Padstow, UK.

Digital Diversions

Media, Education and Culture

Series Editors: David Buckingham is Reader in Education at Institute of Education, University of London, UK and
Julian Sefton-Green is Media Education Development Officer at Weekend Arts College, part of Interchange Trust, UK.

In response to the increasing diversity of contemporary societies and the significance of the electronic media, cultural studies has developed rigorous and exciting approaches to pedagogy, both in schools and in higher education. At the same time, research in this area has begun to pose fundamental questions about the political claims of much cultural studies theory, and about the relationship between academic knowledge and lived experience. *Media, Education and Culture* will extend the research and debate that is developing in this interface between cultural studies and education.

Also in the series:

Teaching Popular Culture: Beyond Radical Pedagogy
edited by David Buckingham

Teen Spirits: Music and Identity in Media Education
by Chris Richards

Wired-up: Young People and the Electronic Media
edited by Sue Howard

Forthcoming:

Schooling the Future: Education 'Youth' and Postmodernity
by Bill Green and Lindsay Fitzclarence.

Contents

Chapter 1

Introduction:
Being Young in the Digital Age

Julian Sefton-Green

Childhood and the Future

Children are at the epicenter of the information revolution, ground zero of the digital world . . . Children have the chance to reinvent communications, culture and community. To address the problems of the new world in new ways.

Jon Katz's (1996) polemical rhetoric encapsulates a sense of momentous and far reaching social change, locating the young at the heart of an on-going revolution. However, his article about the 'rights of kids' in what he calls the digital age, actually rests on far more mainstream assumptions about the young, best summed up in the banal lyrics of a song, recently popularized by Whitney Houston, 'The children are our future'. Children both represent and quite literally embody our, or at least our societies', future. Of course the platitudinous truthfulness of this statement, that children will grow up and become adults in the future, tends to obscure its ideological construction. As Chris Jenks (1996) has recently argued, it is not so much physical children who represent the future but our notion of childhood itself. Modern industrial life has constructed the special and privileged space of childhood not only as a walled garden to keep out the concerns of the adult world but – to pursue the horticultural metaphor – to nurture from seed the adult plant. In a similar vein the historian Carolyn Steedman (1995) has shown some of the literary and artistic ways in which children are conceptualized as icons of growth and development, tracing the history of this construction over the last couple of hundred years. Yet, perhaps the most salient image of a contemporary child in western society is a picture of a rapt face staring entranced at, almost *into*, the computer screen. This image is powerful not just because it encapsulates the hopes and fears within popular narratives of childhood but because it also tells a parallel story, the narrative of technological progress.

Indeed *children* (or *youth*) and *new technology* are terms which are often yoked together in discussions about the nature of contemporary social change, precisely because they both embody similar teleological assumptions about growth, progression and development which underpin late modern society. However, neither of these narratives are without their contrapuntal alternatives. Western constructions of childhood have oscillated between views of the child as savage and innocent; pure and tainted; ignorant and intuitive. Similarly the new technologies – which for the purpose of this volume are primarily defined as the digital information and communications media, such as computer games or the Internet – are also described in terms of binary oppositions. Thus, they are fragmenting contemporary society, yet uniting it; they are destroying education or re-making it; they are transforming culture and communication or merely conferring privilege on a few. Both in the academic disciplines of the sociology of childhood and the newer field of technoculture or cyber theory, these disjunctions and contradictions are being discussed and analyzed (Qvortrup *et al*, 1994; Sardar and Ravetz, 1996), yet rarely are these shared notions of the future analyzed together.

Of course, notions of the future imply either intervention and change or pessimistic determinism; here again these twin narratives of technology and childhood tell similar stories. New technology is seen to offer the hope of transforming contemporary society into a better one, in the same way that adults speculate that their children's lives will be somehow 'better' than their own – as Katz puts it above, addressing the problems of the world in 'new ways'. On the other hand, concerns about the changing nature of childhood – or indeed about its apparent 'disappearance' – have become inextricably bound up with wider anxieties about the impact of technological change. Successive waves of moral panic continuously link the changing nature of young people's lives with an increase in the provision of media technology in the previously enclosed and protected domains of the family and the school. The concept of an 'audio-visual generation' (or what seems to be called at the moment 'cyberkids') seems to have become a shorthand way of labelling these hopes and fears, and it clearly illustrates how each category seems to have become a way of talking about the other.

On one level, this reflects changing realities – for example, the fact that all young people growing up today will work with digital technologies at some point in their adult lives. Yet on another level, it also raises questions about how we describe and conceptualize social change – and indeed, about how we might imagine the future. As I have implied, these debates are inevitably bound up with much broader ideological, moral and social motivations, yet they often float free from any discussion of the concrete realities of children's lives, or of their actual uses of these new technologies.

The central aim of this book then, is to offer some empirical evidence about the multiplicity of ways in which young people are utilizing and appropriating a range of new technologies in the making of youth culture in the digital age. In this process, perhaps, it may be possible to gain a more accurate picture of what the future might actually be like.

Counting the Digital Age

One of the most common ways of defining what it means to be a child (or youth) is in terms of age. However, recent studies of childhood (for example, James, 1993) have examined the ways in which young people themselves negotiate the social meanings of different age boundaries. More significantly they suggest that being a child continuously locates one as being a person who is *becoming* someone else – as opposed to being an adult, where it is presumed one's identity has coalesced into a state of permanence. Yet there is much to suggest that new technologies may be helping to redefine this process. This is not only a feature of the new digital technologies but part of the larger impact 'older' media technologies are still having on our society. Thus, Simon Frith (1993) has shown how 'youth' has been redefined by discourses of taste and by the marketing departments of record companies to cover a biological age up to forty. More pessimistically, conservative commentators such as Neil Postman (1983) or Joshua Meyrowitz (1985) have argued that the prime impact of the mass media, especially television, is to destroy the 'natural' boundaries around childhood and youth, blurring the onset of adult knowledge and experience.

[margin handwritten note: Youth has no age limit. Youth cultures have changed in that adults are welcomed into the culture.]

Digital technologies, or more precisely certain uses of them, continue this process of redefinition in seemingly contradictory directions. Thus on the one hand, they seem to offer a kind of 'adultification', since young people can act in the digital realm with an equivalence of grown-up power. On the other hand, they seem to have continued the process of 'juvenilization' associated with leisure pastimes, and in particular with notions of playing games. Although historians suggest that games and play were proper adult activities in the Middle Ages, changing patterns of leisure (largely due to the impact of industrialization) ended up relegating such activities to the domain of the young. This association of play and childhood was further cemented by the ways in which child development theorists and psychologists in the nineteenth and early twentieth centuries used the metaphor of play in their construction of normativized mental growth. This history seems to have reached a new stage when we consider that the largest area of computer use, and one of the economically most powerful, is that of the computer game and related leisure activities. Equally, much supposedly serious use of the computer, particularly for educational purposes, has become more 'frivolous' with the development of info- or edu- tainment genres. Indeed Haddon (1992) and Murdock *et al* (1992) have shown how the evolution of the domestic PC was rooted in this discourse of home entertainment during its uncertain development in the 1980s.

Playing computer games or even just playing with the computer is thus a central part of its usage: even, for example, the metaphor of 'surfing the Net' carries leisure connotations.[1] However, many of these forms of play are carried out by people who, in terms of age at least, would be described as adults. A further example of this 'confusion' in the UK might be the advertising campaign for the Sony Playstation. This 'computer' is a pure games

(handwritten margin notes: Advertisers use tactics that make things attractive to all ages. Taking on a particular stereotypes)

machine (i.e., not a PC), and was clearly targeted at the mid-twenties consumer. Even if this approach could be interpreted as an advertiser's ploy – to attract late teens to the machine by branding it as a sophisticated twenty-something's plaything – this move clearly signifies that it is reasonable to sell an expensive 'toy' (normally a child's possession), to the upper end of the child/youth age range. On the other hand, many feminist commentators have noted how computer games can be further defined as toys for boys (Spender, 1995:186). This perspective is implicitly critical of the ways in which adult men are socially sanctioned to behave in 'immature' ways, like boys, and encouraged by the content of computer games to retreat into adolescent fantasy (for example, Sardar, 1996:24).

Being an adult in the digital age then, may involve making this concession to one's latent childishness. To echo the proverb, being a man means we can carry on playing with childish things without diminishing our adult status or (and this is just as important) in any way depriving our children of their special rights to play. By the same token, young people can use digital technologies to act in the adult realm, an arena traditionally denied them in economic and social terms. There are many apocryphal and true stories in circulation about young people being asked to design web pages or program machines or act as computer consultants. Similarly, being online is not a body-dependent activity and therefore age is not the barrier it conventionally is in face-to-face social encounters.

Of course, this has led to as much anxiety as it has optimism. Are children going to have unrestricted access to pornography or be abused on-line? Can they participate in adult conversations and have equal access to information compared with their 'adult peers'? Some of the chapters in this collection develop these issues in more detail, exploring young people's actions in public spaces, traditionally assumed to be the preserve of adults.[2] As they imply, the digital age is one in which conventional definitions of childhood and adulthood are being redefined through social usage rather than in terms of biological age. If childhood and adulthood are destabilized by these processes, then it almost goes without saying that youth, the theoretical category occupying a hazy liminal state between these two states of being, is further thrown into disarray.

This argument obviously relates to the ways in which digital technologies are re-configuring the distinctions between work and leisure and – in particular the notion that the home and the workplace are exclusive sites for either. Thus a young person may be working at home while executives play on their machines at work. Indeed, in late 1996, Apple used this 'anomaly' in its advertising slogan: 'And when your children stop working . . . you can play with it.' These and similar scenarios leave us with a number of questions about the potential impact of these kinds of activities on traditionally significant boundaries. If work, leisure, adultness, childhood and youth do not occupy the same spaces that they have conventionally done, what will be the implications for who and what we are?

The Digital and Postmodern Theory

The notion of postmodernism has been at the centre of extensive discussion about the theoretical, political and economic determinants currently influencing contemporary social life. As has been frequently pointed out, this term (and its derivatives) actually covers a variety of different philosophies and modes of academic enquiry. In very broad terms the concept of postmodernity refers to a variety of contemporary 'sea-changes' in the social order at a number of levels, ranging from the organization of the global economy to the organization of individual consciousness. It is argued that changing methods of industrial production, the global homogenization of American consumer culture coupled with a 'new' world order emerging at the end of the Cold War have resulted in a qualitatively distinctive state of cultural, political and economic practices as we enter the new millennium (Harvey, 1989). However, the role of digital culture and technology within this complicated matrix of ideas is far from simple.

One of the key issues here is the precise relationship between modernity and postmodernity. Indeed some critics (for example, Giddens, 1990) argue that it is more accurate to say that the current state of affairs resembles a continuation of the immediate past more than a new beginning. This debate is mirrored in discussion of digital culture, which often fails to consider its relationship with other forms of contemporary media culture. If modernity is exemplified by mass media culture, in what ways does digital culture break with or extend this paradigm? For example, in discussions about the meaning of television in the lives of young people there are a number of unresolved research questions, such as those focusing on the relationships between the context of media use and the meaning of media texts; the specific impact media may be having on young people's knowledge and experience of the world; and the cultural appropriations and resistance to dominant values that might be entailed in young people's readings of TV (Buckingham, 1993a). All of these are 'live' questions that have been re-energized and perhaps refocused by the impact of digital technologies, but it is foolish to imagine that digital culture, in and of itself, invents these questions by virtue of technological specificity. The extraordinary hyperbole surrounding many aspects of digital culture should not distract us from its continuities with more traditional forms of screen-based entertainment (Hayward and Wollen, 1993). In marking out the distinctively new in digital culture it is important not to lose sight of the continuities with older media forms and the sets of theoretical and research questions that surround them.

From this point of view, it is helpful to be clear about the determining role of the technology itself. In general terms, accounts of digital culture find it very difficult to avoid any reference to this question because writing about contemporary change from a 'digital perspective', necessarily tends to rely on technological explanations. Much debate thus falls into a kind of binary determinism. Put crudely, this often comes down to the following kind of question: is it the *computers themselves* which facilitate global communication and our sense of the self (for the optimists) or surveillance and dehumanization (for the pessimists)? These questions vex the cyber theory discussions of art, identity and consciousness, represented in the collections edited by Bender and Druckrey (1994) and Hershman Leeson (1996), and the most politically resistant perspectives on digital culture, as in the essays edited by Brook and Boal (1995). Despite an increasingly sophisticated understanding of the ways in which discourses about scientific progress have permeated our understanding of culture and society (see Ross, 1991), as in the last 40 years of writing about the mass media, it has proven difficult to avoid locating explanations of cause and effect in the technology itself. However, the theoretical perspective developed in earlier accounts of the role of technology in social and cultural change may be just as valid here. In particular, Raymond Williams' (1974) work on television seems to transcend the determinism which increasingly characterizes debates in the digital field. Williams argues that technology cannot be seen either as a wholly autonomous force or as wholly determined by other social developments; on the contrary, we need to look to the complex interrelationships between political, social, institutional and economic interests if we are to explain the ways in which new technologies come to be developed and used.

A second dimension of postmodernity's relation to the modern lies in the changes in economic and political order which go under the banner of post-industrialization. Thus, questions about the role of digital technologies within the emerging global multinationals, and in particular the convergence of communication systems and the entertainment industries, can be seen as part of the on-going transformation of western capitalism's structures and activities. A strong sub-theme in this context is the effects of bringing together the previously discrete areas of making and consuming leisure products. Whereas the paradigm of mass broadcast firmly kept the means of production in the hands of few, the computer, and/or being online, appears to allow the consumer previously undreamed of control and participation in the production of entertainment and culture. Here, there are a set of arguments around questions of ownership, control and access. On the one hand, digital technology seems to be facilitating access through the Internet and increased provision in the home; on the other it appears as if the quality of social life is diminished through increased state regulation and submission to market forces.

In this field, issues of the global economy are discussed in conjunction with theories of commodification and consumerism – not least in terms of the ways in which the computer industries make, market and sell their products. Above all, it is how the computer is now positioned centrally as the 'controlling' technology in a number of fields, especially entertainment, which makes its presence so pervasive in contemporary life. On one level this discussion leads to a consideration of the so-called information society and the ways in which information may be becoming a new form of capital (Webster,

1995). At the same time, these questions about production and consumption are raised in the context of considering the changing face of 'the public sphere', that (possibly mythical) arena of democratic debate (Jones, 1995; Shields, 1996). An important issue here is whether the new electronic forum of the Internet is, in effect, a new opportunity for public discourse. Third, much attention has been paid to the ways in which participating in digital culture appears to be based on the inequalities and discriminatory practices of market forces. The telling phrase, 'the information rich and the information poor' sums up the thrust of much criticism here (Murdock and Golding, 1989: Sobchack, 1996). Yet again however, it is not clear whether these questions of political economy are different in kind or degree from their application to traditional media culture in modern society.

The discussion so far has stressed areas of continuity with broad social and economic features of modern life. I now want to suggest three particular features of digital technology that seem to relate most strongly to young people and which do appear to be reconfiguring personal and social structures. Across each of these three areas, however, I want to note contradictory tensions. Superficially these oppositions might be described in terms of optimism or pessimism, between those who embrace digital culture and those who find it the embodiment of dehumanization and state control. However, this is perhaps not a helpful opposition – or indeed an accurate depiction of critical discussion. In this emerging field there have been few opportunities to synthesize debate, and much discussion in the last five years has, perforce, derived from critics working within delimited theoretical frameworks. As the precise nature of contemporary change becomes more evident to all, it is hoped that these partial positions may engage in productive dialogue with one another.

The Global and the Local – New Communities?

The first issue I want to note is the role digital technologies may be playing in accelerating the contradictory tendencies towards globalization and localization. These terms refer to the ways in which some elements of contemporary society are more connected to, and more reliant on, events in the world economy, at the same time as others seem to be based within a more contracted, localized environment. These opposing yet related movements seem to be bringing together parts of the globe at the same time that parochial and fundamentalist interests are being reasserted. Studies of the world money markets sit next to accounts of how diaspora ethnic communities are developing new hybrid identities in post colonial settings (Eade, 1997). Of course, both tendencies are full of pain as well as pleasure. Thus, it is argued, we are living through a time of local fragmentation and isolation, as evidenced in postmodern geographers' discussions of the wired city (Castells, 1989). However, as life within the home turns inwards, away from the geographically local, so (it is suggested) groups of people are moving towards virtual on-line life, developing and sustaining new forms of community. As the physical family and its setting in the community change, so the international becomes the next door neighbour.

These discussions about the changing nature of community are fiercely contested from a number of perspectives. First of all, there is the question of evidence. In this area the boundaries between academic discussion, market research and advertising seem uncomfortably permeable. Claims about new global communities are rarely supported with the range of evidence – quantitative or qualitative – deemed necessary in traditional areas of enquiry. In a related fashion there appears to be a tendency for critics to extrapolate theories from their own experiences. I may be able to communicate across the world from my desk and participate in an international academic community, but barely five metres from where I write, my next door neighbours – theoretically members of a post-colonial diaspora – don't even have central heating, let alone global communications. This fact also relates to a central problem, noted above, that in constructing a notion of the global village, proponents may have suppressed more traditional arguments around equity and access. Equally, it is argued that notions of urban anomie and fragmentation are as exaggerated and as particular to the industrial city as are any claims for the connected, wired-up global postmodern (Morley and Robins, 1995).

However, young people have often been absent from these discussions despite the central role that the wired, or even the electronic, home – and young people's increasing reliance on it – plays in these scenarios. On the one hand, educational policy-makers are keen to advocate wiring up schools to the Net; but on the other, there is much anxiety about the ways in which the computer appears to isolate and depersonalize human interaction. Members of the same family may be acting alone in segregated spaces, yet they may also be members of electronic communities – a possibility which has significant implications in terms of adults' regulation of young peoples' movements and social behaviours. Rather than hanging out in the park round the corner, young people now 'go out to play' by logging into Internet gameplay services. The young are a key target market for full range of global commodities from Nintendo games machines to designer sportswear and live their local lives in the context of global capitalism (Gillespie, 1995).

Of course, it should be noted that although young people are customarily positioned in these global markets, in practice their power in the marketplace is quite contradictory. The young are both *indirect* and *direct* consumers of new technologies. Although they possess much less direct spending power than adults, young people clearly influence their parents' purchasing power, and this is clearly taken into consideration in the marketing of new technologies. Such advertising is often simultaneously addressed to the young and the adult purchaser, thus meeting multiple objectives. In this respect, the spending power of the young does not directly correlate with their cultural power and therefore it may be inaccurate to see them as the *object* of the global marketplace.

Whatever position one takes in this debate, it is clear that digital culture has become a key site for anxiety about the changing nature of community. Because it offers ways of moving through time and place, access to the computer is thus fraught with possibility and concern. In very practical terms, nearly all young people in western societies do physically participate in school communities; they are not quite so isolated in their homes or (broken) families as is often suggested. However, although the movements of young people may be different from their parents, as is their access to global cultures, it is unclear whether there are discernible patterns of change for youth or childhood. In this respect, analyses are tending towards the plural; it is increasingly recognized that there are now different kinds of childhoods or youths, as distinct from one simple unitary model as can be universally applied even within one society. Thus, studies of the ways in which different groups of young people might be determining their lives stress the elements of negotiation and syncretism which characterize their relationships with preceding generations (Eade, 1997; Gillespie, 1995). To date, however, few of these accounts have focused on the specific role of multimedia entertainment or digital culture.

New Literacies?

The second aspect of the digital postmodern to which I want to draw attention is the difficulty of defining what kinds of relationships the young computer-user might have with the hardware, software and/or online communication. If the preceding section was concerned with questions of how digital culture locates young people's place in the world, here I want to concentrate on a more detailed focus – almost at the level of user and screen. In particular, I want to speculate about the ways in which the user–computer relationship might be implicated in changing notions of literacy. The range of different kinds of 'reading' and 'writing' activities facilitated by the computer and its various multimedia forms suggests that very different levels of skill and understanding, at both psychological and social levels, may be necessary to participate in digital culture. The analogy here is with print literacy. If schooled literacy was a precondition of participation in post renaissance society, then the question remains: what kinds of *new literacies* might be required to operate and participate in a digital world (Lanham 1993; Tuman 1992)? The term *new literacies* deliberately invokes a sense of the *plural* to accommodate the forms and genres of multimedia, in an avowed intent to challenge the orthodoxies of traditional literacy (Buckingham, 1993b).

First of all, I want to consider the rather peculiar position people are in as *consumers*, *users*, or even *producers*, of digital culture. My difficulty in locating the correct term can be further exemplified in the multiplicity of ways that the word *interactivity* is used to describe many key-board/joystick/ screen-based processes. Indeed, defining the *user* of *interactive* technologies raises a number of problems, as these words' conventional usage derives from paradigms associated with print literacy. For example, in relation to computer games, Fiske (1989), notes that playing such games blurs the normal relation between reader and writer: when reading a book the reader cannot influence the course of the narrative in the way one can with games. Indeed, interacting with a game or other digital texts, from CD-ROMs to online World Wide Web sites, is qualitatively different from the relations between reader and writer in the domain of print literacy. Central to this area of concern, then, is the problem of defining *interactivity*. Frequently touted as a new relation between user and producer in the postmodern marketplace, the term is indiscriminately applied to anything from video on demand to 'surfing the Net'. If a fixed relation between writer and reader is the hallmark of the old literacy then an interactive dynamic is at the heart of the new literacies.

This principle has not escaped literary theorists. Recent attention to the construct of the 'active reader' and the application of poststructuralist theory to the new form of hypertext have all contributed to a sense that digital media require a fundamental rethinking of accepted notions of reading and writing (Heim, 1993; Landow, 1992). Indeed, studies of the ways that new and other forms of text and communication is evolving in the digital age suggest that conventional models of consumption as applied to 'older' media forms may also need re-examination. Although this is one area where there may not be as much difference between adults and non-adults, it is frequently assumed that it is the young who are at the forefront of this process of redefinition. To return to the words of Jon Katz quoted above, 'Children have the chance to reinvent communications, culture and community.'

Of course, all notions of literacy have a special relevance for the young; and although young people may not in reality be quite as *hyper-literate* as some theorists fantasize, it is part of the common sense surrounding the computer that young people today are more computer literate than preceding generations. There are two important points to be made here. First of all, a considerable amount of research is needed to ascertain whether or not this is true. Second, we need to tease out the relationships between the traditional and new literacies. The latter clearly does not simply supplant the former and therefore the specific nature of the 'newness' in such literacies needs qualitative investigation.

Knowledge and Learning – New Education(s)?

One of the most pervasive features of discourse around the new technologies, particularly in relation to the young, is that they are inherently *educative*. Yet such an assumption merely raises significant questions about the nature, purpose and meaning of the practice of education. In a number of ways, the use of new technologies begins to question the authority of traditional forms of knowledge. Yet these questions also have to be considered in the wider context of changing educational systems. In first world countries, the effect of the new technologies has to be examined in the context of the state's financial retreat in this area and the move towards greater variety and fragmentation in schooling and training programmes. In the UK and Australia for example, there is fierce debate between so called 'traditionalists' and 'progressives', about how education should be carried out at the same time as the state is more interventionist in terms of national curricula and inspectorial accountability. Yet the economic context for these debates ensures that incrementally fewer resources are directed towards state educational systems. In this context the new technologies are frequently represented both as a solution and a threat.

There are a number of reasons why this might be so, some of which stem from our notion of the computer itself. First of all, the pervasive psychologistic paradigm which has underpinned our concept of the computer persists in seeing the machine as an extension or model of the mind. Thus, whether it is in exercising hand–eye co-ordination or developing the powers of abstract thought, the use of new technologies always seems to imply a particular kind of mental activity associated with learning and development. Whether or not this is true is almost beside the point; using computers appears to be inherently educational. On a more pragmatic level, the relationship of the computer to the so-called information revolution means that the computer is inherently bound up with questions about access to an increased quantity of knowledge – however this may be defined. Thus, for example, it is routinely argued that the World Wide Web possesses the information that will make schools more effective places. Yet, the study of how humans and machines interface also seems to beg a set of questions about the ways in which teaching and learning are currently imagined as social activities (Tiffin and Rajasingham, 1995). Here the child–computer relationship in some ways appears to threaten the pedagogic relationship between adult and child. It is imagined that using computers might replace, or displace, the teacher; or at the least change the traditional ways in which schools are organized. In addition, of course, using new technologies is assumed to be educational in the vocational sense, because many kinds of employment, especially those located in a future world, are presumed to require users to be familiar with electronic technologies.

Furthermore, the changing economic context in relation to schools needs to be seen in direct relation to the increase of expenditure on educational resources in the home and other less formal sites of learning – although of course this does not extend equally to all sections of society. Ultimately, these moves call into question the established body of theory from both right and left perspectives which has cemented authority of the school as the prime mode of entry into democratic society (Green and Bigum, 1993; Plant, 1995). Formal education, it is suggested, is being dethroned from the top of the tree of knowledge. In the fields of formal education, schools, further and higher education, and other knowledge related domains (informal learning, leisure and entertainment interests and hobbies), it seems as if traditional notions of authority and transmission are being undermined from a number of directions at once. On the one hand, ideas of parental authority are clearly changing – the home is not the closely regulated environment conservative theorists fantasize it should be – and the 'independence' afforded to young people by digital technologies is frequently cited as both cause and effect of this problem. At the same time, young people can access other sources of authority which differ from those that adults conventionally believe they control. In this context current concern to implement a moral curriculum, stressing 'family values' in the UK may well be at odds with young people's participation in online chat rooms. Likewise young people who regularly 'surf the Net' at their own pace may well find the regimented structure of a teacher-led curriculum tedious. Real learning, it is argued, takes place outside of the school. Although, schools (and families) themselves may not be fully cognizant of these changes in any theoretical way, except perhaps in the reflex response to censor and repress, it seems again as if this major structural change is impacting on some young people's lives already.

Finally, discussion around youth, digital technology and education raises – albeit in a different form – a number of assumptions about education and cultural capital. Here cyber theorists and postmodern educationalists seem to blend with advocates of the free market. On the one hand, there seems to be a political consensus that the school cannot be the sole resource for educating a future society, but the answer to this problem seems to be that middle-class parents supplement state schooling in their information-rich homes – barely an equitable solution. At one extreme it is suggested that schools cannot transmit the kind of knowledge that can be so easily turned into the cultural and economic capital that sustained the full-employment economies of the past. Yet, this may well be inaccurate and short-sighted in economic terms, and embracing this position merely serves (yet again) to discriminate in favour of the middle class.[3]

Of course, we have to question the idea that it is the digital technologies, the Net or the computer game, which are solely responsible for undermining these power relations. If attitudes to learning are changing, we have to consider an extremely broad range of influences from the intellectual challenges of progressive education to the market's subversion of paternalism, before locating explanations in technological innovation. Yet again we need much more evidence about these changes, rather than allowing theoretical speculation about such changes to stand for the facts. The co-existence of digital technologies and postmodern theory is more than a coincidence obviously, but the matrix of influences that create social change are complex and highly variable between different local situations. For example, the simple but important fact that local phone calls are, to all intents and purposes, free in the US and comparatively expensive in the UK does have a differential effect on the uses of digital communication between these two cultures, despite a shared intellectual culture.

In summary then, it does seem reasonable to conclude that these three dimensions of contemporary change are live processes which affect both the young in different ways from preceding generations. The pull between the local and the global, the reconfiguration of the consumer/user and changing power relations between teacher and taught are key parameters of the conditions in which young people are growing up. Yet, above all, we need to be very cautious about accepting these notions of change because of the absence of substantial evidence in any of these fields. Imagining an electronic future may encompass wide reaching hopes and fears about the trajectory of modern society; but actually mapping its growth has turned out to be a considerably more difficult task.

Youth Culture in the Age of Multimedia: An Agenda for the Millennium

The Research Context

There has of course, been a certain amount of research about digital technology and young people, although most of it has been firmly located within psychological and educational discourses – traditionally deemed the appropriate means of describing the young. One of the earliest studies, *Video Games and Human Development: A Research Agenda for the '80s* (Baughman and Clagett, 1983), produced after a symposium at the Harvard Graduate School of Education, asked a series of questions which still determine a research agenda:

> Do instructional designers consider sex differences in the creative process? Do they promote stereotyped behaviour? Does game playing isolate the individual? What exactly is the place of human relation-ships in the human/machine? Will the tremendous growth of home computers exacerbate the problem of educational equity? (pp. 62).

These questions sound familiar and continue to stimulate debate. In particular they represent a common perspective in educational studies which draws on crude theories of socialization and looks towards technology as a radical solution to the traditional problems of teaching and learning:

> What happens to a school system when the five-year-old is not only computer-literate, but has acquired cognitive information that is normally [beyond] grade two curriculum? How can these cumbersome institutions that we call schools . . . radically change in order to accept new learning? (pp. 63).

In these excerpts the speaker attempts to draw together diverse strands in that conference by implying that the individual child, through use of electronic technologies will make different demands at home and school than in the past. Questions of equity merge with questions about the educational process, the school and the quality of the child's life and experience.

By contrast, these types of questions are frequently contrasted with another kind of agenda, deriving from 'effects' research into young people and the media. Here conservative commentators argue that electronic entertainment is of itself a great cause for alarm. For example, Stutz (1996) suggests that the quality of children's play is 'bruised' through exposure to television and computer games. On the whole the Harvard report is clearly optimistic, for example, carrying accounts of the therapeutic benefits of video games and emphasizing that the technological processes in and of themselves may be cognitively beneficial; indeed, 'experts' from the field of developmental psychology and mental health attest to this analysis. However, research from the effects tradition either sets out to create anxiety (see Newsom, 1996) or to explain and allay concern in the context of moral panics (see Buckingham, 1996). Such work is premised on the defensive, as it were, and frequently offer a familiar binary opposition between parental fears and children's pleasure.

This collision of research agendas brings together sociological and psychological traditions in ways that merely emphasize how little both approaches can have in common with one another. For example, the Australian Broadcasting Authority monograph, *Families and Electronic Entertainment* (Cupitt and Stockbridge, 1996) focuses solely on the social world of the home and respondents' self-definitions of the meaning of electronic entertainment. This report was produced in response to public anxiety about video games and analyzes a system of classifications in the context of detailed accounts of domestic routines. On the other hand, the range of research described in Griffiths (1996) describing the so-called addictive nature of computers seems to have a completely different model of how the individual functions in society.

In addition, the broad range of concern in many of these accounts – home, school and childhood – and the equally broad spectrum of attention from computing in the home to video games actually makes it very difficult at times to be certain that there is one single object or issue that we might be discussing. Of course, the computer as gateway to the Internet or multimedia has to some extent replaced the video game or computer games console as the cause of concern and nowadays we cannot even consider electronic entertainment outside of the convergence of entertainment, financial and telecommunications services and industries. Nevertheless, it is still surprising that one social development, electronic technology, is being used to explain changes in a whole range of social domains – as if the nature of modern childhood could be attributed to a single cause.

This brief history of research in this field also raises the vexed problem of the relationship between the social sciences and broader conceptualizations of social changes. In keeping with its upbeat optimism, the US 1983 publication

(Baughman and Clagett, 1983) indicates that research may answer the questions set by the participants; yet as I have suggested, these questions seem to remain unanswered. Contemporary studies around television and children are frequently batted around in public debate, yet they rarely echo the consensus implied in 1983 report that, 'in the area of television research there is already a history of school, industry and academics working together' (p.2). Ultimately, however, we have to accept that research may not in itself be the solution to the range of social and policy issues associated with children and new technology.

It is for these kinds of reasons that the contributors to this volume have not taken any great sense of concern or public crisis as their starting point. Instead, they attempt to describe and interpret the ways that young people are being addressed by and are appropriating the new technologies as forms of culture. The concerns here are with the ways in which young people are active social agents in the production of youth cultures and in their social and personal uses of new technologies, primarily for leisure use, although, as I have already suggested, one of the features of the new technologies is to make it impossible to escape an 'educational' dimension.

This volume also contains accounts of young people's use of digital technology from around the world. The intention here is to make concrete the dimensions of globalization and modernity which have surfaced in the preceding discussion. Young people at home, school and play across the countries of the first world clearly share similar sets of interests, values and practices. At the same time, the role of biological age is perhaps increasingly less of an issue to these young people. Although I have rather conservatively ordered the chapters in very rough chronological order, relating to the age of the young people studied, the degrees of their independence and powerfulness are not so extremely different. The difference between children and youth are material in some environments, such as the clubs Helen Cunningham describes, but at home, online, playing games or 'working' the boundaries begin to blur.

Finally then, whatever the variety in method or approach, all the chapters in this volume argue from a position of 'informed scepticism'. Although some of the authors clearly have divergent views on the impact, nature and scope of digital technology for childhood and youth, their discussion is based on the close observation and interpretation of children and young people. I am hopeful that it will be a similar combination of empirical detail and theory which will continue to inform speculation about the meaning and significance of the digital revolution. For too long debate in this area has demonstrated a kind of schizophrenia as it has wildly veered between the manic outbursts of moral panic and advertisers' hype. At the least, the authors represented here would hope that their careful and original understanding of the actual ways that young people use and make sense of these new technologies will provide the basis for a policy, research and education agenda for the future.

Outline of Contributions

The volume begins and ends with two accounts of the role of modernity in digital culture. In the following chapter, Helen Nixon provides a systematic critique of the ways in which the family has been targeted in the promotion of new technologies. She explores how the discourses of educational value are tied into the marketing of the home computer and thereby some of the ways in which the home PC is promoted as a solution for the educational and economic problems in Australia. Her account will certainly resonate with readers in both North America and the UK. Nixon's is contextualized within a study of how the global market interacts with local economic conditions, and in this way, it further advances our understanding of the intricate sets of relationships between the local and the global. Her study of the representations of families, young people and computer-related social and educational practices in home computing magazines, suggests how the local continues to be defined in terms of the domestic; yet in pointing to the ways in which entertainment and serious work are meshed together in marketing practices, she indicates how the digital offers a means to bring together traditionally separate categories.

Karen Orr Vered takes as her starting point a long standing concern, namely the gendering of computer technologies. She investigates this complicated question in the unusual setting of a grade three to five classroom at an Apple school in South California. The originality of her approach lies in the fact that she analyzes the ways that boys and girls play at the computer, rather than attempting to follow the customary route of trying to identify ways in which computer games themselves may be intrinsically gendered. The study of the ways in which groups of children play at the computer in the semi-official space of recess time builds on traditions of educational research uncommon in studies of digital technology. Her work suggests other kinds of strategies for intervening in an issue commonly agreed to be a major problem, but which she locates in a broader understanding of gender politics than superficial assessments of the 'sexism' of computer games.

Chapter 4, by Sefton-Green and Buckingham, reports on research into the ways that young people, in this case 11–16 years old, are using computers in the home. It sets up a theme also investigated in subsequent chapters: namely the ways in which the computer might function as a *production* technology for the young and how it may or may not facilitate creative activities. The chapter questions many of the assumptions underlying family investment in the computer and challenges recurrent claims that the technology is inherently empowering the young. In particular, the research attempts to explore the interface between home and school and points to some of the ways in which young people's lives exist in a limbo between adult-constructed communities. The rather romanticized view many adults have of young people's creativity is set against findings which indicate a need for focused programmes of education which explicitly include the home. Such relations between home and school are necessary, it is argued, if structural inequalities between families is not to result in swathes of the population being excluded from the so-called digital revolution.

The following two chapters examine young people's life online, thus engaging with debates about community and identity as well as the interface between formal and informal kinds of education. Abbott's work is one of the first attempts to describe the myriad ways in which young people might be accessing the Net and contributing to the new forms of public discourse found there. His work compares forms of synchronous communication, in the form of real time chat, with asynchronous communication, in the form of home-pages on the World Wide Web. Abbott draws attention to the ways in which the new technologies are offering opportunities for communication and argues that young people are colonizing the Web as they devise and build youth spheres in this medium.

Abbott's chapter also raises some of the methodological problems involved in online research; and no doubt questions here will continue to be addressed in the near future. The second chapter on this subject investigating young people and the Net takes a distinctive approach. Tobin writes from a dual perspective as a parent and an academic. He reflects on his adolescent son's immersion in online life and tries to assess its value. His analysis engages strongly with the theme of the changing relation between informal and formal modes of education. Tobin offers the concept of *otaku*, derived from studies of Japanese youth cultures, as a model of a 'learning culture' to replace the dysfunctional 'hacker' stereotype. However, his picture of family life also asks important questions about the relation of virtual life to the material conditions of its production.

Although she does not use the term, Helen Cunningham might well recognize the concept of *otaku* in her study of the multiple roles of new technologies in contemporary youth sub-culture. Her participant observation of nights out in British dance clubs explores the ways that this subcultural experience allows young people opportunities for both creativity and entrepreneurial training. Like Tobin or Abbott, she stresses the importance of peer learning communities, but her study of older groups of young people shows some of the economic factors involved in young people's inclusion or exclusion from digital culture. Her work shows some of the inventive ways in which young people are appropriating forms of digital culture and in this respect develops some of the ideas from Sefton-Green and Buckingham's study of younger children, whose opportunities for production were more limited. Finally, she also engages with some of the symbolic ways in which young people draw on the wider ideological constructions of new technology; in this respect her approach, despite its different focus, has much in common with that of Nixon.

The final chapter in this collection returns to a consideration of the relationship between digital technology and modernity. Nissen's study of Swedish young men locates what he calls *hackers*, in a comprehensive model of postmodernity derived from the work of Habermas and Ziehe. Again, we find

Nissen describing the work of informal peer networks, but his argument is that using these new technologies is actually a form of engagement with the alienation of modern post-industrial life. In this sense, he situates the subjective experience of youth within the larger political, economic and social changes affecting the modern world. Like Cunningham, his approach also engages with sub-cultural theory. However, whereas Cunningham finds her young people's involvement in club culture broadly progressive, Nissen effectively argues that hackers are recuperated by dominant social values.

There is no conclusion to these discussions; they are after all, ongoing. It almost goes without saying that the diverse phenomena reported, the range of sites and social influences considered are too huge to be neatly summed up. Nevertheless, there is no doubt that digital culture is exerting an enormous influence over young people in a variety of different ways. The experience of growing up in the digital age is both similar to, and subtly different from, the lot of previous generations; I hope that this volume will contribute to a more informed understanding of what that similarity and difference might actually mean in practice.

Notes

I would like to thank David Buckingham for his careful, thoughtful and detailed reading of an earlier version of this chapter. Thanks also to Joe Tobin.

1 Helen Nixon explores these associations further in the following chapter.
2 Accounts of adults at play usually focus on serious questions of consciousness and identity (see Turkle, 1995). There is, as yet, little research into the ways that adults use opportunities for play in terms of their regulation of the work-leisure distinctions, so crucial to these definitions.
3 There may well be a parallel here with current criticisms of progressivist theories of education. The 'technological solution' may well be yet another way of ensuring middle-class advantage, in the same way as the child centered classroom (Cope and Kalantzis, 1993).

References

Baughman, S. and Clagett, P. (Eds) (1983) *Video Games and Human Development: A Research Agenda for the 80's*, Cambridge, MA: Harvard Graduate School of Education.

Bender, G. and Druckrey, T. (Eds) (1994) *Culture on the Brink: Ideologies of Technology*, Seattle, WA: Bay Press.

Brook, J. and Boal, I. (Eds) (1995) *Resisting the Virtual Life: the Culture and Politics of Information*, San Francisco, CA: City Lights.

Buckingham, D. (1993a) *Children Talking Television: The Making of Television Literacy*, London: Falmer Press.

Buckingham, D. (1993b) *Changing Literacies: Media Education and Modern Culture*, London: The Tufnell Press.

Buckingham, D. (1996) *Moving Images: Understanding Children's Emotional Responses to Television*, Manchester: Manchester University Press.

Castells, M. (1989) *The Informational City: Information Technology, Economic Re-structuring and the Urban-Regional Process*, Oxford: Blackwell.

Cupitt, M. and Stockbridge, S. (Eds) (1996) *Families and Electronic Entertainment. Monograph 6*, Sydney: Australian Broadcasting Authority and the Office of Film and Literature Classification.

Eade, J. (Ed.) (1997) *Living the Global: Globalisation as Local Process*, London: Routledge.

Fiske, J. (1989) *Reading the Popular*, London: Unwin Hyman.

Frith, S. (1993) Youth/music/television in Frith, S., Goodwin, A. and Grossberg, L. (Eds) *Sound and Vision: the Music Video Reader*, London: Routledge.

Giddens, A. (1990) *The Consequences of Modernity*, Cambridge: Polity Press.

Gillespie, M. (1995) *Television, Ethnicity and Cultural Change*, London: Routledge.

Green, B. and Bigum, C. (1993) Aliens in the classroom, *Australian Journal of Education*, **37**, (2), 119–41.

Griffiths, M. (1996) Computer game playing in children and adolescents: a review of the literature in Gill, T., *Electronic Children: How Children are Responding to the Information Revolution*, London: National Children's Bureau.

Haddon, L. (1992) Explaining ICT consumption: the case of the home computer, in Silverstone, R. and Hirsch, E. (Eds) *Consuming Technologies: Media and Information in Domestic Spaces*, London: Routledge.

Harvey, D. (1989) *The Condition of Postmodernity: an Enquiry into the Origins of Social Change*, Oxford: Blackwell.

Hayward, P. and Wollen, T. (Eds) (1993) *Future Visions: New Technologies of the Screen*, London: British Film Institute.

Heim M. (1993) *The Metaphysics of Virtual Reality*, Oxford: Oxford University Press.

Hershman Leeson, L. (Ed.) (1996) *Clicking In: Hot Links to a Digital Culture*, Seattle, WA: Bay Press.

James, A. (1993) *Childhood Identities: Self and Social Relationships in the Experience of the Child*, Edinburgh: Edinburgh University Press.

Jenks, C. (1996) *Childhood*, London: Routledge.

Jones, S. (Ed.) (1995) *CyberSociety: Computer Mediated Communication and Community*, London: Sage.

Katz, J. (1996) The rights of kids in the digital age, *Wired* 4.07 (US), 123.

Landow, G. (1992) *Hypertext: the Convergence of Contemporary Critical Theory and Technology*, Baltimore, MD: John Hopkins Press.

Lanham, R. (1993) *The Electronic Word: Democracy, Technology and the Arts*, Chicago, IL: University of Chicago Press.

Meyrowitz, J. (1985) *No Sense of Place: The Impact of Electronic Media on Social Behaviour*, New York: Oxford University Press.

Morley, D. and Robins, K. (1985) *Spaces of Identity: Global Media, Electronic Landscapes and Cultural Boundaries*, London: Routledge.

Murdock, G. and Golding, P. (1989) Information poverty and political Inequality: Citizenship in the Age of Privatised Communications, *Journal of Communication*, **39**, (3), 180–95.

Murdock, G., Hartman, P. and Gray, P. (1992) Contextualising home computing: resources and practices in Silverstone, R. and Hirsch, E. (Eds) *Consuming Technologies: Media and Information in Domestic Spaces*, London: Routledge.

Newsom, E. (1996) Video violence and the protection of children, in Gill, T. (Ed.) *Electronic Children: How Children are Responding to the Information Revolution*, London: National Children's Bureau.

Plant, S. (1995) Crash course, *Wired* 1.01 (UK), 44–7.

Postman, N. (1983) *The Disappearance of Childhood*, London: W. H. Allen.

Qvortrup, J., Bardy, M., Sgritta, G. and Wintersberger, H. (Eds) (1994) *Childhood Matters: Social Theory, Practice and Politics*, Aldershot: Avebury Press.

Ross, A. (1991) *Strange Weather: Culture, Science and Technology in the Age of Limits*, London: Verso.

Sardar, Z.(1996) alt.civilizations.faq: cyberspace as the darker side of the west, in Sardar, Z. and Ravetz, J. (Eds) *Cyberfutures; Culture and Politics on the Information Superhighway*, London: Pluto Press.

Sardar, Z. and Ravetz, J. (Eds) (1996) *Cyberfutures; Culture and Politics on the Information Superhighway* London: Pluto Press.

Shields, R. (Ed.) (1996) *Cultures of Internet: Virtual Spaces, Real Histories, Living Bodies*, London: Sage.

Sobchack, V. (1996) Democratic franchise and the electronic frontier in Sardar, Z. and Ravetz, J. (Eds) *Cyberfutures; Culture and Politics on the Information Superhighway*, London: Pluto Press.

Spender, D. (1995) *Nattering on the Net: Women, Power and Cyberspace*, Melbourne: Spinifex Press.

Steedman, C. (1995) *Strange Dislocations: Childhood and the Idea of Human Interiority, 1780–1930*, London: Virago.

Stutz, E. (1996) Is electronic entertainment hindering children's play and social development, in Gill, T., (Ed.) *Electronic Children: How Children are Responding to the Information Revolution*, London: National Children's Bureau.

Tiffin, J. and Rajasingham, L. (1995) *In Search of the Virtual Class: Education in an Information Society*, London: Routledge.

Tuman, M. (1992) *Word Perfect: Literacy in the Computer Age*, London: Falmer Press.

Turkle, S. (1995) *Life on the Screen: Identity in the Age of the Internet*, New York: Simon & Schuster.

Webster, F. (1995) *Theories of the Information Society*, London: Routledge.

Williams, R. (1974) *Television: Technology and Cultural Form*, Glasgow: Fontana.

Chapter 2

Fun and Games are Serious Business

Helen Nixon

Introduction

Like many people in the western, developed world, Australians in the late 1990s are increasingly surrounded by discourses and texts in the public domain which create or assume a familiarity with the personal computer (PC), multimedia, virtual reality and the Internet. The possible effects on people's lives of digitization, fibre-optic cable and computer networks are described in the features, business sections and leisure liftouts of newspapers; in popular science and current affairs programs on television; and in an expanding range of specialist computer magazines appearing on newsagents' shelves. National press headlines like 'Internet gives us best chance to be Clever Country' and 'Censor to make Internet fit for families'[1] introduce visions of the possibilities and dangers of newly emerging computer-mediated worlds. Young people and families are often central to these visions. They are sought out by transnational conglomerates who construct and market futuristic visions and the technologies likely to realize them. As future citizens, young people are also central to government economic, education and cultural policy which attempts to position Australia competitively within the global cultural economy. Young people, and adults charged with their education and care, are thus at the intersection of technology-related socio-political developments.

What has been popularized as 'the information superhighway' is at once a material, discursive and social construction fashioned by a number of influences: global capitalism, global and national culture industries, government policy and cultural practices. At the heart of the superhighway as projected by commerce and government is the family and the home. At the time of writing, fibre-optic cable rollouts are in progress and pay TV is being established in sections of major Australian cities, with other areas to follow. In addition to the delivery of pay TV, the information superhighway is envisaged as delivering to the home fast Internet access, including online multimedia and computer games. In CD-ROM form, multimedia for information and entertainment are already the subjects of major global and national investment and profit.[2] Although the configurations of networking, hardware, and software likely to make up the online information superhighway cannot yet be specified, it seems certain that telecommunications and the home or personal computer will be central to people's experience of it. In Australia the uptake of the PC has been rapid, with one third of Australia's seven million households having at least one PC in regular use (Hurrell, 1996), and families with children representing the highest category of PC ownership (Elliott and Shanahan Research, 1996).

Techno-textuality, Media Culture and Cultural Pedagogy

Cultural negotiations are necessary to pave the way for the development and adoption of new technologies (Penley and Ross, 1991). How new technologies are named, talked about, and promoted in the media and advertising are integral to the process of cultural negotiation and actual take-up and use. For this reason, Collins (1995) has argued the need for analyses of 'techno-textuality', specifying that close attention should be paid to the cultural mediation of information *about* technological innovation. The study of media culture is key to analyses of techno-textuality. Kellner (1995) argues that in contemporary technocapitalist societies, media culture – a culture common to those who have access to global media – centrally determines social identity and socio-political values:

> A media culture has emerged in which images, sounds, and spectacles help produce the fabric of everyday life, dominating leisure time, shaping political views and social behaviour, and providing the materials out of which people forge their identities (Kellner, 1995:1).

Methods of textually oriented critical discourse analysis have been explicated by Fairclough (1989, 1992, 1995a, 1995b), who argues that discourse analysis of media texts has the potential to explicate the relationship between discourse and social change. Media culture provides representations that mobilize consent to specific political positions through images, discourse and narrative (Fairclough, 1995b). In the contemporary technocapitalist context, media culture thus plays an important *cultural pedagogic* function. As Kellner (1995) writes:

> In a contemporary media culture, the dominant media of information and entertainment are a profound and often misperceived source of cultural pedagogy: they contribute to educating us how to behave and what to think, feel, believe, fear, and desire – and what not to. (Kellner, 1995:2).

Similarly, feminists have argued that media culture and popular culture produce 'the pedagogies of everyday life' (Luke, 1996). For example, in conjunction with the pedagogies of the family and the school, the media and popular culture provide lessons about how to become consumers and how to become boys and girls. Within the intertextual discourses of television, film, advertisements and lifestyle magazines, a matrix of teaching and learning or pedagogic action is produced.[3] This kind of pedagogic work produces lessons about skills and values, and broad socio-cultural and political lessons about gender and social power (Luke, 1996).

In this chapter I will use the contextualized reading of texts of everyday life (television, advertisements, magazines) to focus on parents and young people as discursively constructed subjects and objects of cultural pedagogy in a time of technocultural change. I argue that the discursive tensions which accompany this process can point to dominant and changing socio-political constructions of class and gender. The chapter proceeds in two sections. In the first section I describe the global/local socio-political context against which the texts must be read. Here I discuss how local inflections of global marketing make connections between existing youth cultural practice and the new communications technologies. In the second section I provide a critical reading of representations of families, young people and computer-related social and educational practices in home computing magazines. Here I argue that the family is being constructed as an important entry point for the development of new computer-related literacies and social practices in young people. I argue that what is discursively produced within the global cultural economy as digital *fun and games* for young people, is simultaneously constructed as *serious business* for parents.

The Global/Local Context: Targeting the Home and School

Global economic change has been connected with urgent calls from government and the business sector for Australia to become a Clever Country, for Australians to live and work 'smarter' and to adopt 'intelligent solutions' to increasingly complex economic and social conditions. In a peculiar circularity, new technologies are posited as being both the cause of these social and cultural changes, and as providing potential solutions to some of the difficulties caused by them. In the national economy, embedded within global flows of images, technologies and capital (Appadurai, 1990), the information technology and telecommunications industry (IT&T) is Australia's third largest export category. Analysts predict that multimedia and online services will be the fastest growing IT&T sectors in Australia in 1996. Computer networking, the Internet and multimedia are key to federal government policy in communications, arts and education.

Because of its centrality to the global and national economies, the information superhighway is the focal point of social, education and cultural futures articulated in national policy.[4] For example, alliances have been forged between local councils, real estate companies, computer companies, and *Telstra* – the government-owned telecommunications corporation – to develop experimental techno-futuristic social projects for Australian citizens. In the suburbs of two Australian capital cities, delivery of full broadband online services to the home was trialled in 1996. Networked residents have e-mail access to local businesses, commercial and emergency services, school and council information, and personal bulletins about baby-sitting, odd jobs, community health and family services. While national headlines announce that 'The Net is becoming part of the furniture' this will be reality for residents of Springfield, Queensland, where young parents will raise their children in newly built houses fitted with computers as household appliances[5].

The use of information and communications technologies in educational settings is central to federal and state government education policies. Plans are in progress to co-ordinate nationally the use of interactive computer networks for educational purposes by state governments, non-government schools, the vocational and training sector, the higher education sector and the more informal adult and community education sectors. To this end, an evolving national online directory known as EdNA (Educational Network Australia) was made available on the Internet in February 1996, directing users through hypertext links to educational products and services.[6] The key objectives of EdNA are indicative of an amalgam of educational, public interest and commercial imperatives. These aim to stimulate the use of electronic networks, encourage the development of educational services and high quality Australian content, and provide a new publishing platform for the education and training services industry. At the state level, school systems are funding computer networking in schools and subsidizing computer hardware purchase, arguing that this will be good for the economy, the future workforce, and therefore Australia's place in the world. Laptop computer hire and purchase by parents is on the increase in the school sector, with private schools leading the way in the development of 'the notebook curriculum' (Owen and Lambert, 1996).[7]

Of course any consideration of the Australian IT&T and culture industry context must take into account *global* flows of technologies, images and capital. From the time the term *information highway* came into common use in the usa in the early 1990s, the flows of bytes along cable were seen as 'potential flows of capital' (Henwood, 1995). In March 1994, US Vice President Al Gore made explicit the twinning of the Utopian social vision of global communication, with the White House vision of economic imperialism. Although the Global Information Infrastructure was important for social reasons – as 'a means by which families and friends will transcend the barriers of time and distance' – Gore added 'it will make possible a global information marketplace, where consumers can buy and sell products' (Schiller, 1995, pp. 17–18). The rhetorical and structural pairing of the social with the economic good here serves as a strategy to enlist support for government policies which appear to be about both democratic social participation of citizens, and at the same time, the provision of a democratic right to choose among commodities and establish market competition.[8]

In recent years major global mergers and cross-industry alliances have formed shifting networks of economic and power relations among a limited number of large corporate players – mostly US based   who have control of press, film and television media, software publishing, telecommunications and computing. The new information and communications technologies are now closely connected with established media via patterns of ownership of content and means of delivery (Craik, Bailey and Moran, 1995; Schiller, 1995). Transnational companies invest heavily in technical research, market research and advertising related to computer-mediated communications and entertainment. Their projected vision is a future in which businesses and other workplaces, libraries, schools and homes will pay for fast, high quality delivery of interactive, online services, including delivery of vast storehouses of video, audio and text information and entertainment. The realization of these projections is partly dependent on the take-up of that machine now generally known as the personal or home computer, and the education of the public about multimedia and the online worlds made possible by the Internet.

Local Inflections of Global Marketing: Transnationals Target Youth

But this [youth] consumer is not an alien . . . They find *Ellen* funny. They watch *Melrose Place*, just like us. The only difference is, they admit it.
   They also watch ads just like us. Except they are rather better at it, because they're sharper, faster, and have been practising it almost since they were born Mayes, P. (1996).

Consumption of new material objects such as PCs, CD-ROMs, modems, scanners and digital cameras is an economic phenomenon, entering the cycle of economic exchange. But consumption is also a cultural phenomenon, entering the cycle of symbolic exchange that is contemporary consumer culture (Baudrillard, 1981). As Lury reminds us, consumption is 'to do with meaning, value and communication as much as it is to do with exchange, price and economic relations' (1996:10). The cycle of consumption, central to the economic and cultural infrastructure of late capitalism, is increasingly both global and local, and dependent on the commodification of objects and services which have two key components, information and culture (Hearn and Mandeville, 1995). In this context I want to ask how forms of communication and media culture are embedded within global media economies and cultures: and simultaneously, how the global–local nexus, at the level of economics and culture, is made manifest in everyday texts and practices.
   Although the phenomenon of the global cultural economy is a commonplace, the internationalization of children's culture appears to be taking place according to marketing trends associated with 'the age of flexible specialisation' (Kline, 1995). In these markets, the universalism in global advertising

of the 1980s is being replaced in the 1990s by flexible specialization which responds to local contexts (Ducille, 1994; Kline, 1995; Zhao and Murdock, 1996). Kline (1995) writes that many advertisers of global products for youth now use strategies of flexible specialization, employing 'specific campaigns which are locally produced (by global advertising agencies) that maximise the products' cultural fit by working with local inflections or by addressing known cultural sensibilities' (Kline, 1995:121).

Examples of the global and the flexible specialization strategies of IBM and Coca-Cola, transnational marketers to youth, appeared in Australia in the context of the 1996 Olympic Games – held in Atlanta, Georgia, USA – one of the highest-rating television spectacles of recent times. Billed as the 'World-wide Information Technology Sponsor' for the Games, the IBM trademarked slogan was 'Solutions for a small planet'. Ads for IBM broadcast during the Games exemplified the universalism of global advertising. For example, the ad for *Aptiva*, IBM's multimedia personal computer was a succession of nested computer-screen images which conclude with a voice-over welcoming viewers to 'the future'. In the space of a few seconds, the *Aptiva* ad constructed a final image of a young American boy (in a reversed baseball cap) at his computer as the manipulator of the preceding images and controller of newly created computer-mediated 'worlds'. The ad's mode of address constructs a non-specific, universal addressee – 'Welcome to the Worlds of Aptiva', 'It will open *your* eyes', 'And *your* mind'. But visually, and in narrative terms, it is the young, white American boy in his well-appointed bedroom who is constructed as heir to the multimedia future. Despite IBM's appeal to global diversity and harmony in its generalized 'Solutions for a small planet' advertisements, in the *Aptiva* ad it is not youth in its global diversity who will inherit the worlds of multimedia, but American(ized), middle-class, male youth. This reading is supported by the cultural references in the *Aptiva* ad, indicative of the economic and cultural domination by the US of global popular culture in general (images on the computer screen of the Grand Canyon, an indigenous American, the moon landing, an African-American jazz band), and youth culture in particular (images of a rock group, a film crew, youth in designer street gear, the boy at the *Aptiva* wearing a reversed baseball cap).

In contrast, in an example of flexible specialization, the Coca-Cola 'Always for the fans' campaign broadcast during the Games targeted the youthful subject as sports person, sports fan and as techno-subject in formation. The ads featured pre-recorded videos depicting a cross-section of urban and rural Australians sending messages of encouragement to Australian Olympians via satellite. In the ads, signs of global, US-based culture (now typified by the Coke bottle itself) were inscribed over distinctly local and regional signs of Australianness (people in the outback wearing green and gold colours, waving Australian flags, speaking in the Australian vernacular, and so on). A universal message – 'Coca-Cola. Always for the fans. 1928–1996' – is here inflected by historically specific conditions in which the ad is broadcast. A young, sports-minded, nationalistic, technology-aware, Australian television viewing audience is here the object of cultural pedagogy about the use of the new global satellite technologies to express fandom.

In what follows I discuss two everyday texts which are implicated in global–local webs of capital and youth culture. In each case, transnational companies target youth by combining and commodifying aspects of technoculture and popular culture. In the first example, the addressee is youth; in the second it is youth and their teachers. Both examples illustrate how publishing, the media, advertising and local social networks form part of a 'matrix of socialisation' (Kline, 1995) about emerging computer-mediated cultures. They suggest ways in which text, considered in context, can be understood as performing forms of pedagogical work in the process of technology-related cultural reproduction and change.

Twisties, Soaps and Cyberheads: Popularizing the Internet

In the culture of daily life, everyday texts include promotional and advertising material of all kinds: junk mail, brochures, flyers and food packaging. One everyday text mediating technocultural change in 1996 Australia was the Twisties snack food wrapper. Advertising produced for the Twisties 'Cyberheads surf the Net for free' campaign (April–July, 1996) adorned Twisties packets on the shelves of supermarkets, cinemas and video rental outlets.

The Twisties Cyberheads campaign was produced for the Smith's Snackfood company, a transnational company who targets youth. Young Twisties consumers had previously been targeted in Australia using a set of television ads featuring stars of the youth-favourite American soap *Melrose Place*. In a prime example of postmodern self-reflexivity, the ads feature two of the stars of *Melrose Place* (reported in fan magazines to be off-screen lovers) eating Twisties and watching *Melrose Place*. The narrative line of the ad is enhanced by the placement of the ads as frames to the beginning and end of episodes screened in Australia in 1995 and 1996. In their living rooms watching *Melrose*, young Australians watched the off-duty stars in 'their' living rooms watching themselves on *Melrose*.[9]

The lucrative snack food market is closely connected to the young who are estimated to spend at least AU$75 million each week, mainly on magazines, entertainment and food (Gill, 1995). In the Cyberheads campaign, constructing young Twisties eaters as 'cyberhead surfers' provides a useful associative link between the metaphor of 'Net surfing' and the activities of surfing and skateboard riding – both central to forms of Australian youth culture. Terms associated with popularized, commercial forms of contemporary youth culture – 'check out', 'totally' and 'bizarre' – are also used on the packet to advertise the Twisties Internet site on the World Wide Web: 'Check out the Twisties Net site. It's totally "bizarre".'

The bringing together of snack food, computers and the Internet in this campaign begins to indicate webs of connections between advertisers, products and media. For example, although it is not clear from the packet which Internet service provider is involved in the campaign, the promotion is conducted in partnership between Smith's Snackfood company and one of the world's number one PC-systems retailer, Compaq. Collected packet tokens are entered into a competition to win one of twenty Compaq Presarios (the personal multimedia computer aimed at the home market). The advertised 'free' Internet access comes with the Presario prize.

Not only do texts and associated practices like these arise from a complex of transnational interests which target specific national youth markets, they also begin to establish new connections between the use of information technologies and broad aspects of social and cultural life. In the Twisties Cyberheads campaign, young people's cultural and leisure activities, such as skateboarding, eating and spending time with friends, are commodified alongside newly evolving information related activities like 'surfing' the Internet. In this process, a whole new set of cultural activities are brought together by snackfood, media and computer conglomerates thus creating new possibilities for youth cultural practice.

Surf's up at MLC: Marketing Youth Fiction and (N)etiquette

I have suggested that advertising performs pedagogic work in relation to computers and the Internet. In addition, the 'pedagogical practices of advertisers and corporations' (Giroux, 1994) sometimes intersect with traditional forms of pedagogy to be found in educational institutions. Since 1994 there has been increasing publicity given to the use of the Internet by businesses, schools and the home user in the Australian media and professional magazines. Although computer networking and access to the Internet for school children is a key goal of federal and state educational policy and encouraged by the establishment of EdNA, the use of telecommunications in the curriculum of Australian schools has been patchy since the first reported work was carried out in 1983 (Williams, 1994; Williams and Bigum, 1994a; 1994b). In the main, private education providers, both within and outside of mainstream schooling, have taken the lead in using multimedia and the Internet. The following publisher's promotion targeting young readers and English teachers needs to be understood in this context.

The book *Mosh* by Glyn Parry is a work of fiction about young 'net heads' and 'skate punks'. It tells the story of an adolescent boy's dream in which he appears to move between the matrix of cyberspace on the Internet and the mosh pit of a rock concert (the pit of bodies which forms in front of a band and on which young people 'surf' or are propelled by the audience across the top of the mass of bodies). In *Mosh*, the phrase 'surf's up!' refers to both contexts, surfing the net and surfing the mosh pit. In the Australian context, the 'surfing' metaphor takes on additional meaning for youth because of the popularity of skateboarding and surfboard riding as forms of youth culture.

Random House Flyer

A national education marketing division of a transnational publishing house here targets its young Australian potential audience for a novel by using an information technology related method – an online book launch. Arguably this has already been constructed as culturally salient for young people through other aspects of youth popular culture. For example, in 1995 *The Rolling Stones* held a concert which could be accessed in real time on the Internet, and many other similar concerts have since followed. For some young people an affective link will be established between global Internet rock concerts, the book's title, *Mosh*, and the online launch of the book to 'meet' the author. For young people made aware of the promotion, the Internet and youth fiction are thus associated with existing pleasures of their daily lives.

As well as targeting youth, the Random House promotion performs pedagogic work with respect to teachers, the Internet and social power. The letter accompanying the Random House flyer contends that the decision to launch the book on the Internet was made because that is 'where most of the novel's action takes place'. Although the letter goes on to add that the Internet was 'a natural choice' for the launch, other aspects of the letter suggest another reading can be made of this decision:

We live in an age in which technology can sometimes seem frightening, or at least a little difficult to absorb . . . If the thought of this
seems intimidating please don't let it scare you. Your computer
teacher or information technologist on staff will guide you through the
process. (Random House Education Marketing Manager (1996),
Letter to Housestyle readers).

For assistance with further information, the flyer provides for teachers three
possible sources: a telephone number, an e-mail address and a URL (Uniform
Resource Locator, or Web site address). Thus, despite the supposed 'natural
connection' between the novel's subject and the online book launch, encour-
aging teachers to face *their own* fears of the Internet is part of the campaign.
While the book assumes an interest in the Internet among *young* readers, the
publicity assumes a *lack* of knowledge about it among English teachers and
encourages them to learn more about it.

The central location advertised for the *Mosh* book launch is Methodist
Ladies College (MLC). MLC is a well-established, prestigious, wealthy,
private school for girls in Melbourne. MLC is known in Australian education
as a progressive school in relation to its use of computers in the curriculum.[10]
The school's emphasis on computer education first attracted attention when
each Year 7 student began working with a laptop computer in 1989. MLC has
since embraced computers as the focal point of its curriculum. The principal
and staff are well versed in computers, and the principal has appeared in the
press, magazines and at educational computing conferences espousing the
value of whole-school commitment to the use of laptop computers, multimedia
and the Internet. MLC's recognized authority in relation to 'leading-edge'
teaching and learning using computer-mediated communication serves to
reinforce its already considerable established weight of social and cultural
authority, produced by its church connections, wealthy benefactors and
history of successful alumni.

While the Internet book launch at MLC is an advertising ploy, it also has
socio-political effects. Using the Internet becomes linked to book reading as a
form of cultural capital (Bourdieu, 1986), and both are constructed as more
likely to be the preserve of young people attending private schools. The
publisher's letter and flyer work ideologically to construct non-MLC teachers –
most of whom work in government funded schools – as 'other' to those 'in the
know' about information technology practices integral to Australia's techno-
future. The promotion serves to delimit the 'legitimate' addressees of the
invitation by assuming English teachers will have 'information technologists'
on staff and Internet-literate students, thus discursively maintaining existing
structural relations of unequal social power between private and publicly-
funded state schools (Bourdieu and Passeron, 1977).

Happy Techno-families use Multimedia and the Internet

It should come as no surprise that a lot of the people riding the Information Highway these days aren't old enough to carry a driver's licence.
Raised on a steady diet of TV and video games – and supple-
mented by computer studies at school – children all over the country
are getting online quicker than you can say, 'Stay away from the
Playboy Web site' (Rogers, M. (1995:21).

Parents, teachers and members of the general public are told by the media
that they are entering a new age of high-tech. Politicians, educators and the
newspaper and broadcast media predict that future convergence of telecommunications and computers will bring changes to the way Australians live,
work and play. People are warned that they have to keep up – for their own
sakes, as well as those of their children. In this context, a number of
commercially oriented sites mediate technological innovation for the public.
In 'cybercafes' people can read newspapers and magazines, access the Net,
chat and have coffee. In the retail toy chain *Toys 'R' Us* stores, customers can
browse and chat with 'experts' in Family Multimedia Computer Centres. In the
stores of Australian furniture and electrical store chain Harvey Norman,
computer sections now include Kidscape Creative Learning Centres. These
allow children as young as two to use touch screens in order to 'learn' about the
creative and educational uses of computer technologies and software.
Pamphlets, demonstrations and experts at home computer shows and home
tech exhibitions mediate information about technological innovation to the
general public. In these sites, computer products and services are displayed
and used in ways which integrate them into broad aspects of existing family and
cultural life. They are positioned in spaces and among items already naturalized as 'domestic' such as toys, household furniture, books and magazines.
They are integrated into common forms of the pursuit of leisure and pleasure,
such as shows and spectacles and leisure time browsing. What results is a
complex set of determinants shaping what is taught and learned about the new
technologies, making it difficult, if not impossible, to separate the entertainment, promotional, educational and cultural aspects of such sites and events.
Targeting a more specific audience than cybercafes, retail stores and
home tech shows, there now exists a fast-expanding range of books and
magazines designed to provide a techno-novice readership with an anxiety-
free passage into imagined mediascapes of the future. This is the audience
addressed in series like *For Dummies* published by IDG Communications and
Complete Idiot's Guide published by Que publishers. A subset of the techno-
novice readership are parents with young children and teenagers. Catering to
this market of inexperienced computer users are computing magazines which
construct a parent and child addressee for whom the PC occupies an important
position at home and at school.
Eleven computer magazines targeting novice users were on sale in

Australian newsagents in late 1996. For example, *HomePC*, with the subscription slogan 'no jargon', advertised itself as being 'written for regular folks', promising that 'we will never weigh you down with unnecessary specifications and technical talk'.[11] *Computer Living* had as its cover catch-phrase, 'At last! the computer magazine you can understand.' The editorial of the first issue of *internet.au.* promised to deliver information about the Internet 'in plain English and without the snake oil'.[12] A subset of the 11 magazines specifically targets parents and families, while others target inexperienced computer and Internet users in general.[13]

The magazine titles available in Australia are listed in the table below.

Title and first issue	Place of publication	Publisher
Computer Living November 1994 (preview)	Australia	Pacific Publications (News Corp.) in collaboration with IDG until early 1996. Monthly.
Family PC Australia August/September 1995	Australia	APN Computing under licence to Ziff Communications/ The Walt Disney Company. Bi-monthly until February 1996, then monthly.
Internet Australasia January 1995	Australia	Internet Australasia Publishing. Monthly.
internet.au. November 1995	Australia	Next Publishing. Monthly.
Computer Life	USA	Ziff Davis Publishing Company
Family PC	USA	Ziff Communications/ The Walt Disney Company
HomePC	USA	CMP Publications
Mac Home Journal	USA	MacHome Journal
PC Home	UK	IDG (International Data Group) Media
Parents & Computers	UK	IDG (International Data Group) Media
Easy PC	UK	VNU Business Publications

Table 2.1 Techno-novice computer magazines available in Australia, September 1996 (First issue dates are included for Australian publications only.)

Many of these magazines are owned by or affiliated with transnational communications market researchers and computer publishers such as IDG (International Data Group) Communications, media conglomerates such as News Corporation, and publishing–entertainment alliances such as Ziff Davis Publishing/The Walt Disney Company. Some contain regular sections or features sponsored by transnational computer hardware and software companies, Apple Computer Inc., IBM, Microsoft, Olivetti and Intel. This is not to say that these magazines are directly sponsored by computer companies, nor that the corporations have any say in editorial policy. None the less, when considered in relation to the projected global information highway, patterns of computer magazine ownership highlight that the same few conglomerates have ownership of the means of delivery and projected content, as well as the news and entertainment media which popularize and promote it (Craik, Bailey and Moran, 1995; Schiller, 1994).

Family computer magazines, themselves commodities in the political economy of publishing, exist to sell other publishing commodities such as books and CD-ROM titles, as well as computer-related products and services sold by advertisers. Many of the magazines identify themselves as products of the global cultural economy. Banners on the front covers of *Computer Living*, *Family PC*, *Family PC Australia* and *Parents and Computers* mark them as

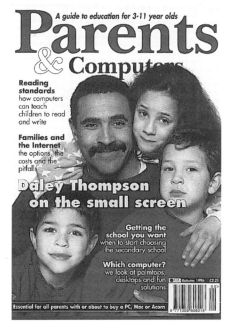

belonging to a postmodern hybrid media and cultural form; part women's magazine, lifestyle magazine, TV fan magazine, and consumer magazine. Cover graphics feature close-ups of TV and radio personalities, and banners highlight reader competitions, special offers, give-aways, poster-inserts, 'True stories' features, and cash prizes to be won.

Home computer magazines construct possible social identities for the computer-using parents and children who are the magazines' assumed 'ideal readers' (Kress, 1985). The bulk of representations of 'the family' in these texts are consistent with the publishers' niche market audience of aspiring adults, (including grandparents, teachers and parents). In advertising and non-advertising photographs, happy techno-families are depicted welcoming the computer 'to the family' (Leo Family PC System, Intel), and invited to share the home computer 'across all generations' (Packard Bell). Photographs of families of staff of *Computer Living* magazine accompany a welcome to readers who are 'joining the *Computer Living* family' (subscription brochure). Readers are provided with reviews of 'family-tested software', and addresses of Web sites likely to be 'of interest to families'. In these texts 'the family' is a monolithic construction; a fantasy of white, heterosexual, married, nuclear, middle-class family happiness.[14]

Smart Parents use Smart Tools to Raise Smart Kids

Providing parental support for children's educational use of computers is the apparent objective of these magazines, as indicated in some of their subtitles and headline banners.

Magazine title	Subtitles
Computer Living	Australia's first family computing magazine
	Fun ● Entertainment ● Education
Family PC Australia	The computer magazine for today's family
	Games ● Multimedia ● Home ● Edutainment
Parents and Computers	A guide to education for 3–11 year olds
Mac Home Journal	For work, play and education
Home PC	Entertainment, education and productivity

Table 2.2 Education in family computing magazines subtitles and slogans, 1995–1996

However, their content and modes of address actually position parents as potential providers for their children of computer-connected educational and life-chance advantages (Bridges, 1994). Parental anxieties and lack of knowledge about computers are invoked in order to be assuaged by what the magazines and their advertisers provide. Readers are exhorted to learn about and use computer-mediated technologies. At the same time, they are constructed as being reluctant to do so, and outmatched by their children with respect to computer competence. A generational gap is first constructed and then enlisted as a marketing tool to convince parents that they need to 'keep up' with the younger generation. Indeed the magazines' stated objectives are to support parents to 'catch up' with their children. A typical example of this construction is *Computer Living*'s subscription slogan: 'Now you can help your children succeed *even though* they know more about computers than you.'

Magazine cover blurbs and promotions encourage parents to enlist the aid of computers in the quest to ensure their children's success: Raise computer smart kids',[15]'Improve your kids' reading skills',[16] 'Give your child a hi-tech head start with the Tomy Comfy keyboard'.[17]*Family PC Australia's* regular section, 'Keeping pace: What's new for families', and its subscription slogan, 'Grow smart together', is typical of the language of competition and progress which abounds in these magazines. Parents want to 'keep pace', 'grow smart' with their children, 'improve' their skills and chances, and provide 'head starts' for them. Parents are reported in the magazines as being supportive of commercial computer learning franchises like *Futurekids* and *Computer Gym* because they provide a service which parents believe is key to the future success of their children: 'Like a lot of parents, I want my kid to have a *better chance* than the next.'[18] An advertisement for ACER multimedia computers makes clear links between access to multimedia computers and competitive advantage in the educational stakes: 'Smart tools for smart kids. Your kids deserve the educational edge of a home PC. And the ACER ACROS multimedia PC gets an A+ . . . gives your kids the advantage they need to stay ahead of the curve . . . moves your kids to the front of the class.' Here the metaphors of grading and references to the normative curve, (common to standardized measurement and achievement in education) ' – gets an A+',' 'stay ahead of the curve', 'move to the front of the class' – are used to persuade parents to consider the ACER brand. When similar language is used repeatedly by journalists and advertisers, what is a discursive construction comes to be taken as a common-sense link between proficiency with computer-mediated technologies and increased chances for educational success. The multimedia computer thus takes its place alongside other educational 'essentials' necessary for academic success.

The use of comparatives without referents – 'better than', 'stay ahead of', 'having more than' – illustrates a form of semiotics common to advertising in which signifiers are open and fluid, and able to stand in for a broad range of desires and competencies (Barthes, 1968, 1973; Williamson, 1978). When the comparatives are specifically linked to educational and life chances, the advertising is performing ideological work by inciting parental fears and desires for their children. At the same time, it also constructs a misleading view of existing socio-political conditions. In Australian society the number of positional goods at each level of education is probably already fixed. Writing about research into education, credentialism and workforce restructuring, Bessant (1993) explains that increasing positional competition for a non-expanding range of credentials and a decreasing number of jobs for young people has the consequence that the demand for education can *never* be satisfied. Parents' desires for their children, partly generated by the commercial sector, must be read against this bleak picture of high levels of youth unemployment and restricted opportunity for the acquisition of educational credentials.

Computer Literacy Joins the Three Rs

Home computer magazines construct young people's contemporary and future learning as being fundamentally different from the past learning experiences of adults. The differences between them are constructed around two axes. First, computer literacy is constructed as a newly established 'skill' essential for future job and life chances of the young generation. Second, the forms of learning supposedly enabled by computer education are ascribed an affective value supposedly absent from previous forms of learning. In this way, difference is first constructed then used as a marketing tool. Learning with computers is promoted as being 'fun' and 'exciting', the antithesis of the supposedly 'boring' education associated with the 'old' technologies of chalk and talk, or pen and paper. Taken together, the argument is made that new forms of literacy and pedagogy are required in the world of today and tomorrow and that they will be superior, stimulating and enjoyable.

The first dimension of difference in the olden days/nowadays construction – that computer literacy is an essential, new skill – is articulated in the following magazine editorial comments:

> Ten years ago you could safely count on packing your kids off to school to learn the three Rs and they'd get a decent job. These days there's this fourth skill – computer education . . . competent computer skills are critical to the future employment of today's students. (*Computer Living*, February 1995:6).

Once it has been established that computer literacy is a necessary new skill, an educational economy of value is constructed within the range of computer-related skills and forms of learning. A pattern well established in relation to children's toys (Luke, 1994) is repeated here in relation to computer hardware and software. Computer-mediated learning is constructed as requiring skills which are first compared with and then grafted on to, traditional skills of early literacy development. What this does is suggest a 'need' for 'developing' young learners to add keyboarding skills to the general motor skills traditionally evidenced in the manipulation of blocks and toys. Skills of co-operation around a keyboard and screen are needed in addition to those traditional socialization skills such as sharing and co-operation during play. Alongside the traditional skills of letter and word recognition in print, the new world 'requires' skills of letter, word and icon recognition on screen. The advertisement for the Tomy Comfy keyboard provides an example of this construction in action. The keyboard promises to provide something for those beginning school and their parents. It will provide the pre-school child with a 'colourful introduction to basic computer skills'. It will be fun, stimulating and safe to use for 4 to 6-year-olds, and will satisfy parents as 'a serious educational system that improves your child's motor skills, enriches vocabulary, teaches basic social values and lots more'. In the educational economy the computer is thus positioned alongside other educational, developmental and socialization toys, promising to be 'accountable' to parent buyers: 'There's even a special evaluation feature that describes your child's performance.'

By contrast, computer games provide a challenge to established hierarchies of educational value. They are also a point of tension in magazines which, while professing to provide educational guidance for parents, are financially reliant on computer software advertisers. In the main, magazines that claim to 'educate' parents about 'quality' software, end up dismissing some games and praising others. Those computer games which can be described as useful adjuncts to learning are given value because they can develop skills valued in the traditional curriculum:

> Unlike your average video game, they require lots of reading, note-taking or research outside of the game in order to play properly. They encourage students to use their problem-solving skills and communicate as part of a group, teaching them to try different strategies and examine the consequences of their actions (*Computer Living*, February 1995:44).

In journalistic forms of pedagogic communication like this, parent–readers learn how teachers and other educational 'experts' describe and value computer-mediated learning. Parents are encouraged to take on the same language and values to educate their children for success. As mediators of 'information' about technological innovation, the magazines thus take on some pedagogic authority. They play a potentially powerful role in the computer hardware and software purchasing patterns of parents, as well as in discursive constructions of the normative computer literate youth subject.

The affective dimension is the second axis according to which the learning experiences of older and younger generations are differentiated in the magazines. Constructions based on the theme of olden days/nowadays suggest that although parents' school learning was not enjoyable, computer-mediated technologies have the potential to change this for their children. In journalism and advertising alike, fun and enjoyment are the privileged descriptors of computer-based learning experiences. Here the pedagogical function of computer games is emphasized: 'Imagine a school where the teachers have to lock the doors at five o'clock to get the children to go home'[19]; 'Think of this CD-ROM as a biology teacher on your computer that you wish you had teaching you at school.'[20] Before CD-ROM, research used to mean 'searching through indexes and ploughing through tomes on dusty shelves.'[21] Now, it is argued, the advent of multimedia and the popularization of Internet has provided new exciting learning experiences. Now, 'for the cost of a local call you can take the kids on a trip to the Louvre Museum in Paris or into deep space from one of many astronomical sites listed in cyberspace.'[22]

Conclusion

the media . . . can no longer be seen as something separate from society; rather they become something within which the social is continuously being defined (McRobbie, 1994:201).

If you were planning 1994's 'in' list, the Internet would be right up there with *Seinfield's* Kramer, Pete Sampras' baggy tennis shorts and gourmet bush tucker (*Computer Living,* November 1994:37).

An emerging media industry which focuses on the computer–human interface, multimedia and the Internet, dominated by what Wark (1996: 105) describes as 'the California based "military entertainment complex" ', is key to the incitement and circulation of fears and desires about electronic futures within mainstream media culture. As Wark (1996) argues, huge investments are being made in unproven products and as-yet undefined new markets in the 'experience industry' (including virtual reality) and multimedia. In such a situation, without guaranteed outcomes, the marketing of multimedia 'fun and games' and educational products to young people and families is a 'serious business'. Alliances between Australian federal and state governments, media conglomerates and computer corporations all contribute to such broad-base cultural mediation of 'information' about the new technologies. This produces a positioning of young people and parents by interlocking and often incompatible discourses of government policy, media culture, popular culture and the school. According to government policy, multimedia and the Internet are the tools which young people will use at home and at school to build Australia's economic and cultural future. At the same time, in media culture – now in the hands of a few transnational conglomerates – the new technologies are aligned with other 'cult' youth media commodities and constructed as 'fun', 'exciting' and 'cool' consumer products for the young. Meanwhile, in family computer magazines media conglomerates and computing corporations construct the PC, multimedia and the Internet as positional goods for parents, aligning them with well-equipped homes, 'good' parenting, and 'quality' education for children. The multimedia, modem-equipped PC is thus placed at the intersection of a full range of political, social and educational interventions within the lives of young people and families: interventions which are complicit in the maintenance of existing structural relations of unequal social power and inequality.

Notes

1 McRea, P. (1995) Internet gives us best chance to be clever country, *The Australian*, 2 May p. 62. Hilvert, J. (1995) Censor to make Internet fit for families, *The Australian*, 20 June p. 29.
2 Interactive multimedia has been singled out for major government-funded development, with the provision of AU$84 million over four years as part of the cultural policy outlined in the Labor government's *Creative Nation* (Commonwealth of Australia, 1994). *Creative Nation* funding supports such initiatives as the Australian Multimedia Enterprise, the Australia on CD program and six Cooperative Multimedia Centres. These projects have continued under the new Liberal–National Party Coalition federal government elected in March 1996.
3 See Bourdieu and Passeron's (1977) theory of the symbolic violence of pedagogic action, according to which the family is the primary site of pedagogic action and the inculcation of the habitus, central to social reproduction. Although the family is the primary site in this process, the school, the media and other forms of entertainment are also posited as sites of pedagogic action central to the production of pedagogic work. Each of these institutions generates forms of pedagogic authority instrumental in cultural production and social reproduction.
4 See three issues of *Media Information Australia* for a discussion of relevant issues: Digital Desires (1996), Given (1995) and White (1994). See also Conomos (1996), Harley (1996) and Wark (1996).
5 Ebbs, G. (1995) The Net is becoming part of the furniture, *The Australian*, 8 August, p. 54. The Springfield proposal is a joint project between Apple Computer Australia, Optus Vision, Springfield Land Corp, IC technologies and George Patterson Bates (Brisbane) as reported in 'At home with an Apple' (1995) *The Australian*, 28 November, p. 47.
6 Established when the Keating Labor government was in power, EdNA's future under the Howard Liberal–National Party Coalition government is uncertain. The EdNA home page on the World Wide Web can be accessed at http://www.edna.edu.au
7 Australian education comprises three sectors: a fully government-funded state school sector, a Catholic education system, and an Independent Schools sector, made up of non-Catholic religious-based schools and other schools which satisfy the conditions for registration as a school. Non-government schools, subsidized by the federal government but generating most of their revenue from other sources, including school fees paid by parents, are known as private schools.
8 Similar rhetorical patterns have an ongoing history in corporate and government discourses in 'developed' countries like Australia and in rapidly developing countries (Atkins 1995; Buckeridge 1995; Weber 1995).
9 At the time of writing, the Twisties Cyberheads campaign has been replaced by a joint campaign involving Smith's Snackfood (Twisties, Samboy, Burger Rings and CCs brands), Twentieth Century Fox, and the Ten Network television series *The X-Files* in the promotion of the film *Independence Day* (*B&T*, July 12, 1996, p. 28).
10 See Spender (1995) pp. 110–114.
11 *HomePC* subscription brochure, 1995.
12 *internet.au.*, November 1995, p. 10.
13 As more Australians have begun using the Internet, *internet.au.* and *Internet Australasia* have been less obviously tailored to novice users. A third Australian

Internet magazine, *Australian Net Guide*, began publication in March 1996. With a subtitle of 'Your complete guide to being online', the first editorial promised that the magazine would provide 'the most practical guide to using the Internet in Australia' (*The Australian Net Guide*, March 1996, p. 6).

14 The work reported here forms part of an ongoing study into family computing magazines and other everyday texts mediating technological change in Australia. The textual corpus drawn on in this chapter consists of the five issues of *Family PC Australia* and fifteen issues of *Computer Living* published in Australia until March 1996, and representative issues of other home computing magazines available in Australia and collected since June 1995.

15 *Computer Living*, May 1995.

16 *Computer Living*, June 1995.

17 *Parents & Computers*, Winter 1995.

18 *Computer Living*, November 1994, p. 39.

19 *Computer Living*, February 1995, p.16.

20 *Computer Living*, April 1995, p.59.

21 *Computer Living*, February 1995, p.6.

22 *Family PC Australia*, December/January 1996, p. 40.

References

Appadurai, A. (1990) Disjuncture and difference in the global cultural economy, in Featherstone, M. (Eds), *Global culture: Nationalism, globalisation and modernity*, London: Sage.

Atkins, W. (1995) 'Friendly and useful': Rupert Murdoch and the politics of television in South East Asia 1993–1995, *Media Information Australia* (77), 54–64.

Barthes, R. (1968) *Elements of Semiology*, (Sheridan Smith, A. M. and Smith, C. Trans.) New York: Hill and Wang.

Barthes, R. (1973) Myth today, in *Mythologies*, St Albans, Herts: Paladin/Granada.

Baudrillard, J. (1981) *For a Critique of the Political Economy of the Sign* (Levin, C.Trans.) St. Louis, MO: Telos Press.

Bessant, J. (1993) *Constituting categories of Youth: Towards the Twenty-first Century*, Discussion Paper Series No 3, National Centre for Socio-Legal Studies, La Trobe University, Melbourne, Australia.

Bourdieu, P. (1986) The forms of capital, in Richardson, J. (Ed.), *Handbook of Theory: Research for the Sociology of Education*, New York: Greenwood Press.

Bourdieu, P. and Passeron, J.-C. (1977) *Reproduction in Education, Society and Culture*, London: Sage.

Bridges, D. (1994) Parents: Customers or partners?, in Bridges, D. and McLaughlin, T. (Eds), *Education and the Market Place*, London: Falmer Press.

Buckeridge, R. (1995) Multimedia, education and export: Industry development issues, *Media Information Australia* (78), 58–61.

Collins, J. (1995) *Architectures of Excess: Cultural Life in the Information Age*, London: Routledge.

Commonwealth of Australia (1994) *Creative Nation: Commonwealth Cultural Policy*, Canberra: Australian Government Publisher.

Conomos, J. (1996) At the end of the century: Creative nation and the new media arts, *Continuum: The Australian Journal of Media and Culture*, **9**(1), 118–129.

Craik, J., Bailey, J., and Moran, A. (Eds) (1995) *Public Voices: Private Interests*, Sydney: Allen & Unwin.

Digital Desires. (1996) *Media International Australia*, 81.

Ducille, A. (1994) Dyes and dolls: Multicultural Barbie and the merchandising of difference, *Differences: A Journal of Feminist Cultural Studies*, 6(1), 46–68.

Ebbs, G. (1995) The Net is becoming part of the furniture, *The Australian*, 8 August, p. 54.

Elliott and Shanahan Research (1996) *The Impact of Computers on Australian Life: The Apple Report Number One*, Brochure order number LB 1420, Apple Computer Australia.

Fairclough, N. (1989) *Language and Power*, London: Longman.

Fairclough, N. (1992) *Discourse and Social Change*, London: Polity.

Fairclough, N. (1995a). *Critical Discourse Analysis: the Critical Study of Language*, London: Longman.

Fairclough, N. (1995b) *Media Discourse*, London: Edward Arnold.

Featherstone, M. (1991) *Consumer Culture and Postmodernism*, London: Sage.

Foucault, M. (1972) *The Archaeology of Knowledge* (Sheridan Smith, A. M. Trans.), London: Routledge.

Gill, T. (1995) Kids have their say on ads and fads, *B&T,* 12 May, 29.

Giroux, H. (1994) *Disturbing Pleasures: Learning Popular Culture*, London: Routledge.

Given, J. (Ed.) (1995) Cultural export: Re-orienting Australia, *Media Information Australia*, **76.**

Harley, R. (1996) Towards and economic future: Australia's multimedia nation, *Continuum: The Australian Journal of Media and Culture*, 9(1), 130–5.

Hearn, G. and Mandeville, T. (1995) The electronic superhighway: Increased commodification or the democratisation of leisure?, *Media Information Australia*, 75(February), 92–101.

Henwood, D. (1995) Info-fetishism, in Brook, J. and Boal, I. (Eds) *Resisting the Virtual life: the Culture and Politics of Information*, San Francisco, CA: City Lights Books.

Hilvert, J. (1995) Censor to make Internet fit for families, *The Australian*, 20 June, p. 29.

Hurrell, B. (1996) Computers rule in one in three homes, *The Australian*, 14 July, p. 4.

Kellner, D. (1995) *Media Culture: Cultural Studies, Identity and Politics between the Modern and the Postmodern*, London: Routledge.

Kline, S. (1995) The play of the market: On the internationalisation of children's culture, *Theory, Culture and Society*, 12(2), 103–29.

Kress, G. (1985) *Linguistic Processes in Socio-Cultural Practice*, Geelong, Victoria: Deakin University Press.

Luke, C. (1994) Childhood and parenting in popular culture, *The Australian and New Zealand Journal of Sociology*, 30(3), 289–302.

Luke, C. (Ed.) (1996) *Feminisms and Pedagogies of Everyday Life*, Albany, NY: State University of New York Press.

Lury, C. (1996) *Consumer Culture*, Oxford: Polity Press.

McRea, P. (1995) Internet gives us best chance to be clever country, *The Australian*, 2 May, p. 62.

McRobbie, A. (1994) *Postmodernism and Modern Culture*, London: Routledge.

Mayes, P. (1996), Get hip and down-to-earth, *B&T*, 7 June, p. 15.

Owen, J. and Lambert, F. C. (1996) The notebook curriculum: An innovative approach to the use of personal computers in the classroom, *Australian Educational Computing*, **11**(1), 26–32.

Penley, C. and Ross, A. (Eds) (1991) *Technoculture*, Minneapolis, MN: University of Minnesota Press.

Rodgers, M. (1995) Kids, cartoons and controversy on the Internet, *Computer Living*, November, 21.

Schiller, H. I. (1994) Media, technology and the market: The interacting dynamic, in Bender, G. and Duckery, T. (Eds) *Culture on the Brink, Ideologies of Technology*, Seattle, WA: Bay Press.

Schiller, H. I. (1995) The global information highway: Project for an ungovernable world, in Brook, J. and Boal, I. (Eds) *Resisting the Virtual Life: the Culture and Politics of Information*, San Francisco, CA: City Lights Books.

Spender, D. (1995) *Nattering on the Net: Women, Power and Cyberspace*, Melbourne, Australia: Spinifex Press.

Street, B. (1987) Models of 'computer literacy', in Finnegan, R., Salaman, G. and Thompson, K. (Eds) *Information Technology: Social Issues, A reader*, London: Hodder & Stoughton.

Wark, M. (1996) In the shadow of the military entertainment complex, *Continuum: The Australian Journal of Media and Culture*, **9**(1), 98–117.

Weber, I. G. (1995) The moral market: Social vision and corporate strategy in Murdoch's rhetoric, *Media Information Australia*, (77), 45–53.

White, P. B. (Ed.) (1994) Superhighway blues, *Media Information Australia*, **74**.

Williams, M. (1994). Telecommunications and Australian schools: Retrospect and prospect, in Ryan, M. (Ed.) *Asia Pacific Information Technology in Training and Education Conference (APITITE)*, (1), Brisbane, Australia: APITITE 94 Council, (187–93).

Williams, M. and Bigum, C. (1994a) Connecting schools to global networks: Curriculum option or national imperative?, *Australian Educational Computing*, **9**(2), 9–16.

Williams, M. and Bigum, C. (1994b), Networking Australian schools: Preliminaries, problems and promise, in Ryan, M. (Ed.) *Asia Pacific Information Technology in Training and Education Conference (APITITE)*, (1), Brisbane, Australia: APITITE 94 Council, (195–202).

Williamson, J. (1978) *Decoding Advertisements: Ideology and Meaning in Advertising*, London: Marion Boyars.

Zhao, B. and Murdock, G. (1996) Young pioneers: Children and the making of Chinese consumerism, *Cultural Studies*, **10**(2), 201–17.

Chapter 3

Blue Group Boys Play *Incredible Machine*, Girls Play Hopscotch: Social Discourse and Gendered Play at the Computer

Karen Orr Vered

In the autumn of 1995, I went from graduate school to elementary school, hoping to learn how children learn about computers. My initial goal was to observe children's social interactions in a computer integrated curriculum: to see if girls and boys demonstrated notable differences in their relationships to computer use and software preference in an environment in which all children were encouraged and required to produce school work with programs and keyboards in addition to paper and pencil tools. For reasons owing more to my own circadian rhythms rather than any scholarly research design, I often arrived towards the close of morning language arts just in time for recess at 10:30. Over a succession of recesses I noticed a pattern worthy of further investigation. At recess, when all the children are allowed to choose from a number of free-time 'play' activities, girls play hopscotch and boys play *Incredible Machine*.[1] The self-imposed gendered segregation about this game playing activity was too incredible to ignore.

Defying the relatively naive allegation that computer use in general, and computer game play in particular, encourages individualistic or non-social practices, the recess play of *Incredible Machine* by Blue Group boys demonstrated a variety of practices we can identify as 'interactive'.[2] The elements of interactivity described here move beyond the limits of 'interface' and its well known player-to-mouse-to-program dynamic. A thorough study of interactivity must include the social dimensions of play, especially when such play is a *group activity*.

While I am not asserting that play is the equivalent of 'work for children', I am suggesting that the social discourse and interpersonal dynamics developed in different play activities serve *as practice* for social actors and reinforce social behaviours which are generalized from one circumstance, computer game play, to others. In this way, computer game play does not merely replicate gendered behaviours and attitudes but actually functions to construct and maintain differences between boys and girls. Computer game play may thus be distinguished from other forms of play, more physical games for instance, because the computer itself and relations developed around computer game play, link-up with academic uses of the computer. Unlike the playground, where the spaces for hopscotch and basketball play may be gendered domains, very few *careers* draw directly from those experiences in the same way as one would expect computer use to influence further academic study or career choice in later life.

To date, most research and folk knowledge suggest that computer game play is a predominantly male/boy activity. While there are many proposals for changing this phenomenon, significant among them those offered by game manufacturers hungry to capture the 'girl market', we must still deal with the present situation in which we find some girls confronting multiple obstacles on their way to the terminal. As the computer increasingly serves a more integral role in education overall, the importance of girls' access to all forms of computer use, including gaming, should concern educators, parents, researchers and policy-makers.

From Interactivity to Play

While some set-top and arcade games allow for two players by providing two sets of controls, most computer games are designed for one player at a time. Consumer hardware employs only one mouse – one mechanism to control screen activity. While this fact is most often ignored by theoreticians and accepted as unproblematic, elementary school children are aware of this contradiction between design intent and player use. Responding to the questionnaire item: 'When you play computer games, how do you play? Do you play alone, with friends, family members? Write down all the different ways you play computer games', many children also answered, that they 'play with the mouse and keyboard'. Putting aside any implied sarcasm, such a response may indicate the user's unwillingness to accept the divide between the social and mechanical dimensions of play. Taking this response seriously, one might read it as an attempt to reintegrate the social and mechanical. Whether third grade sarcasm or real insight, such comments reinforce my belief that a study of activity cannot simply be limited to the dynamics between mouse control and movement of objects on the screen. It must also incorporate the social context in which play is both conceptualized and actualized.[3] Given certain opportunities and constraints, children transform a game for one player into a group activity defined by a sophisticated social structure and activated through play.

In this case, group play at school amplifies our understanding of interactivity and simultaneously suggests a reconsideration of how we might theorize gendered relationships to computer play. From participant observation of boys' play, I identify and classify certain activities as signs of this 'expanded interactivity'. The boys' activities are, however, the very same practices which their female classmates find unpleasant. In interviews with the girls, they cite the boys' behaviours as *their* reasons for not playing *Incredible Machine* at school. My observations of mixed-group play confirm the girls' expressed discomfort with some of the social dimensions of interactivity.[4]

Shuttling between classroom observations, student interviews, and a variety of academic literature from cognitive to literary theory, I propose that insights gained from observations in an everyday environment suggest that *processes of play*, and not the play things themselves, may account for girls' lower interest level in computer games. Moving away from textual analysis of game content and the technological determinism which have strongly influenced theorization about gender and computer use, close observation of classroom behaviour suggests that certain aspects of interactive group play – the social discourse of computer play – affects girls' participation in playing *Incredible Machine*. Thus it is not the game text, graphically or narratively, that is appealing or repelling to girls, but the *social text* developed through group play which provides a context for the game and subsequently serves to enforce gendered segregation at recess play. While the advantages of social interactivity stimulated by computer game play are numerous, it is significant that most girls find these practices unappealing, and that boys, almost exclusively, benefit from such play.

Methodological Significance of Setting

Why or how is the computer-integrated classroom an important environment for studying children's computer game playing practices? Most significantly, it is an institutional environment in which gender equity is ideologically supported, if not thoroughly applied in practice. To date, a majority of observational studies on computer and video game play have been conducted in arcades, science museums, and similar spaces, which are historically male/boy domains.[5] Research like Conn and Marquez's (1983) study of the social context of pinball arcades has been extended to video arcade play. Conn and Marquez argue that pinball play and the arcade setting function as alternative spaces in which generally unacceptable behaviour is accepted. These behaviours include: cheating, display of aggression, breaking away from structured routines of school, in general, a license for 'deviant' behaviour (1983:69). The seedy associations of pinball parlours, and what Conn and Marquez characterize as 'deviant reactions to private property . . . noise, limited space, profanity, violence and gyrating buttocks', designate the space and associated activity as male/boy (1983:72). Precisely what makes these spaces appealing for males makes them inappropriate for females. While the physical 'requirements' of pinball differ from those of computer and video game play – because the mechanical nature of pinball elicits or allows more full bodied movement by players – the arcade environment of video gaming seems to have inherited its masculine character.[6] The school, while not a gender neutral environment, is assumed to be monitored to a greater extent than an arcade. Thus, for researchers, the classroom may be one mixed-gender environment in which girls have equal (if not equitable) access to computer games and applications.

Furthermore, schools differ from homes because when children meet in a classroom, any differences between home environments are suppressed and overridden by the normalizing rules, regulations, expectations and ideologies of the classroom. That is to say, an egalitarian ideology dominates the classroom so that the goal of equal opportunity may be approached. While the home is similarly a highly structured social space, the rules and regulations, social relations among individuals, and access to technology, such as the computer or VCR, differ from those in the classroom. Equal opportunity is not an operational philosophy in all families. Age graded hierarchies and roles of responsibility differ within families and among children in those families. In the classroom, all children are ideally treated with the same set of expectations and given similar opportunities. In this sense, the classroom and its rules for computer use, whether in gaming or academic applications, should provide girls with greater access to computers than they have at home. Previous studies, Giacquinta, Bauer and Levin (1993) for example, have shown that home computers are most often the 'property' of men and boys within the home.

Computer game play also differs from video game play in the home. While many parents of the children in my sample object to video game play and forbid it, they do allow computer games. Such rules imply a distinction and hierarchy of value between the two media. While narrative content and game player activity do not mark computer games as 'bad objects', in fact many of them differ very little in these respects from video games. I am assuming that parents perceive games associated with computer technology as better, perhaps more educational than, games played on other platforms, especially television set-top games. This distinction is reinforced by the fact that set-top games are not likely to be found in classrooms or associated after-school recreational programs, while computers and their games are increasingly part of the recreational fare provided by such institutions.

In addition to the ethnographic studies of game playing spaces, cognitive psychologists contribute a wealth of information to the body of research on computer games and game play, most recently addressing gender differences in game appeal. *The Journal of Applied Developmental Psychology* dedicated a 1994 issue to computer game play. These and other similar studies often observe and measure girls' and boys' skill with respect to game play, accounting for variables such as exposure and practice, age and gender. Concluding that there is no biologically bound, gendered hard wiring associated with computer game playing skill, researchers report that practice improves development of spatial skills for both boys and girls (Subrahmanyam and Greenfield 1994). Confirming the popular belief that boys have more prior experience with such gaming, this study attributed the boys' greater skills to familiarity outside the experimental circumstance which allowed boys to 'learn how to learn' more quickly than girls. While the results of such experiments are valuable, they are still limited by their very design because laboratories do not incorporate the numerous social variables that exist in the everyday social contexts of game play. To this point, Greenfield (1994) admits in the issue's introduction that researchers found it difficult even to attract girls to the experiments.

Although experimental studies are informative, they usually report findings gathered under 'sterile' conditions. Data are not obtained in the mix of social activity under institutional structures which ethnographies of class-rooms suggest are important, especially with respect to how gender operates in schooling.[7] Often, when science museums or laboratories are the test sites, children are grouped by researchers rather than self-selection processes, as they would tend to do in 'natural' play sessions. Such experiments also vary with respect to their valuation of background information on the children. While age and gender are important variables, social class, structure of the living unit (with parents, grandparents, or other arrangement), and what type of school children attend is often not reported. Following scientific experimen-tal methods, cognitive testing seeks to reduce variables rather than embrace them. While this type of research shows that children can improve their spatial skills or motor co-ordination through repeated play, the findings are now generally accepted and it is time for a different type of analysis to be brought to bear on questions of gender and computer game play. For these reasons, the social aspects of everyday play must be addressed.[8]

This work is motivated by qualitative research in general and studies such as Giacquinta *et al* (1993), which emphasized the need for more research to take into account the 'social envelope' in which technology becomes embed-ded because pre-existing social patterns influence structures of use for any new technology. This study also reported that children's computer use is more oriented toward game playing than other applications, despite parental preference for 'academic learning.' Second, computers in the home appeared to be the province of men and boys because the computer was most often located in either a man's study or a boy's bedroom, consequently establishing a male/boy domain for the hardware itself. These findings suggest that studying children's computer game use in coeducational classrooms may provide different opportunities to observe girls' play because the gender and power hierarchies at school differ from those at home. In most elementary class-rooms, the authority figure is female, unlike many homes, and ideally, boys and girls are given the same opportunities in public education.

Blue Group: A Case Study

It is another beautiful day in Los Angeles, Southern California's version of autumn. The sun is shining, 78 degrees Fahrenheit, tomorrow is Hallowe'en and recess has just begun. Two boys ask the teacher if they can stay indoors to play *Incredible Machine*. Within moments the group around the computer has become a crowd. Several boys in the combination third-fourth-fifth grade class gather around the terminal while one controls the mouse. In truly collaborative style the on-lookers advise and point, sometimes touching the screen but never touching the mouse. This was not a one-time event but a ritual. After three days of such play, it became apparent that only boys participated, but not all the boys. Barrie Thorne (1993) argues that the spaces of school are gendered through complex practices of both students and educators. More specifically, Durndell, Glissov, and Siann state that 'a number of studies indicate that in coeducational situations boys dominate the use of computer consoles at school and that some teachers, albeit unwittingly, reinforce these dominance patterns' (1995:220). Blue Group recess play at the computer supports these claims and observations.

The Blue Group boys to which I refer to are classmates in an age integrated magnet school classroom (beginning the autumn term at 6 to 10 years old) in Los Angeles Unified School District.[9] The school incorporates computers across the curriculum within an overall framework of constructivist educational philosophy, best described as a 'hands on' approach to learning. The school's informational brochure describes the program and its educational philosophies as 'interdisciplinary', 'activity-based' and 'thematic'. From 1986 to 1993 the school and Apple Computer, Inc. were closely associated in an effort to integrate computers and other electronic technologies in the learning environment. Each classroom has computers; there is no lab. Teachers give lessons using large screen monitors instead of chalk boards in some cases, and children produce their writing assignments and explore geometry using computer programs in addition to the traditional materials of paper and pencil. This instructional design and practical implementation of computer use meets Seymour Papert's ideals for computer integrated education.[10] Games, however, are available in this classroom only at recess or lunchtime and only those games which the teacher has chosen for educational purposes are allowed. *Incredible Machine* is available because the teacher would like the children to design their own puzzle game and she believes playing such games will familiarize them with possibilities.

These kids are computer savvy to say the least. Indeed this is a special population, but a highly appropriate one for studying children's habits, strategies, and practices with respect to computer games because the majority of children have attended the school from five years of age and are well versed in a variety of computer applications from language arts to mathematics. Several studies indicate that girls' lower interest and skill with computer applications is the result of differential exposure. In this population, however, both boys and girls share a base-line level of familiarity, skill and appreciation for computer hardware and software. Classrooms all use *MacWrite* for word processing, *Canvas* for art construction, and *Hypercard* for programming. For example, Blue Group read the novel, *Planiverse* (by A. K. Dewdney), and then worked in small groups to create animated two dimensional worlds with ecosystems and inhabitants suited to the limitations of a two dimensional environment. Within this context, I was surprised to find recess computer game play was exclusively a boy's activity.

Constructing a (Con)text Through Play

Focusing my attention on the boys closest to the *Incredible Machine*, I suddenly realized the noise level had increased tremendously. Standing up from the table and stepping back for a different perspective, I was amazed to see that the group had grown from the instigating two to a crowd of 12. A dozen students around one computer and one mouse, all playing together without discord. The boy controlling the mouse attempted different moves and on-lookers shouted approval. When he was stuck, a plainly instructive voice emerged from the crowd.

> *Helper*: Click on that arrow over there [pointing].
> *Mouse Clicker*: I can't get it over there.
> *Helper*: OK, get that [pointing]. Put it over there.
> *Mouse Clicker*: Right here?
> *Helper*: Over [pause] over. OK Switch. [With more urgency] Put it
>   down, put it down!
> Mouse Clicker follows the directions.
> *Another on-looker/player*: That'll be great.
> *Helper*: Yeah, I know.

As they completed the puzzle, commentary erupted from the crowd. Praise, questions and a suggestion that someone get control (of the mouse) for the next level were all voiced. They quickly rearranged their seating and a different boy took control of the mouse without a single objection to the turn-taking 'system'.

Throughout the game, in addition to instructions and strategies, some of the boys discuss what they do at home when they play *Incredible Machine*. Others comment on what is 'most fun' about the game and those close enough to the screen point and touch the objects as they are moved around and the construction is assessed. At one moment the Mouse Clicker did not seem to be able to manipulate the mouse with sufficient sensitivity. With gentle care, another boy put his hand on the Mouse Clicker's hand and guided the mouse properly. After the function was complete, the helper removed his hand and the Mouse Clicker was once again the sole manipulator.

Over the course of this first level, as the crowd grew, new arrivals asked, 'How did you do that?' 'John figured it out,' was one response. At this point John is identified as the mastermind but, importantly, he had not been the Mouse Clicker. John was one of the helpers. John confirmed his position by responding that indeed it was he who had figured it out. On the second level attempt, more boys began to function as helpers. Several voices gave directions and suggestions, imploring the Mouse Clicker to 'remember' some previous instance of play and repeat the moves that were successful before. Some boys also speculated that it would be 'nice' if they had more of one item than another. Such a comment indicates that they would like the game to offer other options – in addition to those already dictated by program designers.[11]

As these various strains of meta-commentary developed and focus shifted from the particularities of one puzzle to more abstract analysis of *Incredible Machine* as a game, linguistic representation of game 'ownership' also shifted. As new arrivals asked, 'What are you doing?' no one answered. Perhaps the question was unanswered due to linguistic ambiguity: Southern California's English dialect lacks a plural form of 'you'. Or perhaps the boys were too engrossed in play and meta-commentary. Nevertheless, had the players spoken a language which does employ a plural form of 'you', the newcomer's question might reveal more about the dynamics of individual versus group identity over the course of such play.

As players carried on with the game, helpers began shouting with excitement and urgency, 'We need a fan! Put that fan over there. We need a fan to move. Oh, 'member how we blocked the cat before? You guys need a 'block the cat'. The previously acknowledged roles of Mouse Clicker and Helper seemed to fuse and became indistinguishable through the use of plural first person. Instead of identifying the child with the mouse control and the other with the ideas, the boys began to refer to themselves as a group, using the first person plural 'We'. The new arrivals, coming as they did after the group was far greater than two, acknowledged the group quality of game play and addressed the other boys collectively as 'you guys'. One late arrival even asked, 'Where are we?' Another player responded, 'We're in like level 26 or something'.

While my written description strives for readability, in fact, the activity was complex with up to six or seven boys shouting instructions, assessing strategies, speculating on other scenarios all at once. At any one time there are at least three different foci being addressed by different players. Simultaneously boys give instructions and advice on the game play while others discuss particularly memorable previous games, and still others engage in meta-analysis suggesting design improvements for *Incredible Machine*.

At this particular play session, the Mouse Clicker did not appear to be very well practised at *Incredible Machine* because his ability to manipulate the mouse was low. Despite this relative inability, at the end of recess he expressed pleasure and pride in his accomplishments, smiling broadly and cheering for himself, even though success was thoroughly dependent upon the group dynamics of social play. Without the guidance of the Helpers, the boy probably would have progressed far more slowly, and perhaps not even finished one level during recess. The group completed two levels and began a third.

From an educational standpoint, teachers would be pleased to observe the co-operation amongst the boys. Group game play of this sort provides opportunities for peer tutoring and collaborative learning. Throughout game play no one made derogatory comments, no one claimed superiority (with the slight exception of John's one affirmation of his expertise, but this was quite matter of fact and not what I would call bragging). At the end of recess it seemed that all participants took credit for the success, in a team-like celebratory hoot.

Interactivity

Several types or qualities of interactivity are apparent in the Blue Group boys' play. First there is the social interaction among the boys as they make a group effort to solve a puzzle. They practice giving and taking instruction and direction. They listen to one another as they analyze and strategize for the immediate challenge. Their dialogue also indicates a bridge between play at home and play at school. Importing their home play experience into the classroom, the boys bridge the two spaces of home and school in a process that creates a certain continuity through game play. Discussing previous game playing sessions often includes home play sessions, to which only some boys have immediate reference. Nevertheless, those experiences are incorporated into the group history.

The serial form of play, from one recess to the next, day after day, is vocalized as a history of play. When boys ask aloud, 'remember when we did this or that?' they invoke an oral history and affirm a group cohesion. Self-identification as a member of a group with a publicly shared history may even indicate the existence of a sub-culture at school: 'Blue Group boys who play *Incredible Machine* at recess.'

Speculations like 'wouldn't it be great if it [the game] had' this or that, and references to the difference between *Incredible Machine* and more sophisticated later versions of the game, constitute a meta-discourse about programming in general, and demonstrate a broad knowledge of different games and game genres. The boys are aware that there are other ways to make a similar game and are thinking about elements of game design based on their experience as players.

This summary of interactivity may not be comprehensive, but it does suggest a breadth of considerations in terms of the concept of *interactivity*. In addition to the many activities of interactivity it is significant that many 'players' do not vocalize their participation. The silent on-lookers seem to constitute yet another role in group play, that of 'watchers.'

Seeing one boy standing *behind* the screen observing the excitement of the other boys, I suggested he take my place so he could see the screen. He instantly took me up on the offer but still remained silent from his new vantage point. I interpret his eager acceptance of my offer as an expression of interest in the play, yet his continued silence struck my curiosity. After observing several play sessions I recognized that there is a contingent of participants who assume this role, observing but not commenting nor asking for a turn with the mouse. In-depth interviews with all the children might help to explain these individual choices and the individual to group relationships represented in these play sessions.[12] Some of the boys have the game at home and play more frequently than others. Some boys are new to the school and are not as familiar with computer games or other applications. Still others might not be 'friends' with the group but still stick it out as observers.

The observers' status and function should not be misunderstood as limited because 'watching', in itself has at least two identifiable outcomes. First, those who watch provide an audience for the more vocal and active players. Part of the play may very well include 'being watched', incorporating a notion of *performativity* as part of interactivity. Second, the act of watching may have a transferable effect for other social arrangements. Perhaps watching a game will allow the quiet child to comment on the game in another social context. Such a conversation might serve as the foundation for a new friendship or as entree into a different game playing role at a later play session.[13]

Girls' Play

Observing the boys early in my research, I asked them if any girls ever played *Incredible Machine* at recess. The response was delivered with fourth grade sarcasm, 'Girls play hopscotch and jump rope'. After this comment the other boys burst out in derisive laughter, while I struggled to understand the humour. The comment was clearly a put-down of girls and their play time activity choices.[14]

Later, however, when I started talking to eight girls about their experience with computer games two general trends emerged: some girls play computer games at home but not at school, and some girls do not play computer games at all. Both groups play video games either at their homes or their friends'. Games listed by the girls are among the most popular, *Super Mario Bros*, *Donkey Kong*, and the like. This pattern, girls playing at home or in private, rather than in public spaces as boys so commonly do, is reported frequently by other researchers.[15] Janice, an 8-year-old, said she played at home and was able to supply a long list of game titles she owns. She did not play at school, however, and said this was because she did not know 'there were very many games at school'. Pressing her a bit further, I asked if she knew there was a group of boys who played at recess. She quickly responded, 'Yeah, but I never get a chance to play.' 'Why?', I asked. 'Because everybody else is playing,' she responded.

In light of the social dynamics that I describe as characteristic of recess play among the boys (co-operative and supportive communication, systematic turn-taking, etc.), Janice's comments are provocative. The boys seem to play quite well together in an 'everybody else' environment, to use Janice's term.

They have elaborated rules of play that accommodate the many individuals in the group through turn-taking and an 'assignment' of roles such as Mouse Clicker. Janice's comment suggests a different approach to computer play. While the boys believe they are *all* playing in the group, Janice laments that she 'never gets a chance to play', as if being playing within a group is equivalent to not playing at all.

Another girl, 9-year-old Maria, eloquently described the games she plays at home but said of school play that, 'The boys sort of hog the computer'. Janice confirmed Maria's assessment, interrupting her friend for the first time to add emphatically, 'Exactly, that's why I don't play it'. When asked how the boys 'hog' the computer, the girls both said the boys are 'loud and always yelling', and then they imitated the way the boys shout urgent directions at one another during game play: 'Oooh, get it! Get it! Put this over there!' After the performative account of a boys' *Incredible Machine* session, Janice said, 'It confuses you while you're playing'. She then said that *Incredible Machine* is a good game and she plays it after school with another girl who is 'crazy 'bout *Incredible Machine*'. When asked if she would play at school in a girls' group she excitedly answered yes.

From this sample of discussions with Blue Group girls, it is clear that their disinterest in the game is not based on narrative, genre, graphic or other forms of textual criticism but dependent upon their reading of the social text associated with the game as it is played at school. This gendered nature of play is not exclusive to computer games as I, and others notably Thorne (1993), have reported. But what is distinct about this play dynamic is that it repeats patterns associated with educational activities in the classroom and thus reinforces links between play and 'work'.[16]

Further in my interview with Janice, I asked how a girls' group might play differently from the boys. Stammering for a moment, her reply was more of an objection to how boys play:

> Well, there's these cats and dogs and little animals that you use in it [*Incredible Machine*], and they [the boys] usually try killing them when you're usually 'sposed to like use them, like cats role a ball and dogs, you know. But they try killing, 'cuz there's a rocket and fire and they try killing the animals.

The boys have found the game within the game and are able to accomplish game goals while enjoying moments of subversion by annihilating animals and playing against the grain in other ways. While it is difficult to judge whether Janice's comment is an objection to rule breaking or cruelty to animals, her description of the game's elements, how they 'should' function, and how the boys violate these purposes, reveals her sophisticated understanding of the game. For these reasons, I would not attribute her distaste for playing *Incredible Machine* (at school) to any male gendered orientation *within* the game's content, narratively or otherwise.

Games for Girls

Paradoxically, I suggest, software companies are emphasizing the narrative content of games as they try to discover girls' tastes and preferences in software by forming all girl focus groups to better understand how to capture the missing market share. In both the corporate and academic research orientations, girls are presented with games in all girl groups or are interviewed after playing in mixed groups, and asked what they like and dislike about the games and how they would improve the games if they were programmers. It is commonly reported that girls prefer games with rich character descriptions and well developed stories. In *Billboard Magazine*, Gillen reports that research from Sega's Girls' Task Force indicates that girls are more interested in a 'book-type approach to interactive games, as opposed to a competitive approach' (1994:88). Similarly, Inkpen *et al*. report that games for girls should 'emphasise relationships – including characters, social interactions, stories, and the like' (1994:398). These observations are about narrative text and not about play as an activity. What the software industry and educational researchers both overlook is the social dimension of play, even when their own observations and reports imply its significance.

Indeed, in such studies girls have said they would like more well developed characters and story lines, and their comments should be taken seriously. I would argue that focusing on the game text should not preclude a consideration of what Marsha Kinder (1991) has termed the 'intertextual supersystem' of cross media awareness. Kinder's point is to recognize that while existing games may not have rich character development in the individual application, the histories and geneologies of characters are known to the players, boys mostly, through references to other media sources. That is to say, although the game's story may not be intricate, the background story which contextualizes the game may come from another popular media source, such as comic books or cartoons, and be quite complex. It is not that character and story in computer games do not exist, but girls may be unfamiliar with the background stories and character relationships because they come from other media sources, or networks of associations, which are outside their everyday sphere of reference.[17] Countering precisely this phenomenon, a new series of computer games for girls are just now being marketed and the main character is *Barbie*. Because Barbie is probably one of the most recognized icons in girl culture, it will be interesting to track the popularity of these applications.

Inkpen *et al*. (1994) conducted their study into ways to make games more appealing to girls in order that software may be used to attract girls to science and math disciplines. Ironically, although they conducted participant observation in these mixed gender groups, their overall analysis gives priority to the interview material and virtually dismisses their observations. They report: 'girls would stay [at the computer] if they saw a free machine or if a group of girls were playing a game. Few girls would approach if a large crowd of children were clustered around a particular game' (1994:392). Furthermore, girls did not *ask other players for a turn* but instead waited to be offered a turn at the computer, or asked an adult to secure a turn for them through intervention. Coupled with this, interviews revealed that 'girls play at home, in privacy'. These findings indicate that the social setting and interpersonal dynamics associated with group play significantly influence girls' choices. The implication of this study is that game playing environment may be a greater factor than game content. For this reason it is surprising that Inkpen *et al* (1994) make the leap suggesting that game content should be changed to increase appeal to girls. Even though evidence points to social text rather than game text, researchers and designers still emphasize content when considering game appeal to girls.

Based on the level of game awareness and stated appeal that girls reported in interviews with me and in co-operation with the classroom teacher, I eventually invited girls to play *Incredible Machine* with the boys to see if they would behave differently than the boys, as they claimed they would. It is first important to reiterate that neither I nor the teacher, nor the Blue Room girls consider *Incredible Machine* to be a 'boy's game', even though there are no developed characters in the game, and the only human figures function like the inanimate items – as tools available for building the machines. The game itself does not generate a story but the playing does.

Before this 'experiment' with mixed and all girl groups began, Janine, who had for several weeks passed by the boys as they played, observing from a distance, one day sat down to play with the boys' group. In the swirl of shouting and pointing that characterizes the boys' participation, Janine quietly took a seat in the centre, squarely in front of the screen but only reservedly offered suggestions, almost in a whisper amidst the loud chatter of the boys. The following week we talked about her game playing.

Interviewer: Was that the first time you played with them at recess?
Janine: Uh, no. I played a few other times.
Interviewer: And when you play, do you participate as much as they do?
Janine: No. I just like watching.
Interviewer: How come?
Janine: 'Cuz like, a lot of the times, they're like, they're wrong and stuff, and they're always like yelling at the people that are like wrong. And I don't really wanna' be yelled at because I don't wanna' like be wrong. 'Cuz like whenever I like think of an idea, and then like I tell them, and then if I'm like wrong, then they'll probably like start yelling and going, 'you don't know!' So I just kinda', I just watch.
Interviewer: Do you ever yell at them, when they're wrong?
Janine: No.
Interviewer: How come they don't mind being yelled at?
Janine: Because they yell at other people.

> *Interviewer*: Would you prefer to play with a group of girls or a group of boys, or a mixed group? What's your preference?
>
> *Janine*: I'd like to have like some boys and some girls. Like to have a mixture because there're so many boys there it's weird.

Indeed, subsequent observations of girls at play in both same sex groups and mixed groups revealed that there are noticeable behavioural differences in play style between boys and girls and these differences obtain across both types of groupings. Therefore, contrary to dominant research trends which emphasize the narrative analysis of computer games, I suggest that girls and boys approach computer play differently, irrespective of the software content, including genre and specific elements of narrative such as character and setting.

In one all-girl gaming session two girls sat down at the computer and began a game. Admittedly these girls were not very experienced with the game. They did not know how to 'open' the game, nor did they know there was a crib sheet provided with playing hints. After they started, with help from the teacher, the Mouse Clicker turned to the other girl and asked quite calmly, 'Do you have any ideas?' The other girl had no firm ideas and the teacher intervened, questioning the girls on what they already knew or believed to be the game goal, and ultimately bringing them to an understanding of the goal through question and answer. When another girl arrived, she asked permission of the two girls to 'watch.' They said, 'Sure.' When they finally got some screen activity going, they giggled with excitement at their accomplishment, but quickly returned to their contemplative style of play. They asked one another and the teacher pointed questions, 'How do you get this thing over there?' This is quite unlike the boys' play because the boys never ask, or have the opportunity to ask, specific questions. When the boys play, there is so much direction being given by the Helpers that the Mouse Clicker never has the opportunity to *ask* for instructions. It seems that amidst all the chatter, the Mouse Clicker has enough to do just keeping up with the barrage of suggestions.

Janine finally became excited and said, 'Oh, I got it, I got it!' The teacher asked, 'OK, what are you going to do?' Janine explained her strategy with conviction. Recalling that she is the child who reported not wanting 'to be wrong' or to be 'yelled at' when wrong, it may be safe to assume that Janine felt this group of three girls and the teacher was an environment in which such 'criticism' would not surface. As it turned out, her original idea was not useful for solving the puzzle. After continued discussion with the teacher about why this or that would work, Janine said with some hesitation, 'Well, we could try it.' Throughout this play session, the girls spoke one at a time, asking questions of the teacher, answering her queries, and listening to one another's ideas. Finally, the only behaviour familiar to me from the boys' sessions was the success cheer. When the puzzle was complete, the girls raised their hands above their heads and let out a cheer for their accomplishment.

This play session, while quite different from those characteristic of the boys' play (strongly influenced by the tutorial provided by the teacher), still demonstrates the social dimension of interactivity in group play. An early study (Muller and Perlmutter, 1985, cited in Clements and Swaminthan) indicates that 'children working at a computer spend nine times as much time talking to peers than while doing puzzles'. Considering my observations of children working puzzles at the computer, I am inclined to suggest that this social discourse is the bulk of play.

Granted, my description of this play session indicates how familiarity with the game dictates the style or type of linguistic discourse generated in play. Nevertheless, the girls did not attain similar levels of physical or oral activity that the boys demonstrated from the beginning of the school year. Even with practice and increased expertise, the girls still did not speak over one another, even when one was quite excited about an idea. I never heard several girls at once giving conflicting directions as the boys would do regularly. My observations neither confirm nor contradict Patricia Greenfield's (1994) assertion that boys are more likely to engage in trial and error experimentation. Given certain circumstances, girls will experiment as boys do, albeit seemingly needing more encouragement to do so. The implied question for educators and researchers, as well as other feminists is, what are we doing in our relations with girls that gives them the impression that 'being wrong' is so loathed that it should be avoided at all costs, thus limiting their experimentation? Why do girls find 'being wrong' more distasteful than boys do? The question is not about technology, a particular medium, nor a relationship with narrative development. The question asks us to consider the political dimensions of childhood education as they are embedded in gendered social expectations and practices.

Even after some girls had attained a certain level of expertise with the game, they still demonstrated noticeably distinct behaviour at variance with that of the boys. Recently, after eight months of weekly classroom visits, a mixed group played together with two girls seated nearest the screen, one of them controlling the mouse. As the boys shouted directions and suggestions, Emily let go of the mouse and covered her face and eyes with her hands. I read this body language as a sign of being overwhelmed by the noise and by the pressure to decide whose suggestion to follow. Letting go of the mouse as she did, caused a pause in game progress. Whether a reflex or purposeful action, it had the effect of calling for a re-equilibration, for a return to 'stability'. In addition to the body language that girls express, they often respond to the multiplicity of directions (from the Helpers) by giggling and looking to me (usually the only adult) for guidance or affirmation.

Conclusions

Extensive observation of children's group play with the computer game *Incredible Machine* confirms and extends previous research with respect to the verbal activity stimulated by puzzle/strategy computer games. It also indicates that boys and girls bring different social expectations and norms of behaviour to the game playing situation and that girls find boys' computer related behaviour, like other forms of play, difficult to contend with. As advances in computer game design increasingly replicate the appealing qualities formerly found only in arcade (and set-top) games, and computers are available in co-educational settings, girls have more 'opportunity' for exposure to this popular form of entertainment, but they may also be subject to the male/boy dominance associated with such activities.

Moreover, observations made in a 'natural' play environment reveal more about the given social conditions of play than are accessible in laboratory settings. The socio-environmental factors associated with these contexts may have great impact on the use of computer technology since computer games are one of the dominant links between popular uses of computers and educational applications. If play functions to acclimatize children to tech-nology in general, then computer game play may influence other uses of computers, especially those associated with academic or vocational uses.

Decisions about gender equity and distribution of computer resources in educational settings must take into account the important contextual influences of the social discourses stimulated by and through play. Waiting for the computer industry to produce high quality 'games for girls', or more gender neutral titles is quite simply beside the point. Careful intervention to enforce equitable access in *computer play* is the more manageable and practical option. This may mean establishing 'all-girl' play sessions, or non-competitive round-robin type schedules, to allow access for those students, both boys and girls, who do not usually play computer games. Such inter-ventions are really quite simple, once we have become aware of their necessity.

Notes

1 *Incredible Machine* version 3.0 (Sierra On-Line, 1995) is a computer game of the strategy genre. The object is to create a machine that will achieve a certain end, such as making a ball go through a hoop, using pre-given items. Reviewers often define the goal as building a *Rube Goldberg* machine. The Rube Goldberg Inc. homepage notes: 'Rube Goldberg was a Pulitzer Prize winning cartoonist, sculptor and author. Best known for this wacky inventions . . . which are a unique commentary on life's complexities. They provide a humorous diversion into the absurd that lampoons the "wonders of technology".'

2 Blue Group is the classroom in which these observations were recorded and The School stands in for the actual site name. The children's names have been changed for anonymity. Research observations were conducted over a seven month period from October 1995.

3 Many laboratory studies of children's computer play suggest the need for more research in 'natural' play settings. See Durndell *et al.* (1995); Escobedo (1992) and

Mack (ERIC file no. 383 324). For a history of computer game development and suggestions for broadening the notion of *interactivity*, see Friedman, 1995.

4 For research purposes I distinguish *computer game play* from other forms of play and from other uses of computers. This decision reflects a variety of concerns. First, computers and computer use have become the focus of much attention in educational research and policy because their integration into the classroom is perceived as signalling a number of changes and potential shifts in the way education is conducted. Second, in light of other works about the gendered dynamics of the classroom (see Thorne, 1993), the computer and its use cannot be ignored. Computer game play, however, is related to other game playing traditions such as home and arcade video games. The majority of children's computer use is associated with play rather than *work*. American ideologies about game play tend to separate *play* from other activities because the end goal of game play is purely entertainment rather than a combination of entertainment and production. Hobbies such as woodworking and sewing imply the production of an object and entertainment, whereas game play does not produce an object.

5 Exceptions to this are studies of neighbourhood play groups, such as Kinder (1991).

6 See Myers (1990) for an elaboration of the differences between the physicality of arcade games and computer games.

7 For summaries of a variety of classroom ethnographies see *The AAUW Report: How Schools Shortchange Girls*, American Association of University Women Educational Foundation and National Education Association, 1992.

8 Kinder (1991) broadens the context for understanding game appeal including the cross media marketing of intertextuality. Gailey (1993) adds a different level of complexity by suggesting how social class informs parents' game purchases by genre.

9 The magnet school system was originally developed to support integration efforts across the geographically vast city. To bring children from different socio-economic and racial backgrounds together in the educational environment, the district established neighbourhood schools with specific foci and then drew the student population from outside the immediate neighbourhood, from geographically distant and culturally diverse locations. Parents or guardians must fulfil an application process for their children to be considered for any magnet school, but student selection is not based on prior knowledge of computers nor on overall academic standing. The school is unique in its strong commitment to parental volunteerism. Parents are asked to give the school a certain amount of their time and to participate in fund raising activities.

10 See Papert, 1980, 1993; Nye, 1991; and Clements and Swaminathan, 1995 for descriptions of optimal conditions for computer integrated learning environments.

11 Escobedo (1992) suggests that the genre of puzzle/strategy games elicits the highest quantity of such meta-discourse.

12 In depth histories of the children's game playing habits outside of school is the next phase of this research; it has not been completed at press time.

13 See also Williams and Ogletree's (1992) assessment of computer interest using three criteria: 'proximity', 'observation', and 'working'. While I do not agree with the judgement implied by the separation of these activities, the point that all three types of participation are valid signs of 'interest' is fruitful.

14 When I first began my observations, the jump rope club had not yet been 'formed', but I noticed a boy, Max, and one girl, Janine, would walk through the room and

stand about two feet behind the computer gang, watching the game with some interest but never joining in physically or vocally, by sitting down or speaking. Max has since joined the jump rope club and no longer observes the computer play, while Janine has taken the opportunity to play in both same sex groups which the teacher and I have twice organized, and mixed groups where she is either one of two or three girls or the only girl playing with a large group of boys. See Thorne (1993) for an extended discussion of these patterns.

15 Durndell *et al.* (1995); Giacquinta *et al* (1993); Gilliland, (1990); Inkpen *et al.* (1994), Haddon (1992).

16 When the children are allowed to form their own groups or pairs for computer activities associated with assignments, the teacher reports that they will almost always select same sex partners for research, writing teams, etc. She confirms that given their preference, students will always work in same sex teams, despite efforts made by teachers in keeping with school policy to actively promote gender equity.

17 For an in-depth analysis of gendered marketing practices across media, see Seiter (1993).

References

American Association of University Women Educational Foundation and National Education Association (1992) *How Schools Shortchange Girls: The AAUW Report: A Study of Major Findings in Education*, commissioned by the AAUW Education Foundation; researched by the Wellesley College Center for Research on Women, Washington, DC: AAUW Education Foundation and National Education Association.

Clements, D. and Swaminathan, S. (1995) Technology and school change: New lamps for old, *Childhood Education* 71(5), 275–81.

Conn, S. and Marquez, J. (1983) The social context of pinball: The making of a setting and its etiquette, in Manning, F. (Ed.) *The World of Play*, West Point, NY: Leisure Press.

Durndell, A., Glissov, P. and Siann, G. (1995) Gender and computing: Persisting differences, *Educational Research* 37(3), 219–27.

Escobedo, T. (1992) Play in a new medium: Children's talk and graphics at computers, *Play and Culture* 5(2), 120–40.

Friedman, T. (1995) Making sense of software: Computer games and interactive textuality in Jones, S. (Ed) *CyberSociety: Computer-Mediated Communication and Community*, London: Sage.

Gailey, C. (1993) Mediated messages: Gender, class, and cosmos in home video games, *Journal of Popular Culture* 27(1), 81–94.

Giacquinta, Jo., Bauer, J. and Levin, J. (1993) *Beyond Technology's Promise: An Examination of Children's Educational Computing at Home*, New York: Cambridge University Press.

Gillen, M. (1994) Game makers finally targeting girls, *Billboard Magazine*, 4 June, 88–9.

Gilliland, K. (1990) Curriculum development for gender equity in computer education, in Wanger, C. (Ed.) *Technology in Today's Schools*, Association for Supervision of Curriculum Development.

Greenfield, P. (1994) Video games as cultural artifacts, *Journal of Applied Developmental Psychology* **15**(1), 3–12.

Haddon, L. (1992) Explaining ICT consumption: The case of the home computer, in Silverstone, R. and Hirsch, E. (Eds) *Consuming Technologies: Media and Information in Domestic Spaces*, London: Routledge.

Inkpen, K., Klawe, M., Lawry, J., Sedighian, K., Leroux, S. and Hsu, D. (1994) We have never-forgetful flowers in our garden: Girls responses to electronic games, *Journal of Computing in Childhood Education* **5**(2), 383–403.

Kinder, M. (1991) *Playing with Power in Movies, Television, and Video Games*, Berkeley, CA: University of California Press.

Mack, M. (ERIC file no. 383 324) Linear and non-linear hypertext in elementary school classroom instruction.

Myers, D. (1990) Computer game genres, *Play and Culture* **3**, 268–301.

Nye, E. (1991) Computers and gender: Noticing what perpetuates inequality, *English Journal* **80**(3), 94–5.

Papert, S. (1980) *Mindstorms: Children, Computers, and Powerful Ideas*, New York: Basic Books.

Papert, S. (1993) The children's machine, *Technology Review*, 30 July, 29–36.

Seiter, E. (1993) *Sold Separately: Parents and Children in Consumer Culture*, New Brunswick, NJ: Rutgers University Press.

Subrahmanyam, K. and Greenfield, P. (1994) Effect of video game practice on spatial skills in girls and boys, *Journal of Applied Developmental Psychology* **15**(1), 13–31.

Thorne, B. (1993) *Gender Play: Girls and Boys in School*, New Brunswick, NJ: Rutgers University Press.

Williams, S. and Ogletree, S. (1992) Preschool children's computer interest and competence: effects of sex and gender role, *Childhood Research Quarterly* **7**, 135–43.

Chapter 4

Digital Visions: Children's 'Creative' Uses of Multimedia Technologies

Julian Sefton-Green and David Buckingham

From Creative Machines to Creative Youth

One prominent strand in discussion around the impact of the new technologies is an emphasis on the 'creative' potential of the home computer. Advertisers and other advocates of digital technology have repeatedly extolled the ways in which it brings creative production – whether in written or audio-visual form – within reach of the ordinary consumer. The computer, it is argued, will democratize cultural production: it will *make* children creative.

In many ways this idea builds on a tradition of studies of young people's relationships with older media. Paul Willis's (1990) *Common Culture*, for example, draws a vibrant picture of young people actively engaged in the consumption of media forms, including television, video, magazines and music. While this approach draws on the tradition of ethnographic research on youth culture established by the Birmingham Centre, it also has much in common with the 'populist' approach to Cultural Studies most frequently associated with the work of John Fiske (i.e. 1989), with its emphasis on the popular as a form of ideological resistance to the dominant culture.

While there have been several criticisms of the optimism of his approach, and of the adequacy of the evidence (see Buckingham, 1993a: 202–18), Willis does at least attempt to provide empirical support for what is often a primarily theoretical position. Most significantly in terms of our concerns here, he also goes on to consider forms of cultural *production* by young people across a range of media – for example in music making or magazine production (of the fanzine variety). A similar argument is advanced by Angela McRobbie (1994) in her study of the roles young people play in the fashion industry, through buying, selling, designing and making new and second-hand clothes. Yet while McRobbie focuses on the economic dimension of entrepreneurship, Willis is concerned to synthesize the consumption and production of popular culture into a more over-arching form of 'symbolic creativity'. McRobbie sees creativity in terms of the economic conditions of production and exchange within the marketplace; whereas for Willis creativity is a more generalized dimension of subjectivity or identity formation, in which 'young people are all the time expressing or attempting to express something about their actual or potential cultural significance' (1990:1).

While such arguments offer an important challenge to traditional notions of 'creativity', they may also run the risk of blurring the distinctions between consumption and production – not least in terms of the different economic and institutional constraints under which they occur. Thus, many critics have pointed to the 'creativity' which is entailed in the use of purchased commodities to create new symbolic meanings; and such activity is often seen, in de Certeau's (1984) terms, as a form of 'poaching', whereby the weak resist the power of the strong. Dick Hebdige (1979), for example, offers a classic account of the ways in which groups such as mods and punks appropriated, customized and displayed commodities as part of their broader resistance to social conditions. From this perspective, 'consumption' becomes a form of *bricolage*, in which goods are selected, combined and manipulated in order to define new forms of personal or group identity. These processes are, as we shall see below, interestingly similar to the kinds of creativity offered by some contemporary software packages. Nevertheless, we would also argue that there are distinct limitations in this model of 'creative consumption'; and that there are crucial distinctions – or at least significant differences of degree – between the appropriation or manipulation of *existing* texts and the production of new ones.

Of course, the term *production* as used here typically refers to completed texts destined for consumption by others; although there is no reason why it should not also refer to the more informal – and perhaps unfinished – texts which are generated through more casual forms of engagement. Likewise, *creativity* tends to be used to describe a particular range of formal *artistic* competencies; although it can also refer to much more general qualities of thought or behaviour. In general, we would argue in this chapter that the use of new technologies can blur the distinctions between these *narrower* and *broader* conceptions of production and of creativity: what counts as a 'text' – or indeed as a creative work of art – becomes subject to a wide variety of definitions. On the other hand, the use of such terms can also reflect an enthusiastic fuzziness of thinking promulgated by the market; and it may neglect the distinctive challenges of cultural production for young people in favour of a romanticized notion of children's 'natural creativity'.

In fact, there is now a growing body of empirical research into young people's production of popular cultural forms, both within and beyond the context of formal schooling. For example, the work of the Cockpit Cultural Studies Department, which used photography with working-class young people on the margins of the education system, is now well-documented (see Cohen, 1990; Dewdney and Lister, 1988). There are several ethnographic accounts of young people's creative productions, most notably in the area of popular music, such as the detailed Swedish study *In Garageland* (Fornas, Lindberg and Sernhede, 1995). In addition, action research studies of media education classrooms have also analyzed students' work in a broad range of media forms, including video, photostories and magazines (see Buckingham and Sefton-Green, 1994: Buckingham, Grahame and Sefton-Green, 1995).

While these approaches are complementary, their focus is slightly different. Like Willis, the work of the Cockpit focuses primarily on the cultural politics of style and resistance; whereas the action research studies in which we ourselves have been involved have focused more directly on the question of what and how students might be *learning* from such activities. Nevertheless, all this work points to significant tensions between the skills and competencies that young people might develop by themselves with peers or in other informal social networks, and those that need to be *taught* – whether within the formal environment of the school or the more informal one of the youth club. Such work has also sought to develop a more fully theorized notion of creativity in the context of collaborative media production, which goes beyond the asocial and somewhat mystical terms in which this is often defined.

What tends to remain unacknowledged here is the fact that students will now bring with them into school a whole body of knowledge, skills, competencies and ambitions derived from their out-of-school experience of computers. As we shall see, this can cause practical difficulties in itself; but it also has much wider pedagogical implications. From our perspective as media educators, it requires us to consider the *relationships between* young people's 'informal' cultural competencies (as consumers and users of digital multimedia technology in the context of leisure) and the ways in which these competencies might be used and developed in formal schooling, particularly through the 'creative' uses of technology in arts subjects. Thus, there is a need to investigate the ways in which young people might draw on their 'informal' cultural competencies in their work at school, and how their experiences of the formal curriculum might then impact back on their leisure uses of the technology. It was the first of these issues, framed by the larger contexts described above, which became the focus of the research reported here.

This question of the relationship between home and school uses of computers has been investigated from the inverse perspective, most notably in the study by Giacquinta, Bauer and Levin (1993) on educational computing in the home. Undertaken over ten years ago, when computers were seen by many as a solution for wider social concerns about illiteracy and declining educational standards, this study explored the ways in which computers were used in middle-class American homes for what the authors call 'educational computing'. Their findings, which are in many ways parallel to our own, in fact show little evidence of this sort of activity; and much of their work discusses the relationship between the family and schools as responsible for what the authors see as a *gap*. While our own approach was not so concerned to provide evidence of an educational *problem*, and while the study needs reconsideration in the light of technological change, we will be returning to some of its findings later in our discussion.

The Research Method

We set out to explore the creative use of new technologies within two contrasting school communities. Basing our work in schools met several aims. First of all, as we have noted, we were interested in the relationships between informal and formal uses of the technology – that is, between the context of the home and the peer group on the one hand, and the school on the other. Second, on the basis of previous accounts of computer cultures, we were interested in the role of peer networks; and although friendship groups are not exclusively school-based, they are considerably influenced by schools.[1] Given the discussion about youth and creativity, noted above, we were particularly interested in young people of secondary school age, and we chose two contrasting schools in order that we could investigate the role of social class in determining access to new technology.

The first school (Northfields) is a well-resourced mixed county comprehensive situated in an affluent middle-class suburb of North London. The second (Southfields) is a mixed secondary modern school situated in a traditional working-class dormitory suburb in Kent on the outskirts of South London. Northfields draws from a wide range of ethnic communities, whereas Southfields is substantially white.

We devised an approach which progressively focused on individuals who might be using new technology extensively at home. This technique was devised partially in order to locate such 'unrepresentative' individuals in the first place; but it also enabled us to set them within a more broad-ranging picture of the school populations as a whole. We therefore began by carrying out a survey of the ways in which students in both schools used digital technology in the home. A questionnaire was administered to about 1500 students in total and covered the following areas:

- demographic facts about the respondent (age, sex, class, etc.);
- the availability of media technologies in the home (TVs, computers, etc.);
- their sources of information about digital technologies (magazines, TV, etc.);
- their involvement in 'consuming' digital technologies, for example through playing computer games;
- the nature of their creative uses of digital technology (graphics, animation, music, etc.).

The results from this survey were analyzed and about 45 students in each school were then selected for interview in small groups comprising three or four students of the same age. These were students we identified as being 'high users' of digital technology for creative purposes. In particular we talked to students whose survey responses indicated that they used computers for graphics work, animation and possibly music or video production. These discussions were open-ended in nature, covering issues such as the following:

- exactly how much, and what sort of, digital production work these students were doing at home;
- the particular software/hardware configurations which were being used;
- who had taught them how to use the relevant programs;
- how the use of computers was encouraged or regulated by parents and peers;
- the extent to which digital production as an activity, or the results of it, were shared among wider family or friendship networks.

Finally we were able to visit four homes and observe these students working *in situ*. This gave us a clearer idea of the limitations and possibilities of particular configurations of the technology, and of the social and interpersonal contexts in which the work was carried out. We also talked to their parents to gain a more rounded picture of the family context and to probe their aspirations surrounding their children's uses of new technology.

Each of these three stages – the survey, the small group discussions and the home visits – enabled us to gain different insights into a complex picture. To some extent, the use of different methodological approaches did make possible a degree of triangulation; although our discussion also draws attention to the limitations of information gleaned from only one approach. The following account is organized around the major themes that emerged from our enquiry. Throughout, we attempt to integrate critical commentary with an appraisal of methodological reliability, which remains an especially sensitive issue in any research with young people.

Facts and Figures

The survey was administered during whole school tutorial time to both school populations in the summer term 1995 when both years 11 and 13 had left after taking their terminal examinations. In the end this left us with a relatively equal spread of respondents in Years 7–10: only 4.5 per cent of our responses were from Year 12. We can thus feel confident that our enquiry reflects the perspectives of school students aged 11–15. It will be seen later that the picture of early and mid-adolescent life which emerged is significantly particular to these age ranges. It leaves further scope for looking at both younger children, pre-adolescents and the 16+ age range more generally defined as *youth*.

The overall picture of the sample obtained from the survey is contained in the tables below. Only 1165 of returned surveys (from 1500 administered) were usable in the end, of which a small proportion were incomplete. The lower number of returns for Year 9, and for Southfields, was due to a difficulty in administering surveys to that year group in that school. Answers relating to demographic facts, and to ownership, interest in and usage of new technology were coded. 'Digital production', therefore, refers to the extent of respondents' use of new technology for creative purposes, such as graphics, animation, video editing and music production. The category of 'high interest in technology' refers to a question about the respondents' reading of magazines or TV programmes about new technology and computers.

Age	
Year 7	
(11–12 years old)	26.9%
Year 8	
(12–13 years old)	14.9%
Year 9	
(13–14 years old)	14.9%
Year 10	
(14–15 years old)	25.2%
Year 12	
(17+ years old)	4.5%
Family size	
2–4	60.1%
5–6	29.3%
6+	10.6%
Sex	
Female	49.5%
Male	50.5%
Class	
Working	39.7%
Middle	51.2%
School	
Northfields	56.1%
Southfields	43.9%

Table 4.1 Demographic composition of the sample by percentage (missing observations not reported).

Chi-square tests (which allow one to relate two or more variables to common sense expectations) indicated that there were more middle-class children at Northfields and more working-class children at Southfields $\{X_2. (1) = 75.90, p<.0001\}$. This tallied with staff knowledge and perceptions about the composition of both schools. This was further borne out by the fact that there were significant differences in the quantity of media technology available in the students' homes: respondents at Northfields reported a high level of media technology in their homes, while the respondents in Southfields reported the reverse. These basic class differences reflect national statistics, for example as obtained in the National Household Survey.[2] This pattern of availability has predictable implications for the *use* of technology: our 'high digital producers' – that is, children who claimed they used computers at home at least for graphics work, and possibly for animation and music also – were also those who had a higher than average quantity of media technology in the

	Digital Production			Interest	Access to Technology		
	Low	Medium	High	High	Little	Average	A Lot
Age							
11–12	129	52	72	25	46	155	110
	23.6%	27.2%	32.6%	21.2%	35.7%	24.0%	28.6%
	51.0%	20.6%	28.5%		14.8%	49.8%	35.4%
12–13	140	45	68	38	35	191	104
	25.6%	23.6%	30.8%	32.2%	27.1%	29.6%	27.9%
	55.3%	17.8%	26.9%		10.6%	57.9%	31.5%
13–14	105	37	32	21	8	100	66
	19.2%	19.4%	14.5%	17.8%	6.2%	15.5%	17.1%
	60.3%	21.3%	18.4%		4.6%	57.5%	37.9%
15–16	137	47	45	33	37	165	89
	25.1%	24.6%	20.4%	28.0%	28.7%	25.6%	23.1%
	59.8%	20.5%	19.7%		12.7%	56.7%	30.6%
17+	35	10	4	1	3	34	16
	6.4%	5.2%	1.8%	0.8%	2.3%	5.3%	4.2%
	71.4%	20.4%	8.2%		5.7%	64.2%	30.2%
Family Size							
2–4	349	121	111	66	75	410	212
	63.9%	63.4%	50.2%	55.9%	58.6%	63.6%	55.1%
	60.1%	20.8%	19.1%		10.8%	58.8%	30.4%
5–6	149	54	77	44	40	178	120
	27.3%	28.3%	34.8%	37.3%	31.3%	27.6%	31.2%
	53.2%	19.3%	27.4%		11.8%	52.7%	35.5%
6+	48	16	33	8	13	57	53
	8.8%	8.4%	14.9%	6.8%	10.3%	8.8%	13.8%
	49.5%	16.5%	34.0%		10.6%	46.3%	43.1%
Sex							
Female	300	97	76	17	79	333	161
	55.2%	50.8%	34.4%	14.4%	61.7%	51.8%	41.9%
	63.4%	20.5%	16.1%		13.8%	58.1%	28.1%
Male	243	94	145	101	49	310	223
	44.8%	49.2%	65.6%	85.6%	38.3%	48.2%	58.1%
	50.4%	19.5%	30.1%		8.4%	53.3%	38.3%
Class							
Working	191	78	87	48	68	254	139
	38.5%	44.8%	43.1%	43.6%	58.6%	43.1%	39.7%
	53.7%	21.9%	24.4%		14.8%	55.1%	30.2%
Middle	305	96	115	62	48	335	211
	61.5%	55.2%	56.9%	56.4%	41.4%	56.9%	60.3%
	59.1%	18.6%	22.3%		8.1%	56.4%	35.5%
School							
Northfields	379	119	127	56	37	374	241
	69.4%	62.3%	57.5%	47.5%	28.7%	58.0%	62.6%
	60.6%	19.0%	20.3%		5.7%	57.4%	37.0%
Southfields	167	72	94	62	92	271	144
	30.6%	37.7%	42.5%	52.5%	71.3%	42.0%	37.4%
	50.2%	21.6%	28.2%		18.1%	53.5%	28.4%

Table 4.2 Results of the survey by number of cases observed (missing observations not reported)
The figures refer to:
- number of cases observed
- percentage of column per subsection
- percentage of row per subsection

in that order.

home. As the quantity of media technology in the home was higher at Northfields than Southfields, it is reasonable to assume that children from middle-class homes were more likely to be advantaged in being high digital producers.

However, this apparently straightforward finding is directly contradicted by the fact a higher percentage of respondents at Southfields claimed to be high digital producers than at Northfields. This might suggest that some of the survey responses were misleading; and this was confirmed by some of the subsequent discussion groups – especially at Southfields – where it emerged that some respondents who had claimed to be high digital producers in fact were not. Common sense might suggest that the young people had deliberately misled us, either because young people tell lies as a matter of course (as some of the parents and teachers we came across helpfully pointed out) or perhaps because the administration of the survey may have encouraged students to compete with one another.

However, there is a further possible reason here, which raises some more fundamental issues. In the follow-up discussions, we were particularly struck by the way in which students answered questions about their own activities from the point of view of their machines. When asked if they made animations, they often implied that they did; but when pressed, they admitted that they *could*; and when pushed further, said that their *machines* could, even if they did not actually know how to do this themselves. This is, in our view, symptomatic of the ways in which computers are often talked about: the key concern is not so much what they are used for, or what their users have done with them, but what they are theoretically capable of – according to the market specifications.

Finally we come to the question of gender. Again, our results were perhaps predictable. Males were more interested than females in the broader culture of new technologies; and there were significantly more males who were high digital producers than might be expected by chance $\{X_2. (2) = 27.49, p < .0001\}$. Again this pattern is supported by the other correlates of interest, social class and access to technology in the home.[3] About 30 per cent of the participants in the small group discussions were girls, although none of these volunteered to be visited at home.[4] We were thus left with the picture of high digital producers being predominantly male, even though the spread is not quite as one-sided as some commentators have suggested.

Despite its relatively small size, this survey does offer some suggestive indications about the extent and distribution of computer use in the home. One-third of our students had access to a high quantity of media technology; and a fifth claimed to be actively involved in using digital equipment for media production. On the other hand, only 10 per cent appeared to be avidly interested in the subject, to the extent of watching relevant television programmes, buying magazines or following trends. Perhaps predictably, social class and gender played a substantial role in determining levels of access to, and interest in, these technologies; and in these respects, the new digital elite would appear to be just as exclusive as any other cultural elite. Interestingly, family size proved to be the key variable in that it appears to be inversely linked to digital production, interest and access; although smaller families may well be over-represented among the middle-class group. However, our small group discussions also suggested new perspectives through which we might want to interpret these phenomena.

Inside the Digital Bedroom: Technological Configurations

Some of the students' homes seemed (at least to us) amazingly well-provisioned: a number spoke of having two or three PCs in the house, in addition to games consoles – although this was predictably dependent on social class and on family size. Nevertheless, this equipment was rarely for the exclusive use of the students we interviewed: of necessity, expensive equipment had to be shared with siblings and parents. Although several students had a powerful machine in their bedroom, this was often on loan from the family; or it entailed their bedroom being used as a common space. More often than not, the computer was located in a more public part of the house: a study, annexe or below stairs/spare room space, sometimes specifically demarcated for the children's use.

This shared use of computers often led to a pedagogic relationship between members of the household, where older brothers, dads, and more rarely mums and sisters, taught younger members how to use the equipment. Sometimes older relatives, especially those in full-time employment but living at home, had bequeathed cast-off machines to our respondents. In some cases, shared usage had led to friction and competition; but most of our interviewees implied that this process had settled down, and that guidelines about family usage were enforced through voluntary self-policing.

In general there were two kinds of equipment in use. First, there was the new or newish PC with *Windows* installed, with at least a 386 processor chip. Second, some respondents had an *Amiga* or *Atari ST*, often up to 5 or 6 years old, but nevertheless computers which could double up as production machines or work stations *and* games machines. More often than not, the households had already begun a process of technological specialization, in which particular spaces and machines had been reserved for single purpose use, such as word processing or games playing. This is particularly ironic given the multi-purpose potential of the modern PC – a theme which is strongly emphasized in marketing; but it also shows the way in which the 'moral economy of the household' can influence technological configurations (Silverstone and Hirsch, 1992).

For students with access to PCs, the ubiquity of *Windows* was overwhelming and – we are tempted to add – restrictive. Although many students were fluent word processors, the graphics *Paintbrush* program in *Windows* does not allow the same range of manipulation of shape, colour, form and texture as the

Deluxe Paint program many had installed on *Amigas*. In the case of the latter, many students had also experimented with elementary animations, which are easily added onto the *Amiga* program in modular fashion. On the PC, making music was limited to programs like *Octamed* or *Jukebox*, which allow one to write on musical staves and to get different instruments to play the same notes. Only a few students had their home computers linked up with MIDI and used the computer as a home mixing desk. Some students talked about the ways in which a module on the Nintendo *Super Mario Paint* allowed them to transpose pre-recorded musical sounds onto different instruments, in a similar manner to the PC.

We will return to this issue of the potential implicit within certain technological configurations of program and machine, but three more general observations are relevant at this stage. First of all, many parents (that is, purchasers) saw the potential of computers essentially in terms of hardware. They felt that money needed to be spent once and once only, on the kit. While this is not at all unreasonable in view of the cost and the marketing strategies which are employed, experienced users of computers know that it is the range of software available which significantly determines what the machine can do. This same principle emerged in the study by Giacquinta *et al* (1993) referred to above, which found that parents did not know how to support their children's use of the computer beyond what the child could find out from its peers.

Second, the market strength of *Windows* is effectively a monopoly, and for hard-up young people, this significantly limits their access to a broader range of programs. By contrast, we came to sympathize with the rather romanticised view of the '*Amiga* moment' which looks back fondly at this machine as a democratizing agent of change. The *Amiga* was 'the people's machine', not least because the software was cheap or easily copied, and was often available in the public domain or on the front covers of magazines. This last source had furnished one boy with video titling software and is a good indication of how software might be used and exchanged outside the market hegemony of *Windows*.

The third issue raised by the students' use of software packages is the tension between the easily usable pre-prepared aspects and the ability to produce from scratch. In their graphics work, for example, many students appeared to rely heavily on Clip-Art – in other words, manipulating existing images from a bank of stored illustrations. Students also talked about mixing music in *Stereomaster*, which similarly uses prepared snippets of sound. In neither of these programs are the technical limitations absolute; one can add original material to the image or sound bank. Nevertheless, the students' descriptions of how they used these programs seemed to reflect what we came to call 'lego-creativity': it was possible for them to make things, but the building blocks were factory made. The theoretical reverse of this approach would be to write software for oneself; yet although the 'hacker' is now a standard youth stereotype, we did not find any students who were actually programming computers themselves.

Of course, one of the reasons why home computers have become so popular is that one does not now need the sorts of specialized skills to make the machines compliant in the way one did ten years ago. 'Multi-media authoring', as it is sometimes called, does not necessarily require a fluency in programming languages, although it does require a familiarity with the range of choices which are available. Indeed, it is interesting to note in this respect how definitions of computer literacy have shifted over the past 10–15 years. The emphasis now is no longer on programming, but on coming to terms with the increasing potential and complexity of the software. Indeed, it is conceivable that the processes involved in programming are now possible through working *within* published software programmes, rather than working *underneath* or *inside* the language of the machine itself (see Turkle, 1995).

In this respect, it is perhaps more accurate to say that there is a continuum – rather than an absolute distinction – between 'off the shelf' uses of software and programming or 'authoring' original material. Nevertheless, the students whom we interviewed were very much confined to one end of this continuum – and hence to a limited and somewhat superficial manipulation of the more obvious pre-given options made available by the programmes. This may, of course, be partly a function of age: several students talked about elder siblings or relatives who use the *Amos* programs on the *Amiga*, allowing one to make simple interactive games, but on the whole this age group seemed to find the prepared packages complicated enough.

However, it is misplaced to think of technical configurations as being confined to the main machine; peripherals can be equally important. Interestingly, we did not find any students who had access to graphics pads, thus restricting all artwork to being drawn by mouse. This is, as was noted by virtually all the students we talked to, extremely difficult. A few students had colour printers at home, but here – as with the students who had good quality black and white ones – the expense was often seen as prohibitive. None of our respondents was able to run off or print out images of any quality or quantity, which again had serious limitations for the scope of possible use. Of the students we interviewed, we found only three or four with modems and Internet connections at home. Some of these were mainly used for parents' businesses, and while one boy had had his modem confiscated for accessing pornography, the usual argument here was that they were too expensive to run. On the other hand, quite a few households had scanners – though they seemed to be semi-permanently broken – and other input devices, although we could only find one student who had linked up video input and playback to his machine at home. He was also the most sophisticated user of MIDI and other musical playback devices.

Despite such isolated cases, most of the students here reported some form of disappointment with the technology – and it is worth emphasizing that many of them came from families which were, by any standards, comfortably off. As many of the students recognized themselves, the machines they had at home promised more than they were capable of delivering. Thus, many identified lack of RAM or hard disk size as delimiting the kind of work that they could produce. One student spoke quite poignantly of a Utopian role for the school in this respect:

> if there was a place where you could share your ideas with people and they wouldn't turn you away, like a place where everyone could use a computer, like with massive memory, where everyone could save something and share your work . . .

We are not suggesting that this rather wistful observation implies that these students did not derive any pleasure or sense of achievement from the work they had carried out on computers; but that in talking about it, such pleasures seemed less salient than a sense of frustrated possibilities. This fantasy of a place to share one's ideas, and to play in the luxury of 'massive memory', is one that suggests a fruitful role for schools and other community centres.

'Mucking About with Pictures'

Possibly the most surprising result of our survey was the proportion of young people, especially from the lower age range, who indicated that they were high digital producers. On the basis of casual observations and previous research, we had expected to find no more than a couple of these (across the whole age range) in any school. In fact we categorized nearly 20 per cent of our sample as high producers, on the grounds that they claimed to be using computers for media production of some kind; and this included 26.4 per cent of Year 7 students, as opposed to 5.1 per cent of Year 10. The students we then selected for the small group discussions had indicated that they used computers at home for at least one of the following: graphics work, music production, animation, video editing or surfing the Internet.

What became clear very quickly in these discussions, however, was that our definition of what constituted digital production and the students' were very different. Whereas we were interested in the systematic use of digital technology for production purposes, it became clear that this implicit model was at least somewhat misplaced. Our model was implicitly derived from the descriptions of cultural production in the academic studies of Willis or McRobbie, discussed above; and perhaps, beyond that, from more traditional conceptions of artistic production. However, when we asked students to describe what they had actually *made* on computers the most common response was that they hadn't. They drew 'just for fun . . . when I'm bored'. 'I muck about with pictures' or 'I just mess around' were almost universal responses. Even one of the more difficult animations – a sequence of a train going into a tunnel, which had taken one boy several months – had only been done because, he said, he was 'bored'. Instead of planned or structured production, the picture was of casual, occasional or time-filling activity with graphics or animation programs.

These respondents clearly used computers as a way of occupying themselves when lonely and bored. In fact, they recognized this pattern of usage and to an extent were quite happy with it. The kinds of programs we were interested in were thus valued not because of their enormous creative potential, but because of their 'fiddliness'. They were sufficiently demanding to warrant sustained attention, but accessible enough to use.

This impression that young people used computers as a kind of time filler was supported by several other repeated observations. Many students described when they would use their machines in terms of low points in the week. Thus, the production programs were most frequently used in the evenings and at weekends, when there was little else to do. We will see below how this meshes with parental regulation of the technology, but it is worth noting that these times were especially identified by the younger children (of whom there were more in the first place). Often these students expressed an indifference towards other entertainment media such as television, and it is possible that semi-structured messing about with the computer may have fulfilled similar functions. Indeed, we would suggest that this pattern and type of usage may reflect the changing nature of childhood; as studies have shown, children are now spending more and more time confined to the home, not least because of parental fears of crime and traffic accidents (see Ward, 1994).

Of course, it would be wrong to neglect the potential of such apparently aimless forms of 'messing about' or casual play, either in terms of 'creativity' or in terms of the learning that they afford. A great deal of informal computer use – from the early experimentation of the pioneers to the contemporary practice of 'surfing the Net' – involves a process of unstructured exploration: yet this is precisely how new discoveries or creative possibilities are often identified. As in discussions of children's uses of television, it is important to avoid the implication that the *only* productive uses of the medium are those which are conventionally educational and goal-oriented. Here again, we may need to move away from a notion of production as necessarily involving pre-planned, structured activity – as *work* rather than *play*. Nevertheless, there remain important qualitative differences between making fully fledged productions and this less structured kind of activity, and, we would argue, these differences are often overlooked in the excitement that surrounds new technologies.

On the Bedroom Wall: Marketplaces and Audiences

We made strenuous and repeated efforts to collect examples of work produced at home; but to little avail. We met between 60 and 70 pupils in our small discussion groups, but were given work by no more than half a dozen. There may be a number of reasons for this, some of which are methodological and might be corrected in future research. Some students may have forgotten to give us material, or may not have trusted that we would return it, or may have brought work when we were not visiting the school that day. There were also practical reasons; printers were broken or animations too large to put on disk. More significantly, there is a sense in which the context of the research may have determined what we were able to discover in this respect. Adults conducting research with children – particularly in the context of schools – inevitably invite particular kinds of 'approved' responses, and when the research is concerned with aspects of students' out-of-school culture, children might justifiably be suspicious about its motives (see Buckingham, 1993b).

However, it also became clear that despite the number of students who claimed to use these programs, they rarely seemed to make completed products. Again, some of the explanations here are technical. Frequently there did not appear to be enough hard disk space to store work. However, we felt that the root of the problem was that students of this age generally have little reason for making products in the first place.

In fact, the students' descriptions of what they actually produced were quite varied. Graphics work often entailed 'drawing' planes, comic characters like *Spiderman*, cars and designing dresses. Indeed, students who told us about this work talked about it in terms of 'doodling'; and offered self-appraisals as to whether they were good 'drawers' or not. The animations that were described would also fit into this category: there were stick people falling over, cars crashing, trains going into tunnels. In other words, the narrative content was often minimal, and was frequently an excuse to learn the program. The same attitude was apparent in the case of music. Again, we were given no products, and frequently this was accompanied by the excuse that the student was not terribly musical, but that they were just 'messing about'.

These comments raise quite explicitly the question of technical skill, not only with the computer itself, but also in more conventional modes. What kinds of skills one might need to learn in order to become a digital producer? We would argue that, while children might enjoy 'messing around' with music or graphics programs, they still need access to the conventional repertoire of competencies and aptitudes if they are to produce more complex or meaning-ful work. When compared with older technologies like crayons and paper, the computer can appear to give a degree of polish to one's work; but this is clearly rather different from developing a facility with the forms and conventions of a given mode of expression.

The second kind of work the students produced was in the form of writing, although in fact we did not ask to see any of this. What is more, most of the writing which was described was for school projects. Frequently students identified their 'best' work not as independent creative writing, but as extended projects within the formal curriculum. In this case, the role of the technology itself appeared quite literally to be superficial. The work was neatly laid out; although whether the layout had any formal correspondence with the content is a more open question. Yet even if we were not terribly interested in this work, it is significant that the students were. It clearly met their definition of what constituted *work*, namely that which is sanctioned by the formal school curriculum; it also was rewarding to produce in this form and in this sense, pleasurable to make. By contrast, the *work* we were interested in was their leisure. This would suggest that writing still holds primacy in any hierarchical structure of work and leisure, and indeed that the computer's most salient function remains the production of written text. What is more, writing on the computer is still often seen to be an issue of how the text *appears* – despite the view that word processing has fundamentally changed the cognitive processes which are involved (Heim, 1993; Lanham, 1993).

The final kind of work the students produced or described to us could be seen to belong more fully to the realm of cultural production – and indeed to that of economic production. Again this was varied. Some students helped families with design or layout related to family businesses – and indeed, several were actually familiar with the accounting program *Excel*. Some had made newsletters for local community organizations, churches or football teams. Many had made signs, often no more than enlarging type to direct parents around the school on parents' evening or embroidered names to put on the bedroom door. Within the same domestic framework, the production of birthday cards was also popular, particularly amongst girls (there are in fact dedicated programs for this purpose, which contain a bank of clip-art images).

There were only three students who described making cultural products beyond this limited domestic economy. All were boys. One (Ben, aged 14) ran a band and used a scanner at home to produce cassette box covers and posters to advertise and promote his music. He was convinced that this professional look would have career advantages. He did not use computers for actually making the music: his band is 'punkish' and the aesthetic is of instrumental or vocal authenticity, rather than technological sophistication. He did, however, use his father's *CompuServe* account to join rock music newsgroups. The second boy (Dean, 12) had made a 16 page comic or magazine (of which there was only one copy). This integrated text and pictures based around his favourite comic super heroes, as well as including quite complex animations. The third boy (Andrew, 15) produced music and video on his computer; he had put titles on his family's and friends' wedding and barmitzvah videos, as well as making quite extensive animations (albeit primarily for a friend's Computer Studies GCSE coursework). His ambition was to become a film-maker and he was knowledgeable about 'recording to video' and a number of other complex processes. He described much of this work as a sort of business. He did not get paid per commission but often received payment in kind; and this often seemed to go towards capitalizing more equipment.

Taken as a whole, the nature of these kinds of cultural production forced us to revisit some of the assumptions with which our research began. Our findings clearly do not support the claim – made by marketers and researchers alike – that the advent of the personal computer is enabling young people to become *more* creative (although of course we might well question whether such assertions could ever be proven in any case). At the same time, our research does lead us to ask what we might mean by such a term in the first place. While we would question some of the more populist notions of 'creative consumption', it is clear that the experience of digital production requires a broader, and perhaps less romantic, conception of creativity. In this respect, our conclusions are parallel to those of the Giacquinta *et al.* (1993) study, which found that the sheer availability of home computers did not itself make children use them for educational purposes – although here too, the researchers eventually came to question their received assumptions about what an 'educational purpose' might be.

Neither could we find any examples of the new 'digital aesthetic', proclaimed by some of the more enthusiastic advocates of digital production. The little work that was being done seemed conservative and rooted in older aesthetic forms and conventions. Again, we might ask ourselves whether such expectations are reasonable. Such change often works incrementally, and it will take much longer and require much more sustained attention for any shift in the means of (digital) production to give rise to any change in aesthetic form. Indeed, the notion that the technology inherently dictates a particular – and even unique – aesthetic may be little more than a form of determinism.

On the other hand, the study does suggest that there may be some blurring between the worlds of the professional and the amateur; the newsletters, signs and barmitzvah videos that might have been the preserve of small businesses in the past are now easily within reach of the dedicated hobbyist. Right across our sample, a significant number of parents were working from home, and they were obviously in a strong position to support their children's access to computers in the domestic environment. In this sense, our findings appear to confirm commonly held beliefs about the broader socio-economic processes that have surrounded digital technologies – for example, the increasing 'multi-skilling' of a small elite, and the move away from the small business into the home.

Finally, we need to consider the role of potential audiences and market-places in this discussion of creativity. In all our interviews, we repeatedly asked the students to describe their best piece of work, or a piece of which they were proud. However, very few had answers to this question, primarily because only a few had ever completed products or shared them with a wider audience. Indeed, many students referred to school projects by way of answer here, precisely because school had imposed the discipline of finishing and presenting work. However, outside of school, there are very few opportunities for distributing or exhibiting young people's cultural productions. Beyond the admiring parent, or those who might happen to see a picture stuck on the bedroom wall, there is little sense of wider possible audiences.

To some extent, of course, this is a function of age. Primarily because of their economic dependency, young people of this age are very unlikely to be active in a cultural marketplace in the first place. Although it is not unknown for younger children to be performing or producing work for a wider audience, this largely occurs within the separate province of 'youth arts'. Most studies of music-making, for example, concentrate on older youth, as Helen Cunningham's chapter in this volume and other studies (see Fornas *et al*, 1995; Willis, 1990) testify. Yet music is, in this respect at least, somewhat of an exception, since in this field it clearly is possible for young people to develop an audience for their work and to move into a professional circuit. There is no obvious or easily accessible equivalent for the other kinds of media which might be produced using this technology, at least outside of specialized *avant garde* circles. The public forums or networks simply do not exist – though there may be more opportunities of this kind in other parts of the world (see Smith, 1995 and Nissen in this volume). From this point of view, putting titles on barmitzvah videos, however conservative and limited, is one of the few kinds of opportunities which is likely to be available to young people within a supportive and parentally regulated economic framework.

The role of the school, and indeed of other formal educational institutions, is more problematic, but it may also offer more possibilities for future research and development. We did not have the opportunity to gain either school's perspective on the use of new technology within the curriculum, and this is an oversight we would like to rectify. Nevertheless, we talked to students about this issue, and their perspective was revealing. In a general sense, school is a positive influence. The community of peers and teachers does provide a potential audience for cultural products, and students can receive feedback and learn to work to deadlines. All of these things are necessary to the processes of cultural production. On the other hand, the use of technology is largely constrained and determined by the requirements of the formal curriculum. There are likely to be few opportunities for experimentation with graphics or animation programs; on the contrary, the technology will primarily be used as a means of improving the presentation of existing work. When we talked to students about the work they did on computer within the curriculum, they were predictably – and perhaps unreliably – scathing. On the one hand, they claimed that they were often more fluent users of the machines than their teachers; while on the other, they did not like the dedicated programs, such as those for design and realization, that they were taught. They were critical of front-of-class teaching styles which led them through a program, of large teaching groups and of the lack of compatibility between home and school machines. Many were also dismissive of the slower and less powerful equipment at school compared to the home.

There are many issues here which would repay closer scrutiny. None of the students' criticisms should be taken at face value – but neither should they be ignored. In particular, we were depressed by the overall emphasis in both schools on typing and presentation of written material, when students were talking to us about needing guidance on how to use animation or audio editing software. The constraints imposed by current funding policies and by centralized curriculum planning are obviously a significant limitation in this respect. Nevertheless, we would see much potential in the use of schools and youth service provision to enhance and develop the home use of computers for creative purposes. Schools can provide a form of community patronage by commissioning and showing work, and creating a sense of audience and local culture which would provide a necessary counterbalance to the individualizing potential of these technologies.

Learning the Technology

In the absence of schools fulfilling this function, it has been the family and the home which have provided the most salient context for learning digital production. In this final section, we will explore some of the ways in which the technology was mediated and regulated in the home, and the ways in which this may have hindered or assisted children's learning.

One of the first questions we asked in the small group discussion was about who had taught the students how to use the equipment. Although answers may not have been wholly reliable, two main patterns emerged. On the one hand, we had the notion of the digital autodidact. From this perspective, as some of our parents also implied, the children were seen to learn 'naturally' through fiddling or experimenting, in the same way they are assumed to learn how to speak or eat. One boy, for example, claimed that he had been given a computer when he was four 'to set him on his way'. We would not want to underestimate the potential of this method of learning; and indeed, many of the young people were proud of how much they had achieved through 'self-teaching'.

Nevertheless, they were also quite insistent about the need for a teacher figure. This was more often than not an older 'initiator', who had started off our respondents. The children's accounts of their relationship with these various initiators tended to emphasize the fact of working with an older person, in a way which appeared to reflect upon their own maturity. At Northfields, this role was often fulfilled by a more distant relative, such as a cousin or young uncle or even the friend of a sibling; whereas in the more enclosed working-class community of Southfields, it was more likely to a close relative, a parent or an older-brother or sister. The initiator was usually older except when he or she became a collaborator in middle adolescence. Thus, the older 'high producers' tended to work with friends on projects, whereas the younger ones claimed they worked alone; this was confirmed by our home visits. However, we feel this says as much about peer friendship activities as it does about computers. Mid-adolescents generally have more freedom to stay late at friends' houses than younger children; in this respect, the degree of access to computers is largely determined by other constraints on young people's leisure time.

However, this is obviously an important issue in terms of learning. As has been shown in educational contexts, working with peers enables learners to progress, whereas isolated one-to-one work at the computer screen requires a high level of competence in the first place. Although some students had members of the immediate family who were active users of IT, in general those students with access to wider family and peer networks were in a much better position in this respect. Access to specialized 'professionals' gave middle-class children a distinct advantage here. This could perhaps be seen as a particular instance of the workings of 'cultural capital' – that is, the broad set of social and educational competencies that are differentially distributed between class groups (Bourdieu, 1984).

In addition, we have to account for the role of gender here. As we have shown, most of our high producers were boys. Likewise, with the exception of a couple of mothers who were employed as clerical workers and one who was pursuing a degree in education, the rest of the initiator figures were also male. This was most clear in the case of Ben, the musician, described above. Ben's father, a solicitor, had bought computer equipment for business purposes. This included a modem and a *CompuServe* account, which the father had apparently opened in order to help him find spare parts for his American car. Promoting Ben's use of the technology seemed to provide a way of relating to his son. On the other hand, it was noticeable that where the initiator was female and working with a younger sister, work on the computer tended to be written, in a way which reinforced the role of the computer as a word processor – an extension of the typewriter. It has been observed elsewhere (Wheelock, 1992), that parents have often purchased computers for girls in order to equip them for gender-specific roles as modern secretaries – despite the ironic contradiction that such a role is disappearing (or at least significantly changing) in a computerized workforce.

The other factor affecting access is of course that of parental regulation. Many of the students indicated that buying computers was seen by their parents as a way of securing their children's educational future; this was confirmed by the parents whom we met. However, this desire to invest in their children's future was often mingled with contradiction. At one end of the spectrum, one mother said that computers were 'a necessary evil'; while at the other a father argued that all children should be taught programming. Anxieties about the negative effects of computer games were a significant factor here. One younger boy said he ended up using the graphics and animation packages because his mother would not let him play games except at weekends. By contrast, a voluble and possibly 'imaginative' group of 12-year-olds at Southfields described a keyboard code they could enter to replace the games screen with a page of writing in order to delude the casual parental observer. Another couple of boys said their mothers were concerned about physical damage (such as eyestrain) through excessive attention to the computer. However, only one student reported that his father locked away the computer (which was more strictly used for work purposes), and we only found one boy who had had his modem confiscated because of accessing pornography (or so we deduced from the giggles and embarrassment). By contrast, on all our home visits we found parents who trusted their children, and who were not worried by the Internet except in terms of phone bills. All the older children (14+) described themselves as having absolute freedom as regards when, and for how long, they had use of the equipment.

We noted as a matter of some irony that if *initiators* tended to be male, most *regulators* tended to be female. Yet again, this dimension suggests how our specialist interest raises other, more general questions about the ways in which children's leisure time, thus their culture, is structured and controlled. Equally, we were struck by the ways in which the older, more middle-class boys appeared to regulate themselves, mixing school work 'sensibly' with computer use and clearly diverging from the media stereotype of the 'computer addict'.

Conclusions

It would be at least premature to draw major conclusions from this small-scale piece of research. Nevertheless, we hope that this study will encourage a more general questioning of the kinds of claims which are typically made for the so-called digital revolution. In particular, we would challenge the idea that computers can in themselves transform young people into creative cultural producers. While computers are undoubtedly occupying an increasingly important role in young people's leisure time, factors such as age, social class and gender remain significant determinants on individuals' access to, and use of, such technology. We should look to these larger questions about social inequality before embracing the idea that the digital revolution has come of age (see Murdock and Golding, 1989).

Nevertheless, there are several more specific implications here in terms of cultural and educational policy. Above all, we need to consider the ways in which young people *learn* to use the technology. As we have noted, much can be discovered through unstructured 'messing around'; but at present, many young people are struggling to learn how to use complicated programs and machines. Whether young people can persevere to the extent that they are able to maximize the use of equipment at home would seem to be a comparatively hit-and-miss affair. In terms of creativity, we have argued that the sense of audience – the opportunity to present and exhibit work for others – is crucial. As we have suggested, computers often tend to be used merely to improve the surface presentation of creative work, and they seem to encourage a limited form of clip-art production. These are features that have been associated with postmodern aesthetics; but they could equally be attributed to an absence of skill and of audience. Schools could play a significant role here, but at present they seem to offer an unduly narrow definition of what counts as creative output – in the form of written *work* – and to neglect many of the broader opportunities which the new technology might present.

Access to home computers is possibly as important a part of the distribution of cultural capital as access to books; yet without *support and development* it can easily lead to a reinforcement of the status quo. Many parents think they are buying shares in their children's educational futures, when in reality they are merely reproducing the different levels of labour value current in our society. Without suitable software, without teaching, without opportunities to make and circulate products, young people may end up merely replicating existing social inequalities – and at the same time further feeding the profits of the big computer multinationals.

It may be that we might have uncovered more evidence of creative production work through using other methods. It may be that the creative flowering of the digital revolution has yet to arrive. Yet the authors of the study of 'educational computing' undertaken in the United States over 10 years ago presumably also thought its time had come (Giacquinta *et al*, 1993). Like them, we would argue that without the 'social envelope' surrounding the use of home computers, genuine 'educational computing' will be as rare as the creative uses of computers we set out to discover – for reasons which are to do with limitations of software, with economics and with parental guidance and control. At the same time, we may need to broaden and to rethink our assumptions about what *counts* as 'creative production' – or indeed as 'educational' computing. Yet in our view, these problems will not be resolved through abstract rhetoric, but through creative forms of social and educational policy.

Notes

An earlier version of this chapter appeared in *Convergence: The Journal of Research into New Media Technologies*, 2.2, John Libby Media at the University of Luton Press. The empirical research described here was funded by the Arts Council of England as 'Digital Visions: New Opportunities for Multimedia Literacy'. We would like to thank the Arts Council, and particularly Viv Reiss, for their support for this project; and Abigail Bilkus and Frances Berry, who conducted the statistical analysis.

1 See Cunningham (1995) for accounts of children's computer culture and James (1993) for the role of friendship groups within school settings.
2 See also Murdock and Golding (1989) for the wider argument here.
3 Although girls have less access to technology than boys, it must remain open to further investigation as to the reasons for this: is it largely a function of class or do boys have higher priority in relation to technology in the home, especially in larger families?
4 This may have been due to the fact that they felt uneasy about us visiting their homes (since we are both male); or simply because none of the girls we encountered were highly enthusiastic about working with computers.

References

Bourdieu, P. (1984) *Distinction: A Social Critique of the Judgement of Taste*, (trans. Nice, R.) London: Routledge.

Buckingham, D. (1993a) *Children Talking Television: The Making of Television Literacy*, London: Falmer Press.

Buckingham, D. (1993b) Re-reading audiences, in Buckingham D. (Ed.) *Reading Audiences: Young People and the Media*, Manchester: Manchester University Press.

Buckingham D. and Sefton-Green, J. (1994) *Cultural Studies Goes to School: Reading and Teaching Popular Media* London: Taylor and Francis.

Buckingham, D., Grahame J. and Sefton-Green, J. (1995) *Making Media: Practical Production in Media Education*, London: English and Media Centre.

Cohen, P. (1990) *Really Useful Knowledge*, London: Trentham Books.

Cunningham, H. (1995) Moral kombat and computer game girls in Bazalgette, C. and Buckingham, D. (Eds) *In Front of the Children*, London: British Film Institute.

de Certeau, M. (1984) *The Practice of Everyday Life*, Berkeley, CA: University of California Press.

Dewdney, A. and Lister, M. (1988) *Youth, Culture and Photography*, London: Macmillan.

Fiske, J. (1989) *Understanding Popular Culture*, London: Unwin Hyman.

Fornas, J., Lindberg, U. and Sernhede, O. (1995) *In Garageland: Rock, Youth and Modernity*, London: Routledge.

Giacquinta, J., Bauer, J. and Levin, J. (1993) *Beyond Technology's Promise: An Examination of Children's Educational Computing at Home*, Cambridge: Cambridge University Press.

Hebdige, D. (1979) *Subculture: the Meaning of Style*, London: Methuen.

Heim M. (1993) *The Metaphysics of Virtual Reality*, Oxford: Oxford University Press.

James, A. (1993) *Childhood Identities: Self and Social Relationships in the Experience of the Child*, Edinburgh: Edinburgh University Press.

Lanham, R. (1993 *The Electronic Word: Democracy, Technology and the Arts*, Chicago, IL: University of Chicago Press.

McRobbie, A. (1994) *Postmodernism and Popular Culture*, London: Routledge.

Murdock, G. and Golding, P. (1989) Information poverty and political inequality: Citizenship in the age of privatised communications, *Journal of Communication*, **39**(3), 180–95.

Silverstone, R. and Hirsch, E. (Eds) (1992) *Consuming Technologies: Media and Information in Domestic Space*, London: Routledge.

Smith, G. (1995) 'Digital graffiti', *Wired*, June 1.03, (u.s.) 60.

Turkle, S. (1995) *Life on the Screen: Identity on the Age of the Internet*, New York: Simon & Shuster.

Ward, C. (1994) Opportunities for childhoods in late twentieth-century Britain, in Mayall, B. *Children's Childhoods Observed and Experienced*, London: Falmer Press.

Wheelock, J. (1992) Personal computers, gender and an institutional model of the household, in Silverstone and Hirsch (Eds) *Consuming Technologies: Media and Information in Domestic Space*, London: Routledge.

Willis, P. (1990) *Common Culture: Symbolic Work at Play in the Everyday Cultures of the Young*, Milton Keynes: Open University Press.

Chapter 5

Making Connections: Young People and the Internet

Chris Abbott

Introduction

The history of writing may be complex and obscure but it tells a straightforward story: that the capability to communicate through forms of writing has become increasingly widespread. Although throughout history human beings have made marks or constructed artefacts – the sooty imprints of a human hand on a cave wall, the scratched letters on a medieval window or a letter carefully written on vellum – nevertheless, for most of this time, only those who were privileged in some way had the means to publish widely. Even then the potential readership, writers (or at least publishers) could reach was always constrained by the number of physical copies of the book or other artefact which were produced. Today, however, there is much to suggest that modern societies have reached a new stage in the relationship between writer, publisher and reader with the recent rise of electronic and digital publishing.

The potential significance of this paradigm shift has vexed a number of critics from a variety of perspectives, given the intricate sets of relationships between literacy and democracy as well as wider arguments about how full participation in society may be dependent on access to, or ownership of, the means of production. In this context of 'a struggle between literate and oral worlds . . . between controlling literacy and disenfranchised orality', Richard Lanham (1993:71) has characterized such a shift as 'a democratic movement from big to small, impersonal to personal, citadel to coat pocket' (1993:200). Similarly, Howard Rheingold (1993) has extolled what amounts to a populist revolution in computer linked communities in his extensive account of worldwide Internet use. A strong thread in these perspectives is an attention to the new kinds of participation and communication – even the new kinds of social existence (Turkle, 1995) – made possible by the advent of the Internet and in particular the World Wide Web.

On one level the World Wide Web can be viewed as the latest development of an existing entity, the Internet, but I will argue that it is much more appropriate to see it as a new medium. Where the Internet was largely textual, almost wholly owned by the academic community and serious in tone for the most part, the Web is open to all, uses a wide range of media and is often frivolous, recreational or commercial. The Web is possible due to HTML (Hypertext Markup Language), the language in which Web pages are written and which underpins the Web. Unlike previous programming languages, HTML runs across all computer platforms: a page designed on an IBM-compatible PC and then made available on the Web can be viewed on an Apple Macintosh or even on a British Acorn RISC-OS computer. It is also a genuinely multimedia language in that it can easily combine text, sound, image and moving image. This is particularly important, both because it sets common standards in what is a competition driven market place and because it effectively functions as a kind of global language, thus releasing participants from geographical constraints and allowing easy international communication. Its relative simplicity also enhances the notion of open access for all.

Most of the publicity about the Web, and much of the public perception of its use, has concentrated on the information that can be received through it and associated concerns about inappropriate material. In particular young people have been constructed as potential victims of this aspect of the Net. In September 1996, for example, a children's charity launched an education campaign to protect young users from paedophiles and pornography at the same time as newspapers carried accounts of research by Stockholm University citing 5561 alleged postings of child porn (Beard, 1996). Issues of regulation and control have become a live political concern. These issues connect the Web with a whole history of anxieties around popular culture from novels and comics to cinema and TV, and from this point of view embed its development in very traditional social concerns. The revolutionary side of the Web, by comparison, is the ability it offers writers to become their own publishers. I want to show how it has vastly increased the opportunities available to young people in large areas of the developed world to communicate amongst themselves.

Poetry, autobiographical writing, opinion and polemic have always been generated and transmitted by young people. Yet today such material is being produced and published on the Web, and being read and enjoyed there. This fundamental ability – allowing young people to actually (virtually) reach sympathetic readers – is qualitatively different from non-digital output because publishing on the Web creates *communities* of readers and writers in ways that are very difficult to do in print – especially for this age group. Indeed, this feature of the Web was seized on by young people, particularly in the USA and then in Europe, who were quick to experiment with its more interactive uses; by late 1994 the phenomenon of the World Wide Web homepage had developed. One way of viewing this would be to see it as nothing less than a world-wide boom in vanity publishing on a previously unheard-of scale. However, I want to suggest that it is much more significant than this notion allows.

In general my argument is that publishing on the Web for young people is motivated by the desire to participate in, or create, some kind of 'community'. This chapter will begin by exploring some of the literature which is beginning to theorize the (paradoxical) concept of an online community and find ways of modifying such work for the specific concerns of young people. I will then describe the ways in which earlier uses of the Net developed live communication, paying particular attention to the discursive forms codified in synchronous electronic communication such as Internet Relay Chat. Although taking place in written form, the texts of these conversations, I shall argue, represent the embryonic shape for fully-fledged Web publishing. I will show how this explicitly dialogic dimension to synchronous communication has been recuperated in the textual forms found in young people's homepages – all of which indicate an urge for community, in the sense of being together, of sharing discussion and *communing* with like minded individuals. Publishing here is an attempt to speak directly *with* rather than *to* the audience. In this respect the Web begins to blur the distinction between conversation and publishing as distinct forms of communication: speaking online takes a written form and writing in cyberspace almost has an oral function.

Research into Online Communities

It could be argued that young Web publishers represent an identifiable community which, although not geographically linked, has all the other characteristics of what some writers (Jones, 1995) have come to describe as cybersocieties. Jones quotes Etzioni's (1991) definition of the key characteristics of a community as being 'scope', 'substance' and 'dominance'. If we apply these aspects to Web publishing we find a high degree of compliance. The Web publishing community has a defined scope: it consists of those people who have access to the reading and writing tools and the necessary technology to make use of these. The substance, as has been shown, is highly differentiated and specific to this community, in that it deals with topics and references of interest to readers. Lastly, subtle and pervasive strategies of dominance underpin the community in the form of software upgrades leading to high dominance for those who use the latest plug-ins or add-ons. Even an educational body such as the UK School Curriculum and Assessment Authority tells readers of its Web page that they should have the latest version of the *Netscape Navigator* browser in order to see their site to its best effect. Where young Web page designers are concerned, these pressures are seen in similar references to their preferred browsers, and the team loyalty which has sprung up around the 'battle' between *Netscape Navigator* and *Microsoft Internet Explorer*. Ownership of a page requiring the latest *RealAudio* or streamed video plug-in not only transmits a certain image to readers, it also leads them to feel they should also be using these technologies.

In the preface to his book, Jones (1995) describes computer-mediated communication (CMC) as 'one means . . . with which we can fly in and out of societies' and it is easy to understand the attraction of this for many writers. Much of the book is given up to research into different on-line communities and the rationale for describing them as such. Although writing before the development of the Web, Jones could be talking about the creation of homepages when he says:

> Because these machines are seen as 'linking' machines . . . they inherently affect the ways we think of linking up to each other, and thus they fit squarely into our concerns about society. Media technologies that have largely been tied to the 'transportation' view of communication mentioned earlier were developed to overcome space and time. The computer, in particular, is an 'efficiency' machine, purporting to ever increase its speed. But unlike those technologies, the computer used for communication is a technology to be understood from the 'ritual' view of communication, for once time and space have been overcome (or at least rendered surmountable) the spur for development is connection, linkage. Once we can surmount time and space and 'be' anywhere, we must choose a 'where' at which to be, and the computer's functionality lies in its power to make us organise our desires about the spaces we visit and stay in (Jones, 1995:32)

Nevertheless, it isn't just the ability to move through time and space that defines the computer's communicative abilities so much as its huge range of generated texts. From this perspective, the texts, traces of conversation and writing, are crucial to any analysis of online community. Within this perspective I would identify two important approaches. First, the move away from an emphasis on authorial intent towards reader–response theories within linguistics and textual analysis has lent itself readily to making sense of cybertexts. Where previous researchers have argued that any text is incomplete until it engages with a reader, cybertexts not only do this but can be interacted with to such an extent that they are changed for the next reader. An example of this would be the Guest Book phenomenon, now widely seen on homepages and discussed later in this chapter.

Second, the field of sociolinguistics has much to offer the potential researcher in this area, as has been noted by other writers, such as De Landa (1994). He describes the facility that sociolinguistics offers for studying language variety, diversity and change, and the ways in which sociolinguists have studied group selection procedures:

> Perhaps, once linguists become population thinkers and users of virtual environments, we may witness the emergence of an entirely different type of science of language, one that would be able to explain the dynamic genesis of a new language . . . Perhaps one day linguists will be required to test their theories in a virtual environ-

ment of interacting intentional entities, so that the rules of grammar they postulate for a language can be shown to emerge spontaneously from the dynamics of a population of speakers . . . (De Landa 1994:276–7).

Indeed, McLaughlin, Osborne and Smith (1995) justify their description of Usenet authors (early Internet chat groups) as a virtual community along these lines. They identify the key principles of 'discourse processes' and 'social structures' (p. 94) found within these early forms of computer mediated communication (CMC) and make the case that finding such data constitutes defining CMC as evidence of a kind of community, 'discourse processes generate social structures, which in turn affect discourse processes' (p. 94). Thus, participants in Usenet are seen as part of a common body if they all appear to use particular language terms or phrases, or share a common mechanism for dealing with particular forms of behaviour what the authors call 'conduct-correcting episodes . . . reflecting the self-regulating nature of the network' (p. 95). One of the most common manifestations of this is the practice of 'spamming', the sending of large numbers of abusive or long e-mails to people who post inappropriate or unhelpful messages to a newsgroup. Discussion about whether or not spamming is necessary may take place in the newsgroup and the action that may follow has some of the aspects of a group response, even though it emanates from a series of individuals. Applying the same test to Web authors would appear to be fertile ground for study and this is the subject of ongoing research by the present writer.

However, the central question as to whether Web pages are forms of publication or conversation is also raised by the same writers when they suggest that an alternative way of conceptualizing Usenet is as 'a magazine'. This is despite the fact it is simultaneously a medium for 'talk'. Indeed, it may be that the extension of the concept of 'gossip' into media texts such as soap operas or magazines may be useful here (Dyer *et al*, 1981). Consuming media texts, it is argued has to an extent 'replaced' the dynamic of interpersonal social encounters and therefore changed contemporary notions of what it might mean to participate in a community. For example, McLaughlin *et al* (1995) refer to the large number of 'lurkers', readers who never contribute to the discussion in their discussion. Although they chose not to pursue this line of research, it is impossible to ignore when considering the relationship between Web publishing and its 'community' of readers. The lurkers are part of the community even if they do not contribute in the same way as more active participants. Indeed if we extend the metaphors in use here, we have to also ask whether it might not be more accurate to describe the lurker as a casual reader. The blurring of definitions also raises the further paradox of what happens to talk when it is written down (or transcribed). Can this kind of *talk* actually be described as *writing* despite the fact that many linguists have shown that writing actually utilizes different structures and genres from those used in oral communication (Ong, 1982)?

Multi-User Domains (MUDs)

However, much of the published research to date into the question of online communities (see Dery, 1994; Ludlow, 1996; Shields, 1996) has not actually examined publishing, but has been concerned with MUDs: Multi-User Domains or Dungeons (depending on which author is providing the definition). Participants in these role-playing games adopt identities which may be extremely complex, with fully researched and written life stories. They may assume this identity over many months, with the character in question seeming more and more real to them and to the online participants with whom they interact.

Rather than concentrating on the MUD in terms of writing, much speculation has accrued around the philosophical questions of identity and what is at stake in belonging to a virtual community. Much has been made of the contradictions implicit in the notion of 'being' in a virtual world (Bromberg, 1996), and the most extensive 'ethnographies' in this field, such as Rheingold (1993) or Turkle (1995) have focused on similar kinds of questions. At the same time, well known MUDs like the LamdaMOO and notorious incidents such as the harassment of a female user of one of these MUDs have received an inordinate amount of attention at the expense of sustained investigation of the phenomenon in general (see Turkle 1995:250–4). Indeed, generalizing from exceptional events and attempting to develop a uniform theory about the meaning of MUDs in relation to behaviour IRL – in real life – typifies 'cybertheory'.

The concept of community in MUDs is not therefore built upon evidence about the participants, but more upon extrapolations from the texts themselves. It is important to draw attention to this methodological problem because claims for the significance of MUDs have largely come from privileged investigators working primarily in North America. Equally importantly, although University culture is taken to be central to the MUD community, especially that at MIT, most of the participants studied to date have been adults. Most of the collections of work in this area (Dery, 1994; Jones, 1995; Ludlow, 1996; Shields, 1996) seem to be talking about older university students, the age group most likely to have the time, the inclination and the access to develop on-line lives. By contrast, the study described here is an investigation of publishing by and for younger people; and this difference should make us wary about simply drawing from the notions of community developed in the study of MUDs. My starting point for this discussion of community is not, however, the Web pages themselves but the linguistic forms of real time chat (albeit written) initially developed by young people five or six years ago.

Synchronous Electronic Communication

As I have suggested, one of the areas of the Internet that many young people discovered and found welcoming before the arrival of the World Wide Web was the ability to chat to other users in real time. Synchronous electronic communication has been possible for several years, principally through the use of Internet Relay Chat (IRC). IRC, and other facilities which have been part of the portfolio of utilities offered by on-line information services such as *CompuServe* and *America Online*, were the first sites of real language development and invention on the Internet, with many of the strategies developed then carrying on to Web homepages.

Attempting to codify this language is fraught with difficulties, not least because of the transitory nature of the discourse and the inability of the observer to identify and encode the participants in any meaningful way. All that one has is the text – although this can be a rich and densely packed resource for the researcher interested in language forms, gate-keeping and jargon.

One early development in these synchronous chats was the use of punctuation marks to indicate tone, emotion or intention. *Emoticons*, as they have become known, are constructed from punctuation marks and other keyboard characters. They are read, as it were, with the head leaning on the left shoulder. Although many hundreds have been devised, some of the most common are:

:-)	humour
;-)	indication of disbelief
:-p	putting tongue out
:-D	said with a smile
:-(	unhappy

Acronyms seem more generally understood and used than emoticons, perhaps because they can be typed more quickly and easily. Among the most commonly used are:

BTW	by the way
OTO	on the other hand
OIC	oh, I see!
IMHO	in my humble opinion (used sarcastically)
ROTFL	rolling on the floor laughing

Both emoticons and acronyms were widely used by young people in the early 1990s, the date of the transcript below. By the mid 1990s, however, when many more people of a much wider age-range were using the facilities, most young people seemed to be dropping the use of either emoticons or acronyms except for a few perennial favourites such as :) to indicate that a comment is not totally serious, or ;) if it is flirtatious. One explanation for this could be that the wide discussion of these strategies on the Internet and in some other sections of the media meant that they were no longer effective as gatekeeping devices to keep outsiders away, or as a code to create a bond of common interest. It remains to be seen whether the rapid expansion into other media forms on Web pages will remove the need for textual devices such as emoticons and acronyms.[1]

The following transcript was logged on the CB (Citizens' Band) area of *CompuServe* within a teen chat area. The participants were aware that the transcriber, and many other non-contributing participants, were lurking on the channel. All participants claimed to be male and within the teens and twenties age range, although this may or may not have been accurate. The age range involved, 13–29, is thus almost the same as that involved in my present research into young people and their homepages (12–25 years). The following transcripts were logged in 1993 and 1994.

The transcript begins with the use of an emoticon by *W* to indicate his frame of mind, and a rather desultory conversation about Canada follows, with a healthy disregard for spelling and other rules, apart from the upper case letter C for Canada.

W: i don't care really b'cos this poem is golden:)
S: I'm in Canada . . . don't have states . . . we have provinces
M: oh man
S: Ottawa
G: were exactly in Can

An interesting interjection follows with the dialogue between *S* and *G* being complained about by *M* and then interrupted in novel form by *S*, who sings a line from a Beatles song. To indicate he is singing, he brackets the words with a pictogram of a musical note created from three keyboard characters.

M: you are hurting me *W*
S: o/~ help! I need sombody! o/~

D then arrives and greets everyone with the 'What's up?' salutation which is almost universal in this context. Interestingly, he adds a literary construct regarding his viewing of the CB channel as a trail to wander down.

D: what's up on the CB trail
G: Senato
W: sorry *M* but this is fun
G: your Senators suck
M: can u give me a break
H: whose senators
G: Ottawa

Apparently bored by this discussion of Canadian politics, *S* sings another line.

S: o/~ Help me if you can, I'm feeling down, o/~
W: i dunno mark you brought this on yourself
G: Hockey team

W uses the convention of a pictogram arrow to indicate what he is doing or feeling rather than to say something; *S* goes on singing. *P* and *X* arrive and are greeted as they join the conversation.

W:	<--helping *S*
	:)
P:	hi everyone
S:	o/~ and I do apreciate you being 'round o/~
W:	hi *P*
M:	HAVE PITY ON ME
W:	pitiful is right *M*
G:	H do u support the ways of *G*
X:	hello, I'm *X*
H:	what are *G*
X:	HELLO

It is clear that some of these conversations are between pairs of individuals rather than the whole group, and the full conversation is much more complex than can be shown here. Any two participants can have a private conversation in a separate window at the same time that the rest of the group is chatting publicly, and it seems likely that some of the dialogue above is related to those private conversations rather than the whole group chat.

D:	I'm on my way to old Mexico and I thought I'd sit a spell
H:	hi *X*
S:	hi *X*
X:	what's up
G:	crazy people like me from pittsburgh
I:	hello *x*
	X I mean
H:	yup, I support ya!
	I was born in philly

Since some questions are asked many times by participants, strategies have evolved to make asking them less onerous. Asking for a geographical location is very common, probably as a way of giving some kind of substance to a name which can otherwise seem very anonymous. 'Where are you' is therefore almost always typed as 'Where r u.'

G:	were r u from
M:	I want do it anymore walkman
X:	can you I'm from davis, CA
G:	were r u now??
S:	o/~ yesterday, was such an easy game to play o/~]

5th Feb 1993, 20.12

It is clear, then, that even in 1993 young people were pushing the technology to its limits in order to use it to communicate with each other more effectively. This transcript is rooted in time as well as context: it represents the kind of discourse found in the early 1990s. With the arrival of the World Wide Web in 1993, many of these devices, and their authors, migrated to this new medium. It is to the Web that we should now turn.

Graphical Representation and the WWW

Unlike real time text, creation of a Web page involves assembling the appropriate text, pictures, video and sounds and writing the instructions for the links to other areas of the Web which may be included on the page.[2] These can be designed without being connected to the Internet, so time can be taken to ensure that they are attractive, impressive and fit for their purpose. Expensive software is available to make this process seem easier, but most young people either use the cut-down shareware versions of these programs or they work with the bare text which is at the heart of HTML. As an example of this coding at its simplest, to display the title

Chris Abbott's Homepage

in bold, the user would type in

<b>Chris Abbott's Homepage</b>.

Other features are turned on and off in the same way. Young people seem to discover that the quickest way to build an impressive page is to save one created by someone else and edit it to include their own graphics, text and links. This kind of easy reusability and sharing of textual and graphic constructs is something with which young people are entirely at ease with, but it can bring them into conflict in authority, especially with regard to the laws of copyright. For example, a number of young people who have set up sites as a homage to a favourite television programme or feature film have found themselves threatened with legal action unless they remove copyright images which they have utilized without permission.

Graphics are easily prepared, again for the most part using easily available shareware programs, and these can then be included in the page. In many cases, the evidence for this is straightforward since the software credits are included on the Web page. Indeed, it seems to be part of the growing orthodoxy of Web design that credit for software is given, rather as in the credits for a feature film. Other graphics can be repeated, such as tiles to form a background, or can be used to provide simple animations. Sounds can also be added so that a spoken welcome can be provided to visitors to the page, and, crucially, links can be included to take the visitor on to other areas dealing with associated subjects or prepared by friends of the homepage owner. In this kind of text interactivity is the only possible mode of use.

Throughout 1994 and early 1995 most Web sites were assemblages of text and graphics, with only minimal experimentation in the field of animation and video. Sound was mostly included so that it could be downloaded rather than heard in real time as the site was visited. As streamed audio became available through the use of *RealAudio* and other plug-ins, many young people added sound to their sites – in most cases as a means of providing a musical accompaniment.

By 1996, the development of added software such as *Java* and *Shockwave* meant that the up-to-the-minute Web site could contain animated bullet points, a spoken welcome from the owner, a video clip of a pet cat or an invitation to contact the author via Internet phone or *CuSeeme* low-cost video – all accessed through a local call and a reasonably low-priced modem. Faster modems or other improved links to the World Wide Web such as ISDN and leased lines, along with more sophisticated Web browsers, have all affected the growth of sites.

Many of the first users to see the potential of Web publishing seem to have been young people. On their Web pages authors frequently write about the potential they feel is offered by the Web:

> I once was isolated and lonely, and the 'net really helped give me solace and find some value in a world that sometimes seems tempes-tuous. The advent of home pages gives me an outlet to distribute my thoughts, ideas, and feelings – something so many people on here gave me so much of. Don't begin to think that I believe the net is a supplement for real human interaction. I think its a complement that can sometimes be a little detrimental. Computers are great when you're just beginning to see light and building the confidence to come out of your shell. But one shouldn't stagnate in the Web – it's not some opiate form of human interaction. Computer interaction is so para-doxical – you feel so close yet so far. When one begins to embrace fonts a little too much, it's time to return to reality. (Male, 17 yrs, USA, January 1996).[3]

A further description of the contents of a few Web pages will illustrate the wide range of uses to which this publishing medium is being put. First of all, many Web page authors appear to be building on the features of Internet language previously described in synchronous communication (Abbott, 1996) and have written their texts in an argot which can be almost impenetrable to outsiders. A young British Web user who uses this specialized form of language is also aware of its difficulty for some readers. Helpfully, he therefore provides a summary in standard English:

If any of you have any ideas for a theme to my page, then send 'em in Matee'o's and if ya' 'ave any pics ta go wiv 'em, den by all means giv 'em 'ere! DUDE!

What I meant was, if you can think of a good theme for me to base my page on, then I would be grateful for them. (Male, 14 yrs, UK, January 1996).

The introduction to an American user's homepage is written in a vernacular which is fast becoming, at least in the mid-1990s, the primary mode of textual composition on the World Wide Web:

So you're out surfing, raisin' a little hell with your computer, and where do you find yourself but on my homepage. Not your homepage, see, this place is home to no-one but myself. Beware, ye weak of soul, ye weak of heart, ye weak of ling! Like Lord Byron, I'm mad, bad and DANGEROUS to know. (Male, 18 yrs, USA, January 1996).

Some critics have seen this apparent abandonment of rules as confirmation of the essentially 'insupportable' nature of grammar and spelling. Although not all would go as far as Spender in this approach, many would agree with her that the functional aspects of traditional grammar are increasingly under threat and difficult to defend:

Supposedly proper grammar, dictionary definitions and correct spelling have all been a result of printing press uniformity. The standardised forms did not exist before the advent of the printing press, and they probably won't exert the same hold over our minds as the influence of the printing press declines (1995:xx).

The dismay and distress at the passing of the print era has more to do with bringing to an end a patriarchal presence that has been encoded in communication than it has to do with the loss of print (1995:10).

A student at a Welsh university took a different approach. In early 1996 his homepage was a good example of the kind of literary construct which is often seen on pages produced by young people of student age. Called 'Stoat's Lair', the page is written in an ironic tone, using a literary genre which combines slang, intertextual references and humour. The opening paragraph gives a flavour of the page:

Welcome, weary traveller, to Stoat's Lair. This will hopefully become a hotbed of in-yer-face political radicalism, surfing, anarchy, melo-slice-sharp humour, retro hippy music, environment/direct action demo reports, and neat knitting patterns for old ladies. (Male, 20 yrs, UK, January 1996).

Awareness of the essential US domination of the Web, at least in the mid-1990s, is apparent from many references on the pages, such as that by one 15-year-old Londoner, in which he describes his home country as being 'an island a few hundred kilometers to the east of America'. It is also interesting to note that the writer chooses to write 'kilometer', rather than 'kilometre'. This indicates a desire to conform to a perceived dominant model despite the ironic fact that Americans would probably not use a metric system of measurement.

Self-deprecation or irony is almost the normal mode of transmission on the Web where young people are involved. At the same time, it is striking how honest most of the statements seem to be – as if they were striving for authenticity, although of course, it would be as easy to exaggerate or even mislead:

Peter Thomas. A normal Economic and Social History with Politics second year student at a normal, mundane northern English university. But this is a man with a mission. As soon as he finds out what it is, you'll be the first to know. Here is what he has to say:
Welcome to my new leaner, fitter and meaner homepage. I have been rationalising the concern for the past, oooh 15 minutes, and already it's more efficient, with a less rigid hierarchy, and with all of its flabby and uncommitted staff consigned to income support. Now it is able to kick ass with the best of them in the dog eat dog world (of) corporate finance. (Male, 20 yrs, UK, January 1996).

Perhaps one of the best examples of a text where the writer feels absolutely at home with the medium is that constructed by Peter Dawkins. In his introductory paragraph he manages to pack in a commentary on the reader's intentions and some musings on small-town life in Massachusetts, and then enfolds it all in a comfortable and conversational style:

You must really have nothing to do if you are at my web page. But I'm glad you're here; I don't have much to do. I suppose I should introduce myself and this hot web page. I am Peter Dawkins I am 14 years old and I live in one of the quietest towns in the United States: Belmont, Massachusetts. It has a population of about 25,000, and my middle school burned down over the summer. It's a very suburban, calm life. So one day I decided to make my web page and now here you are. I guess the only thing you need to know about me is that I am a huge sports fan, which is the only excitement in my fairly dull, repetitive school life. I will watch or play nearly any sport. No figure skating or water polo or pro soccer (oh boy, I just love those 0–0 ties!) My favourite teams: in baseball, the Atlanta Braves. In pro football, the Detroit Lions. In College Football, (the subject of my screen name) the Florida State Seminoles. In pro basketball, the Houston Rockets. And finally, my college basketball team is my home-state favorite UMass Minutemen. So now you know just about everything you need to know about me, get out before this page sucks you in forever. Just kidding. I have uploaded a few choice files downloadable to your PC. More are on the way. Oh, by the way, if you have a good sports simulation for the PC or Mac please e-mail me. I can't find any worth having. Also e-mail me if you just want to talk about sports. As you know by now, I am probably really bored and would appreciate someone to talk to about the games. (Male, 14 yrs, USA, January 1996).

Words, the spellings of words, contractions, acronyms, emoticons and appropriate and inappropriate terms all change from month to month or even from week to week. It is important to sustain contemporary knowledge of the appropriate vocabulary according to current group norms. Indeed, Turkle suggests that this is a major strategy for acquiring membership of the group and defining oneself as part of the community:

If we take the home page as a real estate metaphor for the self, its decor is postmodern. Its different rooms with different styles are located on computers all over the world. But through one's efforts, they are brought together to be of a piece (1995:259).

Turkle's analysis pursues the idea that the Web is fundamentally a postmodernist phenomenon in that it allows users to play with and construct multiple identities in multiple worlds. As I suggested in my discussion of MUDs, rather than making such sweeping claims I would argue that for many young users, the Web is not so much an alternative world but a setting where respite can be achieved and issues explored in comparative safety. It allows for complementarity rather than alterity.

Although the construction of fictional worlds, such as the 'Stoats Lair' above, may allow the user the opportunity to work under the guise of a fictional persona, it has also been suggested that the effect of the real world is far more obviously present than storytellers might imagine. In particular, male influence is as marked on the Web as in other areas of the Internet, and male sports and other stereotypical interests such as cars, pornography and computer games are frequently part of the page content. Not all users conform to this stereotype, however, and there are increasing numbers of non-conformers and members of previously marginalized groups such as women, young gays and lesbians, and those interested in non-stereotypical areas. However, it is extremely difficult for any one person to be aware of the scope of this change, since the size of the Web and its constant mutability forever defeats such analysis.

Chris Abbott

Who is Creating Web Homepages?

There has been no large scale reliable analysis of young people's use of the Web to date. Of course, older methodologies do not lend themselves well to research into on-line activity, and bodies such as the Centre for the Study of Online Communities at University College of Los Angeles are attempting to establish appropriate research methods.[4] My investigation of the development of Web sites or homepages by young people aged from 12 to 25 years is part of continuing research into the developing forms of language used by such young people on the Internet (Abbott, 1996). As part of this research, e-mail surveys were sent to 70 young people during the first three months of 1996. These were identified on the basis of random but persistent discovery of Web homepages. Forty-seven of these were returned, a response rate of 67 per cent. The high response rate is itself interesting and could be explained by a combination of ease of reply and novelty, although this is fast disappearing. At that time most of the young people contacted for this survey had never had such an enquiry before.

Approximately half of the respondents were living in the USA or Canada, with the rest in various European countries, particularly the UK but also the Czech Republic, Finland and the Netherlands. All Web sites studied were in English or available in English versions. In some cases, the owner of the page lived in one country but the page was stored in another – a common phenomenon on the Web. This is just one of the ways in which international boundaries have little importance in this on-line community, although languages undoubtedly do. For the moment, as I have suggested, American-English is quite clearly the language of the Internet: a disquieting development for many, especially where home languages may not be spoken outside the country in question:

> Those Icelandic children who learnt to use (computers) in English before they started learning a foreign language in school were being given a silent but unquestionable message which might be phased in the following way: The language of your parents may well be a noble central language which has been spoken for centuries, and may well have its uses for collecting out-of-date and unexciting information about things which happened in the past – but if you want to know about modern things, those things which are presented by the most up-to-date technology, then you are going to have to turn to other languages. (Palsson, 1996:112).

In this respect it could be argued that the Internet has replaced Hollywood as the dominant symbol of US cultural imperialism.

The e-mail survey respondents were fairly evenly spread through the age-range from 12 to 25, with larger groups around the ages of 16 and 20. This distribution could be a historical phenomenon prompted by the easier availability of Web access in higher and further education, since at the time of the survey most of the subjects gained access through their place of education. By 1996 this was changing rapidly, and many young people had a range of e-mail accounts, particularly where they were able to make creative use of the many free for thirty days' offers promoted by the major online services. Most of the respondents, perhaps inevitably, were male, although the 11 per cent who were female marked a larger proportion than might have been expected in a field which has been seen as being heavily gendered in the past.

Many respondents reported, not surprisingly, that they had had a homepage for less then six months. As many as 70 per cent claimed to update their pages regularly, although only a further 24 per cent went as far as claiming to do so at least once a week. The other questions in the survey were concerned with the participants' reasons for publishing on the Web, a question which seemed not to have occurred to many of them before they were asked about it.

This apparent lack of reflexivity may be related to many users' seemingly low opinion of the reasons for their own appearance on the Web, and, as I noted above, the dominance of self-deprecation sometimes results in the use of the third person in order to adopt an air of ironic commentary:

These pages are really a waste of time but this is my way of leaving my mark on the net (Like a dog on a lamppost). (Male, 14 yrs, USA, January 1996).

Darren Peters is a misguided adolescent who spends too much time having fun when he should be doing his A-levels. He is the experimental offspring of William and Shirley Peters. (Male, 16 yrs, UK, January 1996).

This awareness of belonging to a self-defined community is, as I noted above, an important characteristic of a community; it defines itself as something which can be joined. Yet not all of my respondents seemed aware of belonging to such a community. In particular the younger members offered other very straightforward reasons for creating their homepages. Chuck Meadow and Terry Smithson are good examples from two continents:

I am a single male. I am 13-years-old. I live in NY. I am looking for a girl! I'd like one from around East Syracuse, NY! If you want to go out with me, e-mail me! (Male, 13 yrs, USA, January 1996).

Hi my name is Terry Smithson and I am 12 years old. I go to Northamptonshire Grammar School. I live in Northampton England and have a sister who is ten . . . and a brother who is 7 . . . I enjoy three things
   1 Hamsters

2 Cats
3 Star Trek (Male, 12 yrs, UK, January 1996).

The egocentricity of these kinds of statements does not rule out the possibility of an implied reader, but it may be that simply making a statement here takes precedence over a desire to make a connection with others. Indeed when asked why they had a homepage and given a range of options, most respondents to the survey appeared to recognize that their 'reasons were varied'. Seventy-eight per cent agreed that they were using their Web page to communicate with others, and 72 per cent recognized that the design process was a strong motivator. Sixty-five per cent of the total also agreed that the desire to learn how to write HTML code was important. The following kind of explanation (gathered through a later interview) seems to sum up this mixture of motives:

> It looked like a fun thing to have. I am pretty interested in computers, but I haven't had time to really take any programming classes recently. HTML is a great development, because not only is it ridiculously easy to learn but the gratification is immediate and useful. If you write a program in another language, who cares? It has to be very long and complicated for it to do anything of interest to people. But my web page is not very long, code-wise, but produces an interesting and (somewhat) useful product. And the instructions, the tags, are very easy to write since they are often self-explanatory. I also hope to put my resume on my page and some of the humor pieces I've written, so this is free publishing for me. (Male, 18 yrs, USA, e-mail interview, March 1996).

Only 22 per cent admitted that they had a homepage because their friends had one, perhaps an indication of the timing of the survey and the probability that the subjects reached were 'early adopters' rather than the 'later adherents' now filling cyberspace.

When asked who they thought would be reading their homepages, a large majority agreed that they would expect their friends or those with the same interests to be doing so, with 74 per cent agreeing with the former and 78 per cent the latter. A fairly large group of the respondents, 57 per cent, recognized that people with whom they are in e-mail contact may form part of the readership, and 50 per cent recognized the existence of a readership group which consists of people who like to look at homepages. This voyeuristic tendency is supported by the technology and the ability to search across the Internet for interests by name. Only 37 per cent thought that people of the same age would be a significant readership group, and there are indications that age is of little more importance than nationality in online communities, although this may change as online video enables more users to present themselves visually as well as in text and graphics.

An interesting point with regard to readership is that it is in fact possible to know a great deal about who is reading a homepage. Authors in previous media have had to rely upon publishers' returns or market research to assess the number of their readers, but Web publishers can do far more. Many of the homepages I visited have attached a counter to their page, a piece of software which gives a running total for the number of people who have viewed the page. Of course, the mere fact that the page has been viewed may not mean that it has been read (although the same could be said of books). Many Web authors also have access to logs of the people who have visited their page, giving them a profile of their readership according to country of origin and interests. It is, of course, for these reasons that advertising has become so active on the Web. This inbuilt feature of Web writing, that it measures readers, leads to the observation that the Web homepage can be seen as an advertisement for an individual as much as it is a publication.

Further evidence about the interactive way in which readers may relate to writers comes from the facility, common to many pages, to download files, such as stories or poems by the page author or pictures drawn by him or her. This kind of interactivity is further enhanced by the many pages which have taken advantage of guest book software. This allows visitors to comment on the page and invites others to come and visit their own pages.

Like the small pieces of software which count and log visitors to pages, Guestbooks are a way of providing feedback for page owners. Clicking on the Guestbook link leads to a page which can be filled in like a form, with the visitor noting his or her e-mail address and response to the page, although probably not a name or actual geographical situation.

Other pages use Chat software, often freely available itself on the Web, so that users can chat through typed words with other browsers viewing the page at the same moment. A further aspect of interactivity is the almost universal invitation to e-mail the author of the page, a process made easier by the addition of a mail link to the page, clicking on which will invoke the mailer built in to most Web browsers.

Perhaps the most surprising result in the survey was that 93 per cent of respondents stated they were willing to be interviewed individually during the next stage of the process, and these interviews are now in progress using electronic tools such as Web chat and Internet Relay Chat (IRC).

This may indicate above all how much the whole process of Web publication is oriented towards finding a reader – a role writers were as happy I should occupy as the hypothetical peer addressee of their work. Interestingly enough, despite the considerable publicity about offensive material on the Internet, I have seen little of this kind on personal homepages written by young people and my research has been characterized by an open friendliness.

Although I have described the mode of ironic self-deprecation as being most prevalent when it comes to contentious issues it is possible to encounter homepages exhibiting a high level of confidence and self-esteem – especially those prepared by American youngsters. The semi-anonymous nature of the

Web has led some young people to announce their homosexuality to the world in this way even where they have not told their own families.

> Each day of my life has become an inner fight for me, but it is a fight that I will not quit fighting until I win. It is a fight with no way out but winning. I fight against an inner fear, afraid of comments people might make, afraid of discrimination or worse because of who I am. This fear is so strong that it sometimes consumes all of what I feel. Yet this is precisely why I must keep fighting.

> I am bisexual; I am very sure of myself and comfortable with my own identity. But still I fear, every time I come out farther, every time I say something more, will this be my last chance? Will my world fall apart because of the hatred someone else carries? And so I keep talking, I keep coming out, and I keep fearing what might happen. But each time I come out a little farther, I feel an inner success. I have won at least one more battle, and actually I have won two: one outward battle against homophobia and one inward battle against the separation I feel from the world. (Female, 18 yrs, USA, August 1996).

Others feel compelled to share their religious faith with their readers:

> I attend Elton Baptist Church, a independent Baptist church of about 100. There I am a member of the youth choir and treasurer of the teen group. I also serve as an usher during morning services. My belief in the death and resurrection of Jesus Christ, and the belief that sinners may only be received into heaven by God's forgiveness of one's sins is preached by this Bible believing church. (John 3:14–16). (Male, 16 yrs, USA, January 1996).

Conclusion

The imminent convergence of telephony with computers to create the Information and Communications Technology (ICT) networks of the near future is changing the way in which people see each other. It is removing the sense of place from discourse, as physical location becomes not only transparent but immaterial. The language of this post-geographical world is clearly English, but in a form which is different in its component parts and in its rules of engagement from varieties found elsewhere. Current influence is heavily American, but this may change as countries such as the UK, Germany and Holland become heavy users of the technology. Future Internet language may well be multilingual, although it seems likely that for the foreseeable future it is a form of American English which will predominate.

My central argument in this chapter is that young Web publishers such as those quoted here are part of a strongly defined on-line community which is rule-governed, uses gatekeeping language and welcomes newcomers only if they conform to the orthodoxies of the group, a concept for which the term 'netiquette' is only partially appropriate. The shift from Internet Relay Chat towards the multimedia texts of the Web shows a consistent desire by young users to create, sustain and participate in these communities. The preponderance of oral linguistic forms within the semi-written world of the Net continually displays a striving for immediacy, response and dialogue, a sense of communion, which is only partly summed up in the concept of interactivity.

Today extra facilities on the Web extend the possibilities for the kind of synchronous communication discussed above and found in environments such as Internet Relay Chat. The addition of software such as *Shockwave* or *Real Audio* to a reasonably powerful computer and fast modem or other connection produces a Web browser which can transmit sound almost in real time. Internet Phone permits users to talk through a crackly but perfectly audible sound link to users in other countries, but still only paying for the cost of a local call, negligible now in many parts of the world. However, the disguise afforded by written conversations may be more appealing than the ability to talk directly to other putative members of one's community.

Sound is also possible with the low-cost video-conferencing software developed at Cornell University, *CuSeeme*. However, many users have chosen to turn off the sound facility, which is not easy to manage in a multiple conversation, and make *CuSeeme* into a form of IRC with pictures. Opening a Chat window on the screen, participants type their part of conversation in and see the other participants' words scrolling up the window. On other parts of the screen, video windows are opened so that participants can see each other. The video is often no more than a series of still images, with modem access rarely producing anything better than 2 or 3 frames per second, but this is improving. Again, although this kind of facility may be attractive to business, or even the academic community, it remains to be seen whether its real life qualities will really attract the young Web user, for whom partial self presentation, through Web discourse, may be more revealing.

The Web is clearly offering the young people who use it for publication a highly sophisticated and complex means of speaking to their peers, to others interested in the same topics and to those they seek to influence. It is extending their voices, offering them previously unattainable access to other countries and is providing interaction at increasingly complex and sophisticated levels. It is hardly surprising that so many young people have found it to be such a welcoming, engrossing and worthwhile place to be.

Notes

1 These observations are essentially my personal opinion based on a considerable amount of time viewing the field; it is very difficult to back up these kinds of judgements with data in an area which is essentially anonymous and unmeasurable.

2 All that is needed to publish on the World Wide Web is a computer, a modem and a subscription to an Internet provider who is also willing to provide Web storage. Once the computer has been obtained, monthly costs need only be the ten pounds or so subscription to the ISP (Internet Service Provider) although the associated phone calls can become expensive. For some users, especially in the USA and those on cable communications networks in the UK, the calls are free at off-peak periods, lowering costs even further.

3 Pseudonyms are used throughout, but place names and countries are real. Although the creation of a Web page is analogous to the publication of a book, and the author is worthy of the same consideration and referencing as would be any writer of a weightier tome produced by a previous print and paper-based technology, I suspect that this may not have been fully understood by the young people whose pages are the object of study. Consequently, I would contend that creation of a Web page is indeed publication. I have chosen on this occasion to adopt a principle of caution and to preserve the anonymity of the page owners. The precise nature of publication on the Web and the extent to which researchers may attribute quotations is a difficult topic and needs further urgent attention from the world-wide research community.

4 See: http://www.sscnet.ucla.edu/soc/csoc/

References

Abbott, C. (1996) Young people developing a new language: the implications for teachers and for education of electronic discourse, in *Euro Education 96*, Aalborg, Denmark: Euro Education 96.

Beard, M. (1996) Controls tighten on Internet porn, in *Times Education Supplement*, 27 September.

Bromberg, H. (1996) Are MUDs communities? Identity, belonging and consciousness in virtual worlds, in Shields, R. (Ed.) *Cultures of Internet: Virtual Spaces, Real Histories, Living Bodies*, London: Sage.

De Landa, M. (1994) Emergence of Synthetic Reason in Dery, M. (Ed.) *Flame Wars: The Discourse of Cyberculture*, Durham, NC: Duke University Press.

Dery, M. (Ed.) (1994) *Flame Wars: The Discourse of Cyberculture*, Durham, NC: Duke University Press.

Dyer, R., Geraghty, C., Jordan, M., Lovell, T., Paterson, R. and Stewart, J. (1981) *Coronation Street*, Television Monograph 13, London: British Film Institute.

Etzioni, A. (1991) *The Responsive Society*, San Francisco, CA: Jossey-Bass.

Jones, S. (Ed.) (1995) *CyberSociety: Computer-mediated Communication and Community*, London: Sage.

Lanham, R. (1993) *The Electronic Word: Democracy, Technology and the Arts*, Chicago, IL: University of Chicago Press.

Ludlow, P. (Ed.) (1996) *High Noon on the Electronic Frontier: Conceptual Issues in Cyberspace*, Cambridge, MA: The MIT Press.

McLaughlin, M., Osborne, M. and Smith, C. (1995) Standards of conduct on Usenet, in Jones, S. (Ed.) *CyberSociety: Computer–Mediated Communication and Community*, London: Sage.

Ong, W. (1982) *Orality and Literacy: The Technologizing of the Word*, London: Methuen.

Palsson, H. (1996) Multimedia and the language of the Vikings, in *Euro Education '96*, Aalborg, Denmark: Euro Education 96.

Rheingold, H. (1993) *The Virtual Community: Homesteading on the Electronic Frontier*, Reading, MA: Addison-Wesley.

Shields, R. (Ed.) (1996) *Cultures of Internet: Virtual Spaces, Real Histories, Living Bodies*, London: Sage.

Spender, D. (1995) *Nattering on the Net: Women, Power and Cyberspace*, Melbourne, Australia: Spinifex Press.

Turkle, S. (1995) *Life on the Screen: Identity in the Age of the Internet*, London: Weidenfield & Nicholson.

Chapter 6

An American *Otaku*
(or, a Boy's Virtual Life on the Net)

Joseph Tobin

A Postmodern *Koan* (Conundrum)

Japan, the land of Sony, Toshiba and Nintendo; Japan, the world's vanguard post-industrial, information- and technology-based economy, has few computers in classrooms and little media education in the curriculum. To put this observation in the form of a zen *koan*: how can a country be among the world leaders in cutting edge technology and new media when (unlike Britain) media education is not part of their regular curricula and (unlike the United States) their classrooms are not full of computers and modems?

Before attempting an answer, I'll make the conundrum more explicit: Japan isn't just the leader in selling things with computer chips in them – the Japanese are at the vanguard in visualizing twenty-first century life. The Japanese do well in computer programming and computer engineering. But their real forte is in working at the human-machine interface, imagining new commercial, aesthetic and entertainment applications for computer technology and, in the process, re-engineering everyday life. Walking down a street in Tokyo, shopping in an Osaka department store, or watching commercials on Japanese television, one quickly realizes that Japan is on the front edge of the techno-commercial media wave: graphic design, electronic communications, the look, sound and feel of post-modern life can be found in Tokyo a few years before they reach Europe and North America. Japan's role in defining cyberculture is heralded in the West by books such as William Gibson's *Neuromancer* and *Mona Lisa Overdrive* and in the popularity among adolescents and college students the world over of post-apocalyptic, techno-sci-fi *manga*, (comic books such as *Dragonball* and the early *Teenage Mutant Ninja Turtles*), *anime* (cartoons such as *Akira, Ranma* and *Ghost in the Shell*), and video games (*Street Fighter, Tekken*).

This might lead us to suspect that Japanese schools are chock full of computers and flush with new curricula for teaching about computer programming, product design, animation and popular culture. But the opposite is the case. The Japanese spend relatively little on school buildings and equipment, and it shows. Most buildings are shabby. Except for a handful of experimental programs in distance learning and vocational/technical education, Japanese schools have relatively few computers and modems and the hardware they have is often underutilized. Media education courses are rare. Other than the *manga* and Gameboys stuffed in students' backpacks, little popular culture enters the school.

So how do Japanese come to be multi-media experts, if not in school?

Back to Basics

When I posed this conundrum to Yukio Nakashima, a Japanese middle-school principal in Kyoto, he explained: 'Rather than spending time and money on technology and on peripheral areas of the curriculum, we believe in teaching math and science, and other basic academic skills. Giving students a solid footing in the core academic subjects is the best way to prepare them for studying computers and anything else later in life.' This answer is familiar and reassuring to those western educators who believe in 'getting back to basics'. Nakashima's reasoning is based on the logic of scope and sequence, of an orderly curriculum, building predictably and sensibly from preschool to ongoing adult education. This is a conservative position not just because it rejects the need for schools to invest in new technology and for teachers to develop new expertise, but also because it is based on the logic of pedagogical paternalism. We, the teachers and curriculum specialists, will let you students use the computers and modems when we decide you are ready. This logic is consistent with what Sherry Turkle (1995) calls the 'structured,' 'universal' or 'hard' programming paradigm in computer culture, the idea that computer programming is an orderly, logical task that should be based on sound mathematical knowledge and principles. Just as a computer program should be a predictable and logical sequence that any well trained computer engineer could follow and debug, so too should computer education follow a logical sequence, beginning with the basics.

Although I suspect that many educators in the United States would find Nakashima's reasoning familiar and attractive, few American schools are following the Japanese formula of putting off media and computer education until the basics have been mastered. Pressures in American society, including the national crusade to compete with the Japanese in the production of scientists and computer engineers, trickle down to the primary schools, who feel compelled to spend money and energy 'technologizing'. Putting technology in schools is a quick fix. Parent groups organize drives to raise money to buy computers and wire the school to deliver video feeds and Internet connections to each classroom.

Alas, for all of this frenzied spending and activity, American students are not learning much computer and media education in school. There are several problems. One is a dearth of teachers who understand the emerging technologies well enough to teach them. Another is that the computers and modems, in most cases, are used in the wrong way. As Seymour Papert pointed out back in 1980, in most schools computers are programming children rather than children programming computers. Students rarely are given the opportunity to decide what they want to do with computers and modems. Even where elementary schools have their own Web pages, I suspect that the teachers (or some other adults) are doing most of the programming, and the students mostly providing the raw materials and doing only some basic functions (word processing and scanning). The availability of Web-authoring packages combined with the scarcity of teachers who know the newest computer languages and Web-programming, make it unlikely that many students are taught hypertext mark up language (HTML), much less C++, UNIX, or Java in school.

Parents' night at my son's high school is typical, I fear, of how schools use cutting-edge technology. Isaac goes to an elite, well endowed private school. His biology class was held in his school's first 'Internet classroom'. Isaac's biology teacher proudly told us that there were six computers, each with a direct link to the Net. How were these elite students using the net and the computers? The teacher had found a Website that offered detailed instructions on how to conduct a frog dissection. That night we learned that instead of having to follow the directions from a textbook or handout, as we did back in the pre-Internet dark ages when we took high school biology, our children get to follow the same instructions ('with your scalpel, make an incision from the frog's breast-bone to the lower abdomen . . .') on a screen. The only real difference I could see was that in the old days we had to turn over the page to get to the second half of the instructions ('Now remove the heart from the chest cavity.') while Isaac got the opportunity to click on a button (and wait 30 seconds for the screen to refresh).

Experiences like this lead me to suspect that even where the Internet is being used in schools, schools aren't teaching students to work at the cutting edge of the new cyber-technologies. At school, students may learn 'computer basics' (keyboarding, word processing, spreadsheets), and even more current, sophisticated skills, such as how to surf the Web, to scan images into a report, or to use a program such as Page Mill to create a Webpage. But schools are not the primary site for computer/Internet literacy. Which takes me back to my beginning question: if in the United States, as in Japan, students aren't learning to program computers, to hack, and to author Web pages using HTML and Java in school, where are they learning it?

The *Otaku-Zoku* ('The Information-obsessed, "At home" Tribe')

Contrary to Nakashima's reasoning, I suggest that many Japanese youths don't wait until they graduate from high school or college to become computer and media literate – instead they learn outside of school, outside of the formal educational system. In fact, there is a name in Japan for young people with this out of-school knowledge of and interest in computers and popular culture: the *otaku-zoku*.

This is a tough term to translate into English. '*Otaku*' is a polite way of saying 'your home' or 'you'. In the late-1980s the terms *otaku* and *otaku-zoku* (otaku-tribe) came on the scene to refer to young people with an obsessive interest in some aspect of popular culture which they accessed through the emerging computer/Internet technology without ever leaving their bedroom. In some respects *otaku* is equivalent to 'hacker'. But unlike 'hacker', *otaku* refers not just to someone skilled in using computers in nontraditional, unintended, and anti-authoritarian ways, but to someone whose computer interest and acumen is in the service of their obsession with a particular area of popular cultural knowledge. One is not just an otaku, but a *manga*-(comic book-) *otaku* or a *pop-idol-* (pop-singer-) *otaku* or a Twin Peaks-*otaku*. *Otaku* are (typically) young men who spend most of their days and nights at home, at their computers, accessing, processing and distributing information about some very specific aspect of the world of television, music, movies or comic-books.

Otaku are ridiculed by media pundits and psychoanalyzed by social critics. For example, consider the journalist Kyoichi Tsuzuki's description of *otaku*:

> They are easily visible because they don't care about the way they dress. They talk different and look to the ground while talking face-to-face. They are not into physical activities, they are chubby or thin, but not fit, never tanned . . . Computer game programers live on potato-chips that they eat with chopsticks, and on coffee-milk. They have a different rhythm, are awake for 40 hours and then sleep for 12. Computer *otaku* are said to be able to make love with a girl on the screen. But I think many want a girl friend, but can't get one. (quoted in Grassmuck, 1990).

In his *Wired* article, 'The Obsession of the Otaku; Japan's Techo Kids Have Fashioned a World Driven By Trivia – and Barren of Human Contact,' the Tokyo-based journalist Karl Taro Greenfield writes:

> This subculture of kids trades information, trivia and corporate passwords in their bedrooms via modem while their parents down-stairs think they are studying. But they have abandoned schoolwork, sometimes becoming so immersed in the world of computer networks, cracking corporate security codes and analyzing algorithms that they can never come back. And all this just so they can be the first to disclose an upcoming record-store appearance by a low-level pop singer. 'We are the future – more comfortable with things than people,' says Taku Hachiroo, the 30-year-old author of the book

Otaku Heaven and a self-proclaimed Otaku (//wwww.wired.com/ wired/1.1/features/otaku.html)

These comments are characteristic of a genre of Japanese social commentary (mostly spoken or written by Japanese, occasionally by outsiders) that is called *Nihonjinron* (theorizing about Japanese-ness). This genre has two sub-forms: conservative theorizing about the core, essential character of the Japanese character and culture and alarmist theorizing about the way contemporary young people are losing this essential character and undermining traditional Japanese culture and values.

Japanese writings about the *otaku-zoku* are a classic form of the alarmist *Nihonjinron* genre. According to the social scientists and media pundits who describe them, the *otaku* are the antithesis of the idealized Japanese character: they are so unlike what (Japanese) people should be like that they seem to be a new tribe, a new race, a new species of human being. The dysfunctionality of their personalities and emptiness of their souls is inextricably linked to their uncanny knowledge of computers and popular culture.

I have suggested this genre is a culturally specific Japanese discourse. But there are corollaries in the West. Much of the writing in the West about young people and cyber/media culture mirrors the *Nihonjinron* discourse on *otaku*: the new technologies are exciting and potentially empowering, but also dangerous and uncanny. In the West as in Japan, young people who embrace the new technologies are seen to be at risk of losing their core humanness and of becoming alienated, anti-social, apathetic and unhealthy.

Even computer-culture theorists such as Sherry Turkle who embrace the new technologies fall into this trope of newness/danger. Turkle, like the Japanese *otaku*-critics, views cyberculture as a new stage of human life, and hackers, MUDders (computer fantasy-game players), and cyberpunks as new species of human beings. Turkle sees in the new uses of computers 'fundamental shifts in the way we create and experience human identity' (1995:10). She wants 'to know what we are becoming if the first objects we look upon each day are simulations into which we deploy our virtual selves' (1995:22). Her central concern is 'the intense relationships people have with computers and how these relationships are changing the way we think and feel' (1995:22). Her research leads her to conclude that the citizens of cyberculture have a radically new, postmodern sense of self, the multiple windows that can be opened simultaneously and toggled back and forth on their computer screens providing the perfect metaphor for their non-unitary psyches: 'The life practice of windows is that of a decentered self that exists in many worlds and plays many roles at the same time' (1995:14). The core assumption shared by those, like the Japanese culture-critics who write anxiously and those, like Sherry Turkle and the columnists for *Wired*, who write enthusiastically about cyberculture, is that the new technologies are creating people who prefer virtual relationships to real ones, the screen to face-to-face interactions, and information grazing to a focused course of study.

I know these concerns well because they are the ones I have about my younger son. I find Isaac's computer interest and skills to be both wondrous and frightening, simultaneously a source of pride and concern, of vicarious pleasure and anxiety. In this chapter, I am asking the same anxious, existential question about Isaac that the Japanese ask about *otakus* and Turkle about MUDders: is a virtual life a lesser life? In the rest of this chapter, I will toggle back and forth between Isaac and the *otaku*-tribe, using what I know of *otaku* to contextualize and explain Isaac's current life and what I know about Isaac's uses of the computer to shed more light on the *otaku* phenomenon, and specifically on the question of how *otaku* (and their counterparts in other cultures) become cyber-technologically proficient.

Before I start revealing details of my son's life and presenting him as a case study of a category of contemporary young people, some comments on methodology are in order. Clearly, there are methodological problems inherent in a case study of one's own child. The privacy/consent issue is one I negotiated with Isaac. He has read the chapter and generally approves, although he finds it 'kind of weird to be in someone's academic paper'. I play several roles in this chapter including writer, researcher and the research-subject's father, a figure who has a small but important recurring part in this family drama. As in any other methodological approach, the single-case study of one's own child has advantages and disadvantages. I hope that what I lack in objectivity, I make up in insight. Just as many studies of young people's learning in school are conducted by their teachers, studies of young people's learning at home can be usefully, if subjectively, studied by their parents. I do not claim that my report is objective and I cannot know if Isaac is a representative or typical adolescent computer-user. This chapter is designed as a description and reflection on one young man's media uses and pleasures.

As in the case of the *otaku* and the *Nihonjinron* discourse that surrounds them, and MUDders and Turkle's (1995) book about them, the story of Isaac's life on the Internet is a double story, a story of his computer use and of his parents' and teachers' concerns and reactions. Cyberculture is a double phenomenon, a dyadic relationship between young(er) people with computers and old(er) people reacting to them, trying to control them, and worrying about them. Both sides of the phenomenon are worthy of analysis. The two sides make each other possible – the technophiles and the technophobes define themselves through their views of each other.

An American *Otaku*

At age 15, Isaac's life revolves around the Internet and Warhammer 40K (a war-playing game, played with miniature hand-painted metal or plastic figures and dice, based loosely on Wagnerian plots and cosmologies, the writings of Tolkien, and Dungeons and Dragons). The first thing Isaac does when he wakes up each morning is to check his e-mail – he receives around 50 messages

daily and sends replies to about half of them. Keeping up with this correspondence takes several hours a day. On school days, Isaac logs on for 30 minutes in
the morning, eating breakfast at the computer. Whenever he has a free period
at school he uses the computers in the library to telnet to his e-mail account.
He puts in his longest stretches at the computer at home in the late afternoon
and evening.

Most of Isaac's corespondents are members of the Warhammer 40K
gaming mailing list. Isaac posts messages to the list, as well as writing and
receiving letters from individuals. Isaac has formed friendships with several
members of the group. Currently, his closest friend is Thomas, a 15-year-old
who lives in the British midlands. Other e-mail buddies include college
students on the US mainland, a businessman from Nottingham, a librarian at a
natural history museum in London, and several Scandinavians who, according
to Isaac, 'write English better than most aol dot commers.' (Note: 'Aol dot
commers' (or 'A-ols') is cyberpunk for Internet users with accounts on
American-On-Line, whose e-mail addresses end 'aol.com'. *Otakus* and
hackers hate AOL and dislike its customers for many reasons. They accuse the
company of reading and censoring e-mail, overcharging, and taking advantage
of the Internet's most gullible and ignorant clients. They make fun of AOL
users for shouting (USING TOO MANY CAPITAL LETTERS and excla-
mation points!!), sending private replies to whole mailing lists, poor writing
and a variety of other newby (newcomer) Internet faux pas.)

After completing his first check of his e-mail inbox, Isaac checks the
counters on his Web pages to see how many 'hits' he has received overnight (he
averages about 500 a week). He surfs the Web, checking out other Warhammer sites to see if they have been updated and to keep an eye on the
competition – Isaac's page (http://www.aloha.com/~isaac/wh40k-htm) currently is rated number one on the Warhammer rating list. On weekends and
other days when he doesn't have school, Isaac works on his various Web-
related projects. He scans images into the computer. Using his Wacom
(drawing) tablet and Adobe *Photoshop*, he makes original drawings to be used
as backgrounds for his own and his clients' Web pages. He periodically gets
hired to do design work for clients who learn of his services when they come
across his 'Tobin Graphics' page on the Web. Most of these clients are other
Warhammer fanatics, who want Isaac to design original tilable backgrounds,
using Warhammer themes and graphic design, for their homepages.

The Japanese concept of *otaku* provides me with both a name and a way of
understanding my son: Isaac is a Warhammer-*otaku*. He has a fanatic's interest
in the world of Warhammer 40K; he puts more time, energy and emotional
commitment into Warhammer than into any other aspect of his life; he prides
himself on knowing more about nuances of the game and in having higher
quality Warhammer Webpages than anyone else; and the computer and the
Internet are crucial to his expertise.

Isaac was only marginally successful as a Warhammer model-painter and
as a tournament gamer. The breakthrough for Isaac came when we signed him

up with an Internet account. Once on the Web, Isaac quickly found the Warhammer sites. He joined the games' user list, rapidly emerging as one of the most prolific contributors. His background in art (Isaac had won prizes for his painting and sculpting as an intermediate student) served him well in Webpage design. At age 14, as happens with many young people, Isaac reached the point as an artist where he was frustrated with his ability to produce work good enough to meet his own increasingly sophisticated and demanding standards. But the computer gave him a second chance, a new medium. With the scanner, his art-tablet, Adobe *Photoshop* and other drawing, drafting, and rendering software (*Morph*, *Kai's Power Tools*, *Alien Skin*) Isaac was able to produce digital images of a very high quality. Isaac's Webpages were among the first Warhammer sites on the Internet. As the other players on the list gave him praise and encouragement, as well as some constructive critiques and suggestions, Isaac's Webpages quickly grew in size and sophistication. A year after getting his first Internet account (a student account at $20 a month), Isaac had authored 20 pages and subpages on the Web and received approximately 50,000 hits. He had also written over 1,000 e-mail messages to individuals and to the 40k list. He had become a Warhammer 40k celebrity, renowned for his e-mail prolificness, wit and knowledge, and for the quality of his computer graphics. Over the course of the year he had become, before our eyes, a Warhammer-*otaku*.

Otaku Pedagogy

Isaac is continuously upgrading his computer and Web-authoring skills. This summer he plans to begin learning Java programming language, downloading tutorials from the Web. He works on improving his Webpages by adding state-of-the art features such as frames and animation loops. As Isaac sits at the computer, Web-authoring at the outer edge of his knowledge, he lets out a series of epithets and mutterings: 'Doh (in a Homer Simpson voice). What the fuck? That should have worked. Oh wait, I got it. This should do it. What the hell? Why didn't that work? Maybe if I . . . Yeah. Hey, Dad, look at this. It should still look better than that. I don't know why it's running so slow. I'm going to mail David.'

David is David Michaels, a musician, systems engineer, family friend, and Isaac's mentor. In the last two years David has taught Isaac about computer hardware, software, the Internet, and computer jock masculinity. At first, Isaac watched as David installed new devices on our home computer and sorted out logjams in our boot sequence. Gradually, Isaac became a more active audience. David would say, 'Isaac, pull a chair up so you can learn how to do this next time so your Dad won't have to call me.' Sitting side by side at the computer, David would provide Isaac with a running account of his thinking and his mood as he worked on trouble-shooting our problems:

Let's see what this bad boy can do. Does it always take this long for this sucker to boot? Okay, here we go. Now we just go through the file manager and into the setup. Let's just tweak the config.sys here and see if that takes care of the problem. What the fuck have you guys done here? What do you have your interrupts set at? Don't you keep a record someplace? Oh, I see what's happening. I have a hunch that the problem with this puppy is the order of the devices in the the autoexec.bat. If we rem this one out and then, here we go, now were getting someplace.

As Isaac began to follow more of what David was doing and saying, he grew more interested and became more active. Gradually, control of the keyboard passed from David to Isaac as they sat side by side. Gradually, David's ongoing computer-jock monologue became a dialogue.

Little, if anything, of what Isaac knows about computers and the Internet has been learned at school. Isaac is scornful of school in general and specifically of what he sees as his school's misinformed, ignorant, fearful attitude toward the Internet. Isaac and David regularly exchange e-mail messages, producing extended dialogic threads, such as the one that follows, where they complain to each other about the small-mindedness of teachers, bosses, and other authority figures and David gives Isaac tips on how to manoevre around them:

From: Isaac Tobin <isaac@aloha.com>
To: David Michaels <dmichaels@aloha.com>
>My school finally got their network working (kinda), and so now they let people use the net if they attend a special meeting (no freshmen allowed though!).
>What kind of crap is it that, freshmen can't attend? Sheese! If they're going to discriminate, do it by expertise. You could prolly run the 'special meeting'. They are very paranoid about kids going to 'inappropriate' sites, mainly porno, drugs, bombs and anarchy stuff. The freshmen shouldn't be discriminated against. But then again, maybe they are being kept off because they are TOO experienced with computers?
>They don't let us download software, but hey, the stupid computer 'teacher' (she's really a librarian) would not know what Eudora looks like so I am in no trouble. That's what pisses me off the most about these damn rules. I think I'd be a great computer resource teacher but no degree, no job. Maybe if I studied library science . . .
>They don't have any special degrees, AFAIK ['as far as I know']. And they know absolutely nothing about anything. I was setting up their news program (they neglected to set it up!) And I asked the teacher what the domain was for their provider on Maui and she did not even know what I meant! Finally one of the extra nerdy

student volunteers found out the URL of the school homepage and then I could figure out the news server.

>Are you going to do a good Web page for them?

>If I could work out some monetary or grade deal, then I would make em an awesome page, but for now I don't have enough 'school spirit' to stomach a school page. Sorry I'm signing off without a .sig, cus I gotta delete this program when I am done.

>Put your .sig on the flop you're loading Eudora from. Actually, now that I think of it, you could build the sucker so that you loaded a self-extractor into a sub that you created via batch, expand it (with your .sig in the .exe), run Eudora, then when you log out the batch would automatically delete everything for you on the c:. Or if you wanna be really sneaky, you could install eudora on the machine, then make the files and dir hidden with the atttr +h command under DOS . . . Not that I'd advocate any action that might get you into trouble. Just thinking out loud with my fingers. Something to think about: by doing a webpage for them you could get away with a lot of junk! Is there anyone around there who would know what you REALLY need to support a webpage, toolwise? Get the drift? Man, Diane is right. I AM a bad influence! Remember, 'Question Authority!' X-files tonight, Dude.

>You're not a bad influence. You're a rebel!

In addition to learning computer-jock jargon and how to maneuver around his school's draconian computer rules, Isaac has learned from David increasingly sophisticated aspects of Web programming. For instance, in this exchange, Isaac seeks help from David on image mapping, which he needs to understand in order to allow users to click on images rather than on words or buttons as they navigate through his home page:

>I want to dramatically reorganize one of my pages, my Necromunda page, using an image map as the basic list of internal links. The image is a map of the city in which the game takes place . . . I have the image all scanned and cropped, and most of the subpages made up – now I just need to make the image map and tie it all together. I checked out the Netscape site and it talked some about image maps, a html you use to insert them, but it never talks about how you designate which areas will act as what link. I understand that it uses x/y coordinates, but do you just move your mouse over the doc, and read the little coordinate figures on the bottom? Is there a way to 'draw' regions over the image, and say 'okay, that rectangle is a link to page x?'

>>You're really starting to branch out into the more esoteric aspects of web design, eh? I think the map is a good idea. It will be really hot. You're right about the co-ordinate display (as far as that's the only feedback the user sees) so most people use some visual clues on the

map (signs, buildings, etc.). This is a bit more complicated than I can explain via E-mail from work. How about I call you in the evening and we talk it through? Or I could come by and do it in real time if that doesn't work.

In this, as in all of Isaac's exchanges with David, the learning/teaching cycle began with a problem defined by Isaac. Isaac tries to get the computer to do something, struggles to find his own solution, and then writes to David when he gets stuck. David always plays the role of helpful but reluctant (because he's busy) teacher. A key element of David's teaching style is that he is simultaneously generous and stingy with his time: he will make himself available only when he feels the problem Isaac is struggling with is one that Isaac is unlikely to be able to figure out on his own. Image mapping was one of these problems. David comes across on e-mail as a busy, knowledgeable professional, as well as a friend. Isaac is careful not to waste David's time – he struggles to solve problems on his own before turning to David for help because, like the possessor of a magic lamp, he doesn't want to waste any of his allotted wishes.

In other words, David and Isaac's teacher–student relationship is the antithesis of most high school teacher–student relationships. Isaac sets the problem. Isaac decides when class is in session. Isaac decides the scope and sequence of what he learns (although David sometimes gives him advice about setting a long-range course of study: 'I've been thinking about your situation and if I were you I'd take some time to teach yourself some C++ or PERL, because it will put you in better shape for when you get into Java programming down the road'). Unlike high school, David never sets due dates. He never grades. He never tries to teach Isaac anything Isaac doesn't want to learn. He never initiates a lesson.

Otaku Learning Communities

I believe that David and Isaac represent an important but by no means unique node of adolescent cybermedia learning. To return to the conundrum that opened this essay: How do *otaku* learn? Based on my case study of my *otaku* son, I believe the answer is: mostly through self-learning on the Net, learning from their peers, and when they get stuck, through apprenticeships like Isaac's to David. The Isaac–David connection is a critical one, not only for Isaac, but for a large number of his Warhammer-*otaku* peers. Isaac learns the more esoteric and challenging programming lessons from David and in turn Isaac directly and indirectly teaches what he learns to others.

The Isaac–David link in the *otaku* learning community is based on some good fortune. Isaac has a father who knew enough about computers to get him off to a good start – I taught Isaac how to use *Word Perfect*, how to load computer games such as *SimCity*, and how to log onto e-mail on my university account. While not wealthy, we are willing to spend money on computers, software and Internet accounts (our computer equipment, at about $6000, costs more than our two junky cars combined). Isaac thus has unusual access in his home to very high quality equipment, including a Pentium computer with 32mgs of ram, two-gig hard drive, scanner, 28,800 modem, 17-inch monitor, 'video frame grabber', graphics tablet and colour printer.

As important as availability of the equipment is our ability and willingness to support Isaac's computer learning. We care deeply about his learning, but we aren't frantic about his grades, so we don't get on him too much about the time he spends not doing his homework. We are willing to invest time in helping our sons develop contacts with people who can teach them things we cannot – for several years I took Sam and Isaac with me on trips to computer stores and computer expositions and encouraged them to chat with the most knowledgeable salespeople about new products. Whenever I hired consultants to help me with computer or video projects for my work, I invited Sam and Isaac to tag along. It is lucky for Isaac that my closest colleague at work is married to a man who is a systems engineer. But such fortuitous coincidences are much more likely when your father is a professor than a blue-collar worker. Adolescents without well-off, well-educated parents are much less likely to have such access to equipment and knowledge. Unfortunately, this tends to be as true for schools as for homes in poor communities. The cyberculture leaders of tomorrow, as today, are likely to come largely from the privileged classes. Bill Gates (of Microsoft) and Stephen Jobs (of Apple) are examples of industry leaders with Isaac's sort of pedigree and disposition: they came from relatively well-off family backgrounds, attended good schools, and spent a lot of their time as young men messing around with cutting edge media and popular culture.

My hunch is that in every *otaku*-tribe, there are such nodes, such pairs as Isaac and David, who serve to funnel knowledge from one generation to the next, from professionals to hackers. In almost every *otaku*-tribe someone will have a family friend, an uncle or a neighbour, who has expertise the group needs. If such expertise is not readily available through such propinquitous connections, it can be systematically sought out through locating experts on the net or by cultivating relationships with knowledgeable clerks at computer stores. One way or the other, *otaku*-tribe members get the information they need individually, and then disseminate this knowledge laterally, to their peers, when their peers seek assistance. They disseminate information generously because such sharing is part of the ethos of the computer-, Web-, and *otaku*-cultures and because it gives them a chance to show off. Unlike most school settings where students compete for grades and teacher approval, *otaku* tend to be lavish in their praise of work they admire, direct in giving constructive criticism, willing to admit their ignorance when they need advice, and generous about helping each other:

From: The Dark Angel<daveyt@argyle.com.uk>
To: Isaac@aloha.com
Re: Your kickass page
I just had a look at your Warhammer Page and What can I say but
FUCKIN BRILLIANT!

From: Brad Humphrey@igloo.com
To: Isaac@aloha.com
Subject: backgrounds
>Greetings. I bow before the eternal might of your page! I was
traversing the net when I stumbled across your Warhammer site. The
background art was excellent. I believe you said you create your own
so I was wondering if you could give me a little help. I'm currently
working on my own home page and have been having a very difficult
time finding an appropriate background. The page is based on H.P.
Lovecraft's mythos with pictures of the macabre adorning it. With this
setting, finding a background worthy is very difficult. I made the
attempt at creating my own, but just couldn't create anything that
complemented the page. I would greatly appreciate if you could assist
me in creating a suitable background, or helping me come up an idea
for one. Thanks for your time and keep up the superb art.

>>I'd be glad to help. What graphic program(s) do you have? I make
all my backgrounds in Photoshop. I usually start off with a square file,
about 1' by 'inch, at 72 dpi. Then I paint in the image. The best way to
make something tile is to use the filter called offset, and then to blend
the edges with the smear tool. For the HPL background I would go
with something very dark. Maybe an almost abstract black and dark
green mass of tentacles.

From: Celia Howard <choward@camelot.co.uk>
>Dear Mr Tobin,
>>Isaac is fine (I'm only 15 after all),
>I think your web page is COOL! My self being into Citadel stuff I
particularly likeyour Necromunder things and the freak gallery.
>>Thanks! What armies do you play?
>This is the first E-mail message I've written to any body so don't
mind if it's a bit dodgy!
>>Nah, its fine.
>got your E-mail, thanks! You wanted to know about what armies I
collect, well firstly for Warhammer 40,000 I've got an Imperial guard
army (don't laugh). For Epic I've also got an Imperial guard army (sad
isn't it!?).
>>Its not sad, it shows your devotion to your army! And BTW, is
your name Celia? If you aren't Celia, maybe you should sign your
emails with your name to make things less confusing.

>Another thing is that my name isn't Celia (she's just the one that pays the bills) my name is Nigel, her son. By the way, how did you get her name?
>>E-mail programs have a feature that says the name of the person who sent the e-mail. Your's is set for Celia Howard..
>P.S. Check out http://members.aol.com/bubklaus/start/misc.htm it's about Wallace and Gromet and if there's nothing else there you like you have got to hear the sound samples (.wav's). Cool. A little slow, but cool.
from Nigel

Otaku-tribes are genuine learning communities: the Websites and user lists make it clear to all who among the group has the most advanced knowledge in particular domains (game rules, painting techniques, e-mail conventions, Web programming). When the expertise is present in the group, they turn to each other for help. When the expertise is lacking in the group, someone goes outside, gets the knowledge needed, and brings it back. The Warhammer-*otaku* learning community embraces a great variety of ages and levels of knowledge and expertise. People help each other learn crossing boundaries of age, education and geography. This *otaku*-university requires no dean, no curriculum committee, no registrar, no attendance sheets, no grading or testing. For all of these reasons, I suggest that it is a more effective educational institution than high schools and colleges.

This Boy's Virtual Life?

Thus far I've waxed rhapsodic about Isaac's experiences on the Internet and the quality of interpersonal interactions in the Warhammer-*otaku* learning community. But I have two lingering concerns: (1) Is Isaac's time on the Internet well spent? (Is this authentic alternative education or glorified Nintendo playing?) and (2) how worried should I be that most of Isaac's social interactions are 'virtual' as opposed to 'real?'

Wasting Time or Writing across the Curriculum?

To answer the first question, I've spent the past few months charting and analyzing the variety of activities Isaac pursues on the computer. This inquiry was fuelled more by parental concern than by my need to get data for this paper. For a very bright boy, whose parents are paying a great deal of money for him to attend an elite private school, Isaac's grades and overall school performance are only so-so. A typical evening in the Tobin household: Beth, Isaac, and I finish dinner in front of the television and then move to the couch to watch the next show that comes on. Beth asks Isaac, 'Do you have your homework done?' Isaac replies, 'No, I guess I better start,' and he slouches off to the computer room (Sam's bedroom when he's not at university). Isaac sits down in front of the computer desk and flips on the small television that is on the shelf next to the monitor (television is always on in our house, but that's a topic for another paper!). After thirty minutes or so, I drift in to see if Isaac is doing his homework. As I look over his shoulder, as I had expected, I find him reading and responding to e-mail. When Isaac is writing a school essay on the computer, he keeps his *Eudora* (e-mail) program open in a hidden window. He has set the system to alert him of incoming mail. If Isaac is in *Word Perfect* and mail arrives, Windows automatically toggles him into his mailing program. 'Isaac, how's your paper coming along?' 'Not that great.' 'Then why are you reading e-mail?' I know the answer: he finds reading and responding to e-mail more meaningful than writing assigned essays for school.

In this ongoing homework drama, I play my part ambivalently and halfheartedly. I feel as if an amateur playwright has handed me a script to follow that doesn't make much sense, but I read my lines anyway, with as much conviction as I can muster, which isn't all that much, since I can't really get into my part. 'You've already spent all afternoon on e-mail. You should have written your essay first, when you had more energy in the afternoon, and then you could have messed around with your e-mail at night, instead of getting yourself into this situation where you are tired and running out of time and you've only written a page and if you stay up much later you'll be exhausted in the morning.' As I recite this monologue, I sneak a look over Isaac's shoulder, at the e-mail thread that fills the screen. Some words catch my eye: 'metaphysically speaking', 'vengeful gods', 'theologically consistent'. 'What's this thread about, Isaac?' 'It's sort of a metaphysical debate about the motivations of the Eldar. Lots of people think that Eldar are just good elves. But I think they are not good. Evil, in fact. They are a dying race, who are incredibly arrogant, who are thoroughly selfish and depraved.' 'Are the Eldar supposed to be some actual culture that once existed, or they from Tolkien or someplace or did the Gamesworkshop guys just make them up out of thin air?' 'They are not taken directly from any one culture, but they are a good mix of ancient Celts, ancient Egyptians, Melniboneans, who are a fantasy race created by Michael Moorcock, and even a little bit of the British empire. They are mainly Melniboneans who speak Gaelic, use Egyptian hieroglyphics, and worship Celtic/Norse gods.'

Isaac eventually gets his more important homework items done well enough to earn Bs at school, with an occasional A. Our conclusion, as concerned parents, is that Isaac is making good choices about where to invest his time and energy. The writing he does on e-mail and for his Webpage seems, on the whole, to be more interesting, varied, authentic and satisfying than the writing he does for school. Isaac writes thousands of words each day on e-mail, several hundred words a week for school. The letters he sends each day to members of the Warhammer, X-philes, Space Ghost Coast to Coast, and

Mystery Science Theater mailing-lists and news-groups get multiple, lengthy responses within 24 hours. In contrast, his essays are returned a week or so later with a letter grade, some corrections, and two or three sentences of evaluation. His mailing list respondents engage with the content of what he writes; his teachers focus on the form.

Isaac's e-mail writing is in several genres: chatty letters to friends, arguments about Warhammer rules, anthropological/theological debates about the world views and character traits of the various Warhammer armies, and critiques and commentary on the television shows he follows. Although we worry a bit about his grades and about the quality of his academic preparation for college (is writing about the Eldar, air-brushing, and Mulder and Scully an adequate preparation for writing research papers and essays in college?), on the whole we have concluded that writing online is excellent preparation, and thus that his time on the Net is well spent. In our judgment, Isaac's choice to work hard on his school essays, but not very hard on daily homework and thereby to free up time for him to spend on the Net makes good sense as preparation for getting into a good university and doing well once he gets there. Isaac's *otaku* activities complement rather than compete with his academic studies. His academic work would be less rich without his Internet life, and his Internet life would be less successful without the knowledge (of history, literature, religion and anthropology) and skills (as an artist and writer) he has learned in the sporadically worthwhile classes he has taken over his years in school.

Isaac's writing on e-mail and the Web is a model of writing across the curriculum. His letter writing to the friends he's made on the Web represents a renaissance of the epistolary form. E-mail has its own conventions and 'netiquette': don't SHOUT; don't over-use acronyms; reply promptly; and most importantly, don't flame (remember that there is a reader, with feelings, on the other end of the line and the written word, even when digitized, lingers longer and has the potential to carry more sting than a spoken comment). The letters to and from friends that Isaac has allowed me to read are funny, informative, and empathetic. For example, he and his English friend Thomas exchange a thousand or more words a week in letters that cover the progress of their individual and shared Warhammer activities: reports on games they played on the weekend, ideas for an article they are planning to co-author for the Warhammer magazine *White Dwarf*, complaints about their teachers and school, and an ongoing discussion of linguistic and cultural differences between their countries.

Virtual or Real?

The above discussion makes it clear that we are satisfied that Isaac's life on the Net is intellectually and cognitively rich. But we are less sure about the emotional quality of this electronically mediated social life. As his parents, we are racked by the questions of whether Isaac's life on the Net is emotionally satisfying for him now and if it is preparing him adequately for interpersonal relations in his future. Is Isaac happy? Will the self-confidence and interpersonal skills he is developing on e-mail translate into real life? Is this just a phase he is going through, a period of withdrawal and preparation that will be followed by a social blossoming, a time in the future in which he will have 'real' (that is, face-to-face) friends? Do *otaku* grow up and become happy, normal adults?

Being nudgy as well as concerned parents, we have posed these questions to Isaac on numerous occasions. Although his answers don't completely ease our anxieties or resolve the debate, they are interesting and compelling. For instance, a recent dinner-time conversation:

> *Beth*: I got word from my dean that my exchange to Leicester has been approved. So I guess that means it's really going to happen. We're going to be in England next Spring!
>
> *Joe*: So Isaac, that means you'll be able to visit the Games Workshop headquarters. And to meet Thomas. Won't it be great to actually meet him after writing back and forth for so long?
>
> *Isaac*: Not necessarily. I often find it disappointing to meet someone in person who I first got to know through e-mail. People are usually better on e-mail than they are in person. Why do you guys automatically assume that meeting people face to face is better? Face to face, you get too focused on how people look and how old they are and other trivial stuff.

A conversation with me looking over Isaac's shoulder as he checks his mail:

> *Joe*: Is that message from an adult or a kid?
>
> *Isaac*: I don't know.
>
> *Joe*: We can figure it out from his address. Bjk@gau.edu. G.A.U. I bet that's Gustaphus Adolphus University. That would mean he's probably a college student from Minnesota. See, you can figure out a lot about people's age and what they do from their addresses.
>
> *Isaac*: Why would I want to do that? Why is it so important to you to figure out his age and where he lives? Those things don't mean anything. Those things have nothing to do with our conversations. I know the people I write to from what they write to me and the list. That's all that matters to me.

Turkle (1995) argues that the key feature of the Net is that it gives its users the opportunity to be someone other than who they usually are, or to explore multiple sides of themselves. Isaac's take is just the opposite. For Isaac the Net is the place where he feels that he and others can be most truly themselves, where he can present the most coherent version of himself to the world. While reading Turkle's *Life on the Screen*, I told Isaac her central thesis. His critique was scathing:

> I hate people who have the idea that when you write on e-mail you are being different than you really are. That's like the idiots at my school who run the computer lab who are all worried about people doing weird stuff on e-mail. Unless I am playing a role playing game, I'm always myself on the Net. I never lie or make stuff up when I write to the list. I'm sure there are some people who do, but I despise them, just like I despise people who lie and boast in real life. There's nothing different about e-mail that like magically turns people into liars. It sounds like the author of that book has got Internet users confused with the people who play on MUDS. The MUD guys are just like DandDers (Dungeon and Dragons players) or those Mediaeval fair people or community theater people. Some dorky people just like to put on costumes and pretend there something they're not. You can do that without the Internet.

Isaac, as an e-mail user, is less the post-modern, playful, non-unitary self posited and studied by Turkle than a very earnest transcendentalist, less a creature of Baudrillard and Jameson than of Hawthorne and Emerson. Isaac rejects the notion that who one really is can or should be reduced to one's origins, or to essentialized sociological categories such as one's life stage, race, class or gender. On the Net, Isaac writes only to connect, not to mislead or dissemble. On his homepage, he writes from the heart, with Holden Caulfield-like intensity:

> things I hate:
> stupidity, religon, capitolism, cool poeple, aol, forrest gump, star trek: generations, steak, republicans, physical exertion, petty tyranny (most high-school teachers fall under this category), physical violence, pretentous stuff in all lower case, all these fruit flies that have landed on my monitor, plaid, most of humanity, big throngs of stupid sheep-like poeple – they make me feel like travis bickle.

> I spend most of my time slaving away doing busy work that will have no effect on my life, watching tv, reading e-mail or usenet, painting and converting miniatures, playing 40k, eating, and sleeping. When I can I like to read, draw, paint, and sculpt, but I have not been able to in a while.

> I dont have any plans for life. I suppose I will end up in academia, either in english, some form of social studies/history, or art. High-school is very frustrating, and I hope college is better.

> Well, I hope I did not bore you to much. I wrote this late one night
> when I could not sleep, and so I was very pissed and mad (view this as
> stream of consciousness writing).

Except for the section on his homepage where he includes a 'morphed'
(distorted) photo of himself and some biographical information ('I'm a 15-
year-old 10th grader at a private school in Honolulu. I was born in Chicago. I
lived in Japan for a couple of year before moving to Hawaii'), Isaac's Web and
e-mail writing avoids (he would argue rises above) mention of the insignificant
and accidental biographical details of his life and physical appearance.

Isaac makes a persuasive case for the quality of his e-mail life. His
arguments are almost convincing. And yet we worry that there is something a
bit defensive, compensatory, and sad in his argument that he doesn't
particularly need or want more face-to-face social interactions. However,
asking if Isaac's life on the Web is meaningful implies we could and should do
something about it if it is not. The questions we ask about Isaac thus belie the
tendency of parents, teachers and other adults to play god/social engineer with
the adolescents whose lives we presume to control. All that is clear is that the
computer, the Web, e-mail, and Warhammer 40k are sources of great pleasure
to Isaac and that his life on e-mail and the Net is helping him carve out a
relatively coherent, functional gender and class identity, providing him with a
workable sense of who he is and how others see him at this juncture of his life.
If cyber-culture functions this way for Isaac, it is possible it functions similarily
for other *otaku*, who thus may not be as bizarre and interpersonally
handicapped as Japanese popular culture and social critics have made them out
to be.

Hackers are From Mars, *Otaku* from Venus?

In *Life on the Screen*, Turkle (1995) suggests that there are two kinds of
computer users: the PC/Windows-types who like to mess about with the
hardware and hack into programs, and the Mac-types who just want it all to
work. The PC-types exemplify a masculine engagement with the computer –
an urge to take machines apart and master them. This hacker/handyman
mentality has been articulated most eloquently by Seymour Papert, who writes
in *Mindstorms* (1980) of tearing the backs off clocks and other machines as a
child to see how the gears work and of wanting to give contemporary children
this same opportunity to get inside and mess about with computer hardware
and software. The Mac-types exemplify a feminine engagement with cyberspace captured by the advertisements that feature both famous and ordinary
folks telling us all the things they do with their Powerbooks. Sandra Bullock's
character in *The Net* notwithstanding, hackers are masculine, PC-types. And,
although they are mostly male and although their lives are centered on hyper-

masculine interests (war-gaming, comic books, pornography), *otaku*, at heart, arc more Mac-like and feminine.

Consider Isaac's correspondence with Thomas and the other members of the list. Although an invention and convention of the end of the twentieth century, Isaac's e-mail correspondence harkens back to the heyday of letter writing in the pre-electronic era. At times, when I contemplate Isaac eagerly checking his mail each day, and then typing away diligently on the computer, busily keeping up his daily correspondence, he strikes me as being part twenty-first-century hypermasculine cyberpunk, part eighteenth-century Jane Austen heroine. One of the ironies of e-mail is that it merges masculine technology with feminine correspondence.

Alternatively, the hacker and the *otaku* can be seen to represent not masculinity and femininity, but rather two modes of masculinity: the hacker's masculinity is centered on a fetishizing of tools; the *otaku*'s in a fetishizing of information. Hackers belong to a larger group that includes guys who customize their cars and ham-radio operators. *Otakus* belong to a larger group that includes trivia experts, sports fans and Trekkies.

The key difference between hackers and *otakus* is that *otakus* are more interested in information than in computers. Contemporary Japanese slang distinguishes between *computaa izon-shoo* ('computer-addict') and *info izon-shoo* ('information addict'). Isaac and his fellow *otaku* are both computer and information addicts. But their attachment to computers is secondary. They love computers because computers connect them to information. Information processing is not (just) data processing: it is exchanging, re-purposing, remaking, personalizing not just data, but also feelings, opinions and desires. The Japanese are ahead of the rest of the world in grasping the implications of life in an *info-shakai* – a post-industrial, information society. The new jobs will be found not in production but in consumption; not in engineering, but in advertising and graphic design; not in making machines, but in working at the human-machine interface; not in hacking but in organizing *otaku* communities – virtual communities linked by machines, but held together by shared passions.

Isaac, who isn't particularly interested in sports, cars, rap or rock, has formed his male identity largely around Warhammer 40K, the computer and the Internet. His *otaku* life provides him with a male performative identity, but also, simultaneously, with a way to pursue less macho interests, including art, corresponding and even interpersonal intimacy. Warhammer and computers are the subject, but not the purpose of Isaac's correspondence with Thomas and David and others in his *otaku* community. Wargames and computers, like hot rods, football trivia and babes, function as organizing principles/excuses/sites for 'homosociality' (Sedgwick, 1990). *Otaku* life is about relating to others while seeming to care only about one's obsession. Sometimes, in Isaac's e-mail correspondence, the focus on Warhammer and computers temporarily recedes to the background, and the conversation turns to other topics and more interpersonal concerns: problems at school and at work, talking-through of aspirations and sharing anxieties about future plans. To mark these departures from the rule of writing to each other about Warhammer and computers, Warhammer-*otaku* use the acronym 'Ob-40k.' As Isaac explains,

> 'Ob-40K' means 'obligatory 40k material.' The same convention is used on other lists, too, like 'Ob-Xphiles,' or just 'Ob-list.'. If one of us sends something to the whole list or an e-mail to a list member and we put in a bunch of stuff that has nothing to do with 40k, that is kind of against the spirit of a mailing list. Sometimes a list maintainer will even warn people to stay on the topic of the list. Every once in while he might even delete a message that isn't mostly about 40K. So if I write a couple of paragraphs that isn't about 40k, I start the next paragraph with 'Ob-40k,' meaning, 'Don't worry, I'm about to get back to the obligatory focus of our group.' It's sort of serious, to let the list maintainer know that at least some of the message is on topic, and sort of humorous, kind of making fun of yourself, acknowledging that you've been off-topic in your message, and that you've been using the list for something other than strictly 40k concerns.

Zen and the Art of Media Teaching

Where does this leave us media educators? Some Zen answers to a chapter that began with a *koan*: How do we professional educators teach young people to use cutting edge media? By not teaching it. We should hire more high school teachers who, like David Michaels, aren't teachers. We need teachers like David who hated school and did poorly in formal educational settings, but who are accomplished lifetime self-learners. We should offer more courses which, like the curriculum of the *otaku* learning community, have no one instructor, no syllabus, no grades, no scope and sequence. We can teach them to master cyberculture by getting out of the way in the classroom and inviting them to teach us and each other. We can best teach our high school students to become producers rather than just consumers of cyberculture by letting them out of high school sooner and more often, into apprenticeships with people who really know what they are doing.

We media educators need to accept the fact that we are not the key players in media literacy. Schools, with their budget problems, cumbersome purchasing procedures, technophobic staff and morally panicked parent groups, can't keep up with the new technology. Inevitably, the equipment and textbooks in schools are made to teach last year's new media. It is not just a problem of equipment and books, but of professional knowledge as well. Teachers, including media education teachers, know best what they learned when they were in college. With each year of tenure in their school, they risk growing another year behind professionally. This is less a problem for a teacher of history or Shakespeare than it is for a computer or media instructor.

There are instances, of course, where students learn to use the Internet and computers at school. My hunch is that in these situations teachers and students interact much as David and Isaac do. The students pose the problems and pursue their interests. The teachers facilitate and learn alongside their students. They don't stick to an orderly curriculum. They don't fill students' time, dragging out lessons. I suspect that such teachers are rare, but certainly not nonexistent. My point is not to criticize teachers or to suggest that it is their fault that they aren't doing more and better media education. Rather, I've tried to explain why I believe that most teachers are neither well suited nor situated to be key players in cyberculture learning. To understand the acquisition of media and computer literacy, we need to shift our focus to nodes and networks of learning that function outside the parameters and vision of formal schooling.

References

Grassmuck, V. (1990) 'I'm alone but not lonely': Japanese *otaku*-kids colonize the realm of information and media. www.race.u.tokyo.ac.jp/RACE/TGM/Texts/otaku.e.html

Greenfield, K. (1993) The incredibly strange mutant creatures who rule the universe of alienated Japanese zombie computer nerds (*Otaku* to you), *Wired*, US 1.1.

Papert, S. (1980) *Mindstorms: Children, Computers, and Powerful Ideas*, New York: Basic Books.

Sedgwick, E. (1990) *The Epistemology of the Closet*, New York: Routledge.

Turkle, S. (1995) *Life on the Screen: Identity in the Age of the Internet*, New York: Simon & Shuster.

Chapter 7

Digital Culture – the View from the Dance Floor

Helen Cunningham

Technology's New Image

Most young people have grown up with technologically based entertainment media in the form of television, video, teletext, arcade games, CD players, record-decks, mixers and samplers. Increasingly this entertainment technology is computer based. Indeed, the computer is becoming the all round home entertainment system, with a growth in the number of homes who have a CD-ROM drive, or even an Internet connection. The range of technologies aimed at the home market is ever expanding. New combinations of hardware such as the TVPC (CD player, TV and PC all in one unit) are now being marketed as an ideal package for a teenager, and new software packages aimed at the home consumer appear on the market with almost weekly monotony – for example, photo discs enabling the user to store their holiday snaps on CD-ROM, and low cost image manipulation software such as Kai's *Power Goo*. A number of software packages aimed at the educational market are available enabling the user to draw, paint, manipulate images and make simple animation or music tracks. Computer technology is now sold alongside puzzle games in toy shops, such as TOYS 'Я' US and alongside pens and paper in stationery shops.

The image of technology has certainly changed since the 1970s when computers were perceived as mathematical machines, used primarily for business applications and data storage. Knowledge of computers was seen as an extension of maths and science. Computers required a knowledge of programming languages, and using one involved extensive periods of inactivity while programmes loaded from tape cassette players. By the 1990s computers were no longer purely associated with work environments. The concept of the computer as an artistic and musical tool has become naturalized in the minds of young people. This is partly due to the extensive media coverage of the use of technology in the production of popular entertainment. Children's television not only carries items on the making of films such as *Roger Rabbit* and *Toy Story*, but often explores the possibilities offered by computer special effects in the making of films such as *Terminator 2* and *Lawnmower Man*.

From this point of view teenagers have grown up regarding the computer as a creative instrument. As Andrew Goodwin (1990: 263) puts it 'We have grown used to connecting *machines* and *funkiness*.' However, as Sefton-Green and Buckingham further explore in this volume, the creative potential of this age group is frequently not realized due to the lack of an economy in which young people's productions might circulate: 'the absence of an audience for much of this work meant that it [is] always limited and constrained . . . There [is] no obvious reason to make artefacts and in most cases nobody to make them for' (Buckingham and Sefton-Green, 1995). I want to suggest in this chapter, that when these adolescents enter 'club cultures' in a few years time, there exists both a reason to make these cultural products, a cultural economy in which to distribute them and an appreciative audience for this type of work.[1]

The participants in contemporary youth subcultures have been brought up on 24-hour TV, music videos containing non-narrative visuals, interactivity within computer games, and adverts that are computer generated and manipulated. In many ways the technological gadgetry that surrounds young people has been naturalized, but this is not to say the effects of this technology go unnoticed. This chapter examines how technology is being used within club culture, how access to this technology (hardware, software and technological knowledge) is gained, and looks at the role of youth subcultures as a training ground for the cultural industries. Empirical data will then be advanced in order to critique current debates about the democratizing potential of these new technologies.

Methodology

This research developed out of my own involvement in club culture – in Manchester and London – over the past eight years, and of course, my own position as a participant within the club scene has no doubt affected the research process. I have been studying club culture from the inside having been involved in the club scene for many years prior to writing this chapter. In the last few years, primarily due to the explosion of interest in computer games and the Internet, alongside the continued popularity of computer based music, I became inquisitive as to how the image of technology was changing and the impact this may have on young peoples' relationship to these new technologies. I found myself becoming more and more interested in these new technologies and their creative potential.

Over the past two years (1994–6) – when interest in new technology within club culture has been at its most intense – I have attended clubs regularly with my friends as part of my normal lifestyle: they are the main meeting spaces and social playgrounds for my circle of friends. On one level then, my identity as a clubber with natural friendships with cultural producers from within the underground club scene pre-existed my becoming an academic and certainly enabled me to gain an insight into new occurrences within club culture. The research I describe here consisted of going out to clubs, mainly in London, in particular to 'techno nights', and more recently 'jungle/drum 'n bass' nights, in an attempt to gain an overall picture of what was happening both musically and visually. Further data are drawn from the music press, style magazines and fanzines; again I read these regularly. On average I attended one club each week, although some nights out consisted of visiting up to three different clubs on the same night. Many of my friends work within the club culture industry and its related fields, and so, for me, work and leisure blurred, given that my social life regularly consisted of actively seeking out the new, the innovative and the experimental fields within the club scene. These nights of research were part of my everyday (or night) life and this obviously raises a number of complex methodological issues around the objectivity of the ethnographic researcher.

Andy Lovatt and Jonathan Purkis discuss in detail the role of ethnographic researchers who 'are already immersed in their chosen culture prior to intellectual engagement', asking, 'are they a fan, an interpreter, a researcher, an essayist or all four?' They go on to suggest that these new researchers are 'called upon to adopt many different "tactics" and identities during the course of their various research activities' (1996:250). When doing this research I have been both a participating fan of dance music, while simultaneously attempting to interpret and analyze the changes within the club scene. Although the lack of analytical distance between myself and the object of study may for some be seen as problematic, I believe that the insider position that I have occupied has benefited the research in that a position of trust between myself and others, for example, the visual producers, enabled me to discover some of their more unorthodox ways of gaining access to the technologies. I don't believe I could necessarily have gained this insight into their working practices if I had been an outsider from a university who had come along and formally interviewed these people.

While attending these clubs I collected data for this research through informal interviews, or 'ethnographic conversations', with promoters, DJ's, visuals producers, musicians and clubbers themselves. In general, the informants I interviewed had usually met me a number of times before I began to chat about my research. Again I would argue that my position as an insider within club culture enabled me to chat to these people in a relaxed way. Their response to me was clearly direct; I was seen as an interested and involved participant within the club scene rather than an academic.

After noting these methodological issues concerning my own position within the research process I also want to mention a number of practical problems involved in carrying out research in club culture. The interviews took place in a club venue where the sound system was usually at full blast. The usual rules for interviews – such as find a quiet place and tape record the process – were understandably impractical. When interviewing the promoters, DJs and visual producers I sometimes suggested we stand somewhere quieter, such as the bar or 'chill-out room', where I could take notes; but often within a popular club night no place is quiet and all spaces are crowded.

As well as the specific questions and issues that I discussed with the producers within club culture, I also wanted to talk to the participants – the clubbers. I was keen to get their views on the music, the visuals, their experience of technology and whether or not they had access to other technologies, such as the Internet, outside of these spaces. These interviews were less formal and often took the form of 'chattering' with people at the bar and chill-out rooms. In these situations it was impossible to take notes; I had to rely on memory. These conversations are, by their very nature, only with a random sample of clubbers; and although I was keen to gain the views of women in particular, I make no claims about the representative nature of my research. When talking to people within club culture it is inappropriate to ask direct questions about class, income or background. However, in my conversations with the cultural producers I was keen to find out about their background and did try to ascertain how they had trained in their chosen field.

My research identified four main areas within club culture in which computer technology was being used. These were the creation of music; the production of visual art for display within the club night; the production of promotional 'subcultural media' such as fanzines and flyers; and the use of technology as an entertainment/communications medium in itself, that is using the Internet in club venues. There has also been a major interest in the use of Internet as a promotional medium by the music industry, with an increasing number of Web sites set up by clubs, festivals and record labels. Club culture provides the audience and the venue in which much of this creative work (both visual and musical) can be displayed, as well as providing the reason to utilize desk top publishing skills to produce flyers and fanzines to promote and discuss the club scene.

Digital Music and Club Culture

The combination of the club scene and technology is not really surprising when one considers how the dance music scene has developed. The dominant musical form amongst youth culture in the 1990s is *dance music*, a wide generic term for all forms of what Thornton has termed *disc cultures*.

In the 1990's, records have been enculturated within the night life of British dance clubs to the extent that it makes sense to talk about *disc cultures* whose values are markedly different from those of live music cultures. What authenticates contemporary dance cultures is the buzz or energy which results from the interaction of records, DJ and crowd. Liveness' is displaced from the stage to the dancefloor, from the worship of the performer to a veneration of 'atmosphere' or 'vibe' (1995:29).

The music is produced in recording studios and played in vinyl form. Indeed, the technology is so central to one specific genre within dance music that the genre itself is named 'techno'. By the mid-1990s computers were integral to dance music production. The record decks, a mixer (and sometimes drum machines and samplers) are the instruments with which the DJs perform their set for the club crowd. The young people who grew up playing *PacMan* on their *Atari* games consoles in the 1980s have now entered club culture, and are the first generation to view computer technology as the natural instrument on or with which sounds can be created, played and reproduced. As Goodwin notes, 'Manipulating a record turntable, or programming a drum machine is, for this generation of musicians, the equivalent of learning an instrument' (1992a:94). Just as participants within punk subculture picked up an electric guitar and created their own sounds, youths within club culture have also had a go at DIY (Do It Yourself) music technology.

The technology with which these forms of music can be created has become increasingly accessible. Many older teenagers have access to a pair of record decks and a mixer on which they perfect their mixing skills. PCs are increasingly common in teenagers' bedrooms, whereas keyboards and samplers are the add-ons which these youths save up for, or purchase jointly with a friend. Bedroom mix tapes have become one form of 'subcultural' promotional media, as aspiring DJs record tapes showing their mixing abilities; these can be sent off to promoters and passed round to friends. Most of the new DJs and musicians on the dance music scene have taught themselves mixing, sampling and other computer skills in the same way that young people within previous subcultures may have learnt how to play bass guitar or the drums. Andrew Goodwin comments on how computer technology has now been accepted as an instrument on which music is made: 'today's pop musicians are often technicians who have learned to program every bit as skilfully as earlier generations learned to play' (1990:264). However, before I discuss recent developments in club culture, I need to contextualize them within the history of the club scene.

DJs and Technology

The DJs' adoption of the mixer is central to club culture. As Tony Langois argues in his study of the British House Music DJ, 'The key role in the House scene is that of the DJ. It is his own transformation from passive "record player" to (virtual) musician that gives the House event its significance' (1992:230). DJs took on the role of musicians, creating a seamless mix of sound. The importance of the creative and technical skills of the DJ is also acknowledged by Ross Harley who points out that, '. . . house would never emerged without the rise of the DJ as technical innovator and (later on) as fully fledged producer' (1993:222). By the mid-1980s the creative (if not institutional) distinctions between DJs, musicians, producers and sound engineers had collapsed. House music DJs knew that this music was produced technologically, and they learnt to use this technology. Indeed many of the DJs from the late 1980s have now become producers. Goodwin states:

> If the new technologies herald a further shift in power relations away from musicians and towards producers and mixers, it is also the case that many musicians . . . have noticed this and . . . have opted to train themselves in this new skill (1992a:94).

It may have been the case when Goodwin was writing that existing musicians retrained and learnt technological skills; but for those currently entering club cultures, who have grown up alongside House music, Rap and Hip Hop, the computer is just another tool alongside the record decks. Today's aspiring musicians know that music is produced in ways that dissolve conventional distinctions between technical skills and musical creativity.

Writing about the 'New Pop' of the 1980s Goodwin (1992b) discusses the controversy around the notion of 'authenticity', when bands began to create music in the studio which they were unable to perform live, i.e. without the use of machines. But 'throughout the 1980's, pop, rock, and rap audiences became habituated to the idea that some of the music being heard "live" might be on tape, or might emanate from a machine, and/or might consist of a sample of music recorded elsewhere' (Goodwin 1992b:32). By the late 1980s with the birth of 'Acid House' it became the norm for music to be produced on a computer and played in vinyl form.

Club nights usually consist of DJs mixing records, and this is how the majority of dance music is consumed; although as Thornton (1995:83–4) discusses, some of the most successful dance acts also go on tour playing live: 'their record labels see touring as a main means of building the artist identity essential for big sales'. She further identifies how the 'lines that previously demarcated the gig, the PA and the club have been blurred' but the examples she gives are of successful dance music groups who put on live club tours combining the live act with a club night feel. The scale of these events is very different to the experience of an 'underground' club, but these types of events have introduced more technology into the club night:

> Acts like . . . the Orb, 808 State and the Prodigy have toured clubs playing with computers, samplers and 'improvised' keyboard parts, vocalists and other guest instrumentalists (not to mention turntables). These artists create events that have been hailed as 'live' (Thornton 1995:84).

This attempt by successful dance acts to bring elements of the studio into the club night has blurred the lines between studio and club still further. DJs are now including effects pedals, drum machines and samplers in their DJ sets. As this combination of mixing records and live performance becomes more widespread, the influence of this approach is filtering down. Increasingly old Atari's or lap top computers are being seen in clubs linked up to both samplers and keyboards. The ambitions of teenagers in the late 90s is not only to mix records and to DJ, but to also make their own tracks. The nineties dream is of becoming a digital musician, more than just a DJ.

There may be more opportunities now for young people to create their own tracks, but the problem still remains that it is very difficult to get tracks played. Music is being produced by young people but as yet it is not easy to get this music heard in a club venue. The music industry is still an extremely difficult one to break into. However, new technology does provide some new methods of getting your music heard. A new club night, Abacus at the ICA in London, which aimed to focus on the innovative and experimental, did not want to have established DJs but asked for people to send in DAT tapes of their own creations and was hoping to create a club night using these new unreleased sounds.

However, although young people are producing music using home based technologies there is still not a cultural economy for these musicians to plug into. Personally I am optimistic that this may gradually change as technology comes down in price. For example, the dance music industry is based on 12″ single releases unlike the rest of the music industry which is based on album sales. These 12″ singles are distributed to DJs through mailing lists and specialist dance music record shops. A record by a previously unknown musician could become very popular when only a limited number of copies have been pressed. As club culture is based on 12″ singles rather than albums, there has been a massive increase in the number of small labels which put out records for this specialist market. Thus when the technology comes down in price, and as the market becomes ever more specialized into niche sub genres, the cost of pressing a record has come within the reach of many more people.

In overall terms, of course, music is just one area within club cultures where young people are using the new technologies in creative ways; yet perhaps music is also the one area in which it is the most difficult for people to find an audience. A second aspect of club culture where technology is being used in innovative and experimental ways is in the production of club visuals.

Creating a Visual Environment

Contemporary youth culture often has the reputation for being less creative than previous eras of youth cultures. Indeed, 90s culture is frequently described as a 'cut 'n' paste culture' in which nothing new is created, fashions from previous generations are recycled and music is merely the assemblage of samples. It is only recently, in 1996, that Club culture and its associated art forms has at last been recognized as a truly creative culture by sections of the Arts establishment, acknowledged by the 'Jam, style +music+media' exhibition at the Barbican Art Gallery in London:

Jam seeks to give a platform to a diversity of creative people working outside the fine art arena, chosen for their empowering attitudes, a contemporary non-retro approach to image making, with 'sample-delia' – an eclectic spirit – often the defining characteristic. (Jam, Barbican Art Gallery, London, 12 September–15 December 1996).

New technology is often accused of diminishing the creativity of young people. However, in this section I will argue that club culture is providing the motivation for young people to use this new technology in innovative and creative ways.

In economic terms, club culture has relied on promoters hiring venues for their weekly or monthly club nights. The venue may play host to a number of different club nights in any one week. Each promoter wishes to create a unique identity for his or her club night and this is achieved not only by diverse musical policies but increasingly through club decoration. The same venue space might have a completely different look each night of the week as different visual teams transform the walls and divide off the space with drapes and sheeting onto which images are projected. A few years ago the prevalent form of decoration in House music clubs were home painted banners, with psychedelic colouring and UV paint which glows under the UV lights.

Although painted banners still exist, they are often accompanied by moving images in the form of slides or video footage. The aim is to provide visual stimulation which blends in with the music. In clubs playing 'techno' music the visuals often continue this techno influence. The iconography of computer games and other interactive forms such as CD-ROM is prevalent. These computer graphics, psychedelic screensavers and fractals are often mixed in with images 'sampled' from sci-fi films and popular television. Tony Langois describes the visuals used in club culture as: '. . . constituting something of a post-modern idiom, consisting as they do of collage, "cut-up", and distortion of time and colours' (1992:237). The club is a site for displaying this new art form. The images are frequently computer generated, and both manipulated still images and video footage are photographed or filmed directly from the computer screen. These videos are often simple animation sequences or screen savers.

In general club visuals tend to utilize low grade technology such as slide projectors or super 8 film footage, but often produce some of the most innovative and exciting results. The club visuals team I observed doing some of the most interesting work, have a number of tricks in which they use *low tech* equipment to simulate *high tech* images. At one of the club nights I attended they projected a slide onto a record turntable which was covered in mirrors. The image reflected off the mirrors onto a large wall and created the effect of a moving rippling image and many presumed it was produced using a computer graphics package. This same group also had a black and white video animation which they projected onto walls in club spaces. When asked how this was produced, they revealed that it was not an animation package but consisted of a number of files created in a simple drawing package on an old slow PC. The animation effect was achieved simply due to the slowness of opening and closing graphics files. There were many more examples of how they were using low tech in an innovative way so as to simulate the appearance of high tech creations.

Indeed youth culture has often used low tech to produce innovative results, although some critics, such as Ross Harley, have a romanticized view of why this is so:

> Echoing the punks of the 1960's and 1970's, today's renegade producers and consumers are more likely to refer to DIY 'garage multi-media' and 'street tech' than the lustre of hi-tech, arguing that the only position worth occupying is that of low end technological improvisation and electronic monkey-wrenching. 'The street has its own use for things,' as cyberpunk luminary William Gibson once wrote (1993:224).

This romanticized notion of low tech does not question or criticize the economics of an industry in which many are denied legitimate access to the technologies due to lack of finance. Youth cultures' use of low tech is often out of necessity rather than choice, and high technologies are appropriated and used whenever possible.

Appropriation of High Tech: Strategies to Gain Access

Young people have demonstrated many ways to get round these problems. Machines such as scanners and samplers, combined with the cut 'n' paste abilities of computer software, have transformed the ways in which we think of ownership of sounds and images. The distinction between old and new images is blurred. In this field it is very clear that copyright is both an outdated and unworkable method of property control. One prominent graphic design team working within the music industry, The Designers Republic excuse their infringement of other peoples copyright by stating:

> . . . we've always had this thing about visual sampling. If you draw parallels with music, you sample something put it into your own track and use it differently. You don't sample something and make it sound the same. (The Designers Republic, 1996:28–30)

Within the peer networks of club culture, lack of access to software is not that great a problem. As well as the freeware and shareware available on the Net, there is an underground economy of piracy in which most programs can be swapped for other software or games. If the software you wish to use is not available as a pirate copy, there is usually an alternative program which someone within your peer group will pass on to you. It may not be the latest version, but it will usually do the job.

The ideologies of the digital age stress the need for new improved software and hardware upgrades. The fast pace of change in the computer industry means that any investment made in hardware or software may quite quickly become obsolete. Ross Harley discusses how:

> As part of the logic of capitalism . . . the music industry's own continuity is stored up by an ever-changing array of fetishistic commodities exchanged for profit. Put simply, new technologies enliven flagging consumer interest and initiate fresh desires that promise to be fulfilled by the acquisition of new objects, in the form of what is now commonly referred to as 'hardware' and 'software' (1993:212).

These ideologies have been actively resisted by many within youth cultures who have developed strategies to gain access to these technologies. Of course, the principle underlying copyrights and licences for programs focuses on the loss of income to the holders of these licences, if such products are pirated. Many users of pirated software defend their actions by condemning the excessively high prices of the professional programmes. When these programs are pirated and swapped between friends, it is frequently argued on a political level that such actions are attempts to even up the inequalities of access to these technologies. After all, the logic goes, software companies are not actually losing any money as these users could actually not afford to purchase these products: yet without piracy they would just be denied access to them.

Strategies have also been developed to enable new software programs to be used in club visuals. New versions of professional software are often obtained from demo discs which are given away free on computer magazines. These demo discs are often fully working programmes, the only drawback being that the work cannot be saved. These discs, of course, are intended to tempt the user to purchase the software package. As the price of these new packages is often out of the reach of these young clubbers, work can be created using the demo software, but as it cannot be saved it is then filmed direct from the computer screen. The file is then discarded and the work is lost but the images are stored on video.

Even when these images are created with expensive high tech multimedia computers using software such as Adobe *Photoshop*, or multimedia packages such as Macromedia *Director*, there is often a problem of how to display such visual products in the club as the nature of the club spaces and clubbing activities cause practical problems. Although the images can in theory be directly projected from the computer screen, this is an expensive option; computer projection equipment is very costly and would be vulnerable to theft and damage in this milieu. Underground clubs often run on very tight budgets, and equipment hire and insurance would often be beyond the means of most of these club nights. Again, as a way around this problem, the computer screen may be videoed (with a borrowed camcorder) and the video then projected onto the wall of the club space. I have also seen video footage transferred onto 16 millimetre film for projection using even cheaper second hand film projectors.

Some of the young people I interviewed were using computer hardware which had been originally bought for the purposes of school work, whereas others found ways of gaining access to the computers and scanners available in local colleges. An important development in terms of the democratization of access to these technologies is the opening up of computer rooms in a number of libraries across London. These facilities provide top end machines and software which can be utilized for an hourly fee.

Typically the biggest problem reported by the people I interviewed in relation to equipment was the perennial one of memory (RAM) and storage of files, as storage drives and memory are so expensive. However, in recent months both of these products have come down in price. Another major problem for many young people is insurance, as the majority of companies will not insure computer equipment in a 'multi-occupancy' household, especially if the occupiers are unemployed.

High Tech Dreams

Cyberpunk fiction has had a extensive impact on contemporary youth cultures, in particular within the techno subculture. As cyberpunk is set in the not too distant future, many of the gadgets and technological instruments dreamt up by these authors as fictional devices are now appearing in high street shops. However the performance of these devices in 1996 is often below their level of usefulness in cyberpunk fiction. As Philip Hayward explains

> Gibson's work, and the Cyberpunk genre in general, have principally served to excite interest in newly developing interactive computer systems . . . Whatever Gibson's (best) intentions, his work has created a desire for cyberspace technologies in advance of their production (1993:186).

New technology is facilitating a new wave of creativity amongst youth as new developments in technologies are tried out and pushed to their technical limits. But of course, as I have already shown, the creativity within youth culture is being held back in some instances by the technology. The projects attempted in club nights are often beyond the limits of what is currently technologically possible. The new technologies and the hype around them, along with the fictions of cyberpunk writers, have given people dreams of what they want to achieve with this technology; but in some cases these projects cannot be realized. Mike Featherstone and Burrows sum up these implications of cyberpunk:

> The term cyberpunk refers to the body of fiction built around the work of William Gibson and other writers, who have constructed visions of the future worlds of cyberspaces, with all their vast range of technolo-gical-fix visions of the future, with a wide range of post-human forms which have both theoretical and practical implications; theoretically, in influencing those who are trying to reconstruct the social theory of the present and near future, and practically, in terms of those (largely young people) who are keen to devise experimental lifestyles and subcultures which aim to live out and bring about selected aspects of the cyberspace/cyberpunk constellation (Featherstone and Burrows, (1995:3).

When these young people get their hands on these newly emerging technolo-gies, they seem to expect them to perform as they do in cyberpunk fictions, but sadly they are often disappointed.

For example, a number of clubs have attempted link ups between different club venues or to broadcast the club night live on the Net using *CuSeeme* links and *Real Audio* technology. Dance music bands have per-formed in one venue and hoped to transmit live over the Net to clubs elsewhere. Yet many of these attempts at Internet link ups have frustrated the club goers. The developments in Internet technology have been hyped in the media but when it is actually tried out, the technology does not live up to the expectations. Many within the club scene want to incorporate these new technologies into club culture but are frustrated by the slow development of the technology. The underground club culture 'zine *Phasis* (issue 4) summed up this frustration in an article reviewing a club night put on by 'Digital Diaspora' under the headline 'Digital Diasporation!':

> Dance music and club culture should be seizing new technologies and pushing them to their limits – that's the essence of the culture. The potential for enhancing the club space through digital video, computer animation, the Internet, is huge. But it's not a simple process. There are many problems, not least the high cost of the technology itself. With much of the innovation in club culture coming from low-budget operations, the cost alone will keep the high-tech stuff out of most clubs for a while yet. So anyone who's prepared to try it out deserves praise, whatever the outcome. But, in pushing technology to its limits, it's important for promoters and clubbers alike to accept that limits do exist . . . The truth about the Internet and software like CUSeeme and Real Audio, is that it simply doesn't work properly yet. It's still

the exception rather than the rule for these kind of links to come online, and stay online, trouble free . . . Keep pushing the limits.

These technologies may not yet be able to deliver the dreams promised by cyberpunk fiction but they will continue to be tested out within club culture.

For example, night-clubs may not be the first place to spring to mind when one thinks of places where one might access the Net; but as well as attempts at live link-ups between club nights, a number of clubs have also provided computer terminals for clubbers to use. There has been one weekly club night in Central London, Megatripolis, where Internet access has been available for over two years. Once Clubbers have paid their entrance fee into the club – which is only £1 before 11 pm if you have a UB40 (unemployment benefit) or student card – they can surf the Net until 4am, for no extra charge. The terminals are all linked to the World Wide Web, and also have software installed such as *Cubase*, *Photoshop*, and *Quark*. There is frequently a technician on hand all night to supervise and help out with any technical problems. This room is always full of people using this opportunity to e-mail their friends, or to surf the Web. Another monthly club in London, 'the big chill', contained two terminals, supervised by an Internet service provider who was also on hand to give technical support.

Some clubs are host to Internet providers and have Internet access; there are also Internet cafes which play host to 'club nights'. In central London there is a monthly club 'The Sprawl' whose venue is an Internet cafe/bar in London. For a modest entrance charge of £3 club goers can have a beer, listen to the DJs and have half an hour of free Internet access.

The reasons why Internet access has became available in clubs are complex and contradictory. On one level the Internet has become romanticized as an anarchistic, subversive technology. Philip Hayward discusses how:

> Euphoria over the revolutionary nature of cyberspace technology has often been expressed in decidedly 'mystical' tones echoing the 'spiritual' concerns of 60's hippie psychedelia and converging with aspects of those beliefs and practices which have come to be known as 'New Age' (1993:197).

New Age youth cultures have embraced digital technology and for the past few years many music festivals such as Glastonbury and Phoenix have had a computer tent and a web site with *CuSeeme* links to the activities of the festival.

The two clubs in London where Internet access was provided were both clubs which could be described as embracing this new age philosophy. They were clubs which attempted to bring the feel of a festival event into an urban club space. They included not only the music which was central to the festivals, but also the other aspects of the festival field, such as the many stalls (selling such things as jewellery and clothing), and services (such as aromatherapy massages, hair braiding), as well as the computer access which could also be found at the festivals. These new Age philosophies embrace both mysticism and the entreprencurial spirit. These ambiguities are best expressed by Philip Hayward:

> the [New Age] world order is posed as fundamentally post-materialist and it promises to fill the perceived spiritual void of Western society. New Age is, however, nothing if not contradictory. In particular, New Age is big business (1993:197).

Of course the companies producing the new technologies now being sold to young consumers are also new expanding businesses. The presence of computer technologies within New Age club cultures could also be seen as a good marketing strategy by the new Internet service providers who see festivals and clubs a way of gaining a credible profile for their companies and a youthful street-wise image.

The Creativity of the Underground – Training and Youth Enterprise

My research has documented how technology is being used within the *underground* of London club culture. The use of high tech equipment for displaying visuals or for Internet access has been relatively limited due to the lack of finance for equipment, but not all clubs operate on such tight budgets. Indeed, some clubs have a turnover of millions; although in my view these clubs have not incorporated technology in the same innovative ways as the smaller, less financially successful clubs. Perhaps due to size, these 'corporate clubs' have related to youth culture interest in new technologies in very different ways. For example, club venues such as 'The Ministry of Sound' and 'The Complex' in London have both obtained sponsorship from Sony and have games rooms within the club containing Sony Playstations.

This provision of games consoles is very different from the experimental uses of digital technology which I have documented in the previous sections. The corporate clubs who can afford to invest in the technology perhaps lack the motivation to be experimental. Although no one definition of underground or mainstream exists, the underground itself often sees creativity and inno-vation as primary characteristics of itself, whereas the mainstream is seen to be primarily concerned with commercial opportunities. This is not to say that underground club nights can not be commercially successful: the difference between underground and mainstream is more one of attitude. Underground clubs, being more committed to innovation and experimentation in all aspects of the culture, are perhaps more willing to experiment and introduce new elements into the club experience – for example to include new musical sounds or more experimental visual arts – whereas mainstream nights perhaps have developed a successful financial formula and do not want to run the risk of changing this.

Nevertheless, I would argue that the underground clubs are doing more, producing highly experimental work within smaller budgets, often on low tech formats than some of the larger club venues. It seems to me that within the smaller underground nights the club promoters and DJs are more in touch with the skills and creative abilities of their crowds. The promoters and DJs are themselves part of that crowd and know friends, or friends of friends, who will help out with the various aspects of putting on the club night, such as the flyer design and the club visuals. Within underground club culture I would suggest that there is more crossover between producers and consumers, as increasing numbers of young people turn their club culture activities into a whole way of life, earning money for their cultural productions.

I have detailed a number of examples where young people are utilizing new technology and producing cultural goods for use in their own subcultures. These goods have an economic value as well as a cultural one. For many the motivation to work within these youth cultural industries is not just the desire to make money, but a desire to do something they enjoy. Over the past eight years as the dance music scene has evolved, many of the young innovators within this culture have been able to make a living through their subculture. Club culture thus becomes a whole way of life, giving people not just a lifestyle and an identity but a means of making money to support that lifestyle. A small but significant minority have been able to turn their subcultural activities into employment opportunities, and this is an area within club cultures that needs further research.

Angela McRobbie points out how work on subcultures in the 1970s concentrated on the 'signifying products' and the meanings produced by these images and did not question the day to day activities of cultural production within those subcultures. McRobbie (1994: 161) has begun to examine these questions in relation to contemporary youth cultures:

> my concern . . . is with the way in which the magazines produced by the fans, the music produced by DJs, the clothes bought sold and worn by subcultural 'stylists', do more than just publicise the subculture. They also provide the opportunity for learning and sharing skills, for practising them, for making a small amount of money; more importantly, they provide pathways for future 'lifeskills' in the form of work or self-employment. To ignore the intense activity of cultural production as well as its strongly aesthetic dimension (in graphics, fashion design, retail and music production) is to miss a key part of subcultural life – the creation of a whole way of life, an alternative to higher education (though often a 'foundation' for art school), a job creation scheme for the cultural industries.

McRobbie's findings are especially true in relation to club culture and the cultural production that is occurring using digital technologies. Formal training in digital technologies is available either at a very high cost through private training courses or is available free to a relatively small number in universities where demand for practical courses is very intense. The informal training in these new skills that is taking place within these subcultures is extremely important in equipping people with transferable skills and enabling them to obtain employment in this quickly changing field of digital media. Many of the people who are producing goods for use within their own subcultures have trained themselves and then pass on these skills to others within the subculture.

In the course of my research I became aware that the London subcultural scene, that is those who are involved in the underground, experimental aspects of digital music and art, is a relatively close-knit community. Most of the cultural producers I interviewed personally knew many of the other musicians and artists working in this field. At many of the club nights the same groups of people were present, as the clubbers went to check out what was happening in other club nights similar to their own. As I enquired into how these people knew each other, it quickly became apparent that many were friends. Some of the artists in the visual teams had originally worked for free to gain work experience, learn new skills and make valuable contacts. Within the music industry contacts and networking are all important. Promoters, DJs and visual teams pass on their knowledge and contacts to others. Often equipment and studio space was shared by a group of people. Indeed during the course of my research, I was actively incorporated into this process. When I was chatting to people about technology in chill-out rooms I was often asked 'have you got a Mac? . . . what software have you got? I can get you a copy of . . . if you want.' When computer technology was being used, people were keen to discuss with others what they had done and how they had achieved this. Katie Milestone describes a similar situation in her research into Manchester youth culture:

> As the eighties progressed people with no formal training began to become involved in record and flyer design. Inspired by the existing Manchester network a new breed of designers realised that in this city not only did you not have to have formal training to become a pop star . . . you could also become a graphic artist as well (1996:106).

Many of the people who are working in this hidden economy of club cultures, producing visuals, lighting, flyers, music and fanzines have been denied access to training on digital media by the formal training sectors. For many the traditional notion of the work ethic is no longer an option with the decline of the steady 9–5 job for life. De-industrialization and high youth unemployment have meant that many young people are disillusioned with the jobs which are available. To quote McRobbie again, 'Subcultures are often ways of creating job opportunities as more traditional careers disappear' (1994:162).

In many ways the philosophies encouraged by the proponents of digital media – small scale business, working from home, flexible working hours, the absence of a 9–5 routine, being your own boss – all appeal to those who have rejected (or been rejected by) the dominant culture. Digital media has perhaps provided even more opportunities for this hidden entrepreneurial economy. Working from home with a computer and a modem, on a freelance or self-employed basis, is becoming more common. In this way club cultures provide training in business skills as well as in producing the cultural goods. There are increasing numbers of small businesses often set up by one, two or three like-minded people, who produce goods to sell in the cultural economy of club culture. These businesses range from graphic design, Web site production, video production, through to the production of flyers, independent record labels and DJs.

Digital media are being used to facilitate changing working practices in this country, but it is within the subcultures that young people are offered motivation and opportunity; they often operate as testing grounds for new skills. These day-to-day working practices of club cultures need further examination and research, along with the range of mechanisms for training young people in digital media.

The Potential for Democratizing Technology?

Digital technology is often talked about in celebratory terms, as if the technology alone will lead to a more egalitarian society. What I am arguing is that the coming together of the new digital technologies and the dance music scene has provided the incentive for many young people to have a go themselves. New technology has enabled people to become producers as well as consumers within these subcultures. Writing about this relationship between technology and society within the context of popular music Simon Frith (1986: 278) has put this clearly:

> Technology . . . has certainly been the necessary condition for the rise of the multinational entertainment business, for ever more sophisti-cated techniques of ideological manipulation, but technology has also made possible new forms of cultural democracy and new opportunities of individual and collective expression . . . Each new development in recording technology enables new voices to be heard and to be heard in new ways; and pop voices are systematically denied access to other public media.

In principle the wider availability of technology means more people can be involved in musical and artistic creativity as more people have access to the tools of production such as computers and camcorders.

However, Goodwin has three reservations about this argument for the democratizing potential of music technology. First, he states that:

> new technologies are not nearly as classless as they might appear to be
> . . . there is a world of difference between a Casio sampler bought in a
> department store and the hugely expensive sampling computers that
> sit in pre-production studios (1992a:91).

There may still be a world of difference between these two technologies but this gap is rapidly closing to the point where his concern may no longer be valid. Similarly in the same piece he also argues that:

> the expertise needed to operate the more sophisticated computer is
> such that they have bred a new generation of technicians, engineers,
> and programmers who are often hired along with the equipment to
> implement the ideas of musicians who in fact have little or no idea how
> actually to use this supposedly democratising technology (1992a:92).

Again this may be true for certain musicians, but there is a growing and ever-expanding new generation of artists who have always produced music on computers and who have taught themselves how to operate them. Here again, I would dispute the relevance of this concern within the culture I have studied.

Goodwin's third reservation concerns the gendered nature of this technology:

> the democratising function of the new technologies of pop seem to
> stop short of opening up the new forms of composition and engineer-
> ing to women – probably for socially complex reasons having to do
> with the identification of technology with masculinity. In other words,
> it is the boys, still, who are playing with the toys (1992a:92).

Goodwin is right in saying that the dominance of men in this area of music production is due to 'socially complex reasons'. However, he then goes on to lay the blame for women's lack of participation in music production on an 'identification of [the] technology with masculinity'. To expect new technologies to reverse decades of female inequality in the workplace and male dominance in both the world of technology and of the music industry may be just a little too much to ask in such a short space of time. Within contemporary club cultures, it is still primarily the boys who are playing with these toys, but increasingly there are more and more women who are working within club cultures and working in ways that use these technologies. However I would agree with Benjamin Noys that:

> It is difficult to judge whether the subculture itself is more or less sexist
> than other subcultures or the dominant culture. There are female DJs,

including DJ Rap who has started her own label, Proper Talent, and Jo who is the artist who created the abstract Jungle track 'R-Type' (Awesome Records, 1993) . . . So certainly there are spaces for female expression (1995:329).

Further empirical research is needed to explore this question fully. Although dance music club cultures have been the prevalent form of youth culture for less than ten years, within this relatively short history the number of women DJs has increased significantly. In the early days of Acid House it was very rare to see a female DJ, but now women DJs are far more common. Within the new and developing genres within dance music, such as jungle/drum 'n bass, many of the DJs within the London underground club scene are female. This may be just the beginning. As I discussed earlier many of the DJs within club culture go on to become record producers; I hope this new generation of female DJs will go on to become the producers of tomorrow.

Through this limited account of the use of technology within underground club cultures in London I have suggested that club cultures play a vital role in providing the peer networks in which access to technology is gained. Many people find within these cultures the incentive and opportunity to use the technologies to produce 'media-art'. Club culture provides an economy in which these cultural goods circulate and provides the motivation and contacts to learn these new skills. The artists who are working within club culture often have no formal training (i.e. paper qualifications) in these technologies. Many of the musicians and visual artists I came across while researching this chapter have not attended university, and others who were at university were not being specifically taught how to use these technologies. The technical knowledge and competencies developed within club culture are being passed on to others. Increasingly events are being organized, such as Muzik Masterclass hosted by the dance music magazine *Muzik*, where studio equipment is available for people to experiment with. Club culture is, to a great extent, democratizing access to technology and is providing training in ways not covered by the formal education system. Subsequent motivation to work within these sectors of the economy has led people on to training schemes either within further education or within the government's Training for Work schemes.

Club culture is incorporating new developments in technology into its club nights in exciting new ways. The underground club night has become a testing ground for new technological projects, where young people can try out new ideas and new forms of art. Club culture provides not only the motivation but also the space in which to display this art work. Much of the creative artistic talent within club culture goes unnoticed by wider society, even though it provides training ground and initial motivation for many of those now working within digital media arts.

Notes

I would like to thank the club visuals team at CORE, the promotions people at *Sapour*, and the editors at *Phasis* for their help, advice and support in the writing of this chapter. Their contacts within the world of club culture and their commitment to it have proved invaluable to my research.

1 'Club Cultures' have been defined as

'the colloquial expression given to youth cultures for whom dance clubs and their eighties offshoot, raves, are the symbolic axis and working social hub. [They are] associated with a specific space which is both continually transforming its sounds and styles and regularly bearing witness to the apogees and excesses of youth cultures (Thornton, 1995:3).

References

Buckingham, D. and Sefton-Green, J. (1995) Digital visions: New opportunities for multimedia literacy, project report for the Arts Council of England, London.

Featherstone, M. and Burrows, R. (1995) Cultures of technological embodiment: An Introduction, in Featherstone, M. (Ed.) *Cyberspace, Cyberbodies, Cyberpunk*, London: Sage.

Frith, S. (1986) Art versus technology: The strange case of popular music, *Media Culture and Society*, **8**, 263–79.

Goodwin, A. (1990) Sample and hold: pop music in the digital age of reproduction, in Frith, S. and Goodwin, A. (Eds) *On Record Rock Pop and the Written Word*, London: Routledge.

Goodwin, A. (1992a) Rationalisation and democratisation in the new technologies of popular music, in Lull, J. (Ed.) *Popular Music and Communication*, London: Sage.

Goodwin, A. (1992b) *Dancing in the Distraction Factory: Music Television and Popular Culture*, Minneapolis, MN: University of Minnesota Press.

Harley, R. (1993) Beat in the system, in Bennett, T. *et al* (Eds) *Rock and Popular Music*, London: Routledge.

Hayward, P. (1993) Situating cyberspace: The popularisation of virtual reality, in Hayward. P. and Wollen, T. (Eds) *Future Visions: New Technologies of the Screen*, London: British Film Institute.

Langois, T. (1992) Can you feel it? DJs and House Music culture in the UK, *Popular Music XI/2*.

Lovatt, A. and Purkis, J. (1996) Shouting in the street: Popular culture, values and the new ethnography, in O'Conner J. and Wynne, D. (Eds) *From the Margins to the Centre, Cultural Production and Consumption in the Post-Industrial City*, Aldershot: Arena.

McRobbie, A. (1994) *Postmodernism and Popular Culture*, London: Routledge.

Milestone, K. (1996) Regional variations: Northernness and new urban economies of hedonism, in O'Conner J. and Wynne, D. (Eds) *From the Margins to the Centre, Cultural Production and Consumption in the Post-Industrial City*, Aldershot: Arena.

Noys, B. (1995) Into the 'Jungle', *Popular Music 14/3*.

The Designers Republic (1996) *Blueprint*, March, 28–30.

Thornton, S. (1995) *Club Cultures: Music, Media and Subcultural Capital*, Cambridge: Polity Press.

Chapter 8

Hackers: Masters of Modernity and Modern Technology

Jörgen Nissen

Although many might think that the Internet, or virtual reality or indeed cyberspace are important, it is in fact only a select few who would seem to know what these terms actually mean – who truly understand their deepest significance. This kind of knowledge is restricted to a self electing elite – hackers – who as long ago as the late 50s have had the reputation as the 'masters of computer technology'.

However the term *hacker* frequently causes a number of problems as it has been used in many different ways. For example, nowadays the hacker epithet is associated both with illegal trespassing and with social recluses who sit in front of a computer screen rather than socializing with other people. In 1976, Joseph Weizenbaum described what he called 'compulsory programmers':

> Bright young men of dishevelled appearance, often with sunken glowing eyes, can be seen seated at computer consoles, their arms tensed and waiting to fire, their fingers already poised to strike at the buttons and keys . . . Their rumpled clothes, their unwashed and unshaven faces, and their uncombed hair all testify that they are oblivious to their bodies and to the world around them. They exist, at least when so engaged, only through and for computers (1976:116).

They have also been portrayed as young computer geniuses who, with their brilliance alone have penetrated all of the world's computer systems. However, these pictures are misleading in many ways. First, the hacker epithet was in fact created by the 'computer-interested' themselves and is, if anything, an honorary title bestowed upon a person who has done something admirable – for example, finding a good solution to a programming problem. Secondly, neither the idea of illegal actions nor the image of social recluses corresponds to the real activities or the personalities involved. Therefore throughout this chapter I will sometimes use the expression *computer captivated youth*, although the reader should bear in mind that these young people may regard themselves as *hackers* in all or several of its possible meanings.

The main purpose of this chapter is to understand the interest in computers which captivates these young men. My principal argument is that it is fruitful to view all the hours spent in front of the computer screen not only as a way of learning to grasp a modern, complex and currently much-hyped technology, but also as a question of handling modernity itself. It is a question of dealing with the modern in two ways: a modern technology *and* the process of modernity. This combination is not surprising as the development of new technology is itself a part of the process of modernity. Moreover, the new information and communication technology (ICT) is not just any new technology. It is *the* technology which, it is argued, will lead us into a new society: the information society. This is a revolution that has been compared with the transition from agricultural to industrial society.

In order to bring together an analysis of computer captivated youth with a discussion of the evolution of modernity, this chapter breaks down into four sections. First, a general account will be given of the concept of modernity and the specific theories about how the evolution of modernity affects youth. Secondly, I will discuss the culture of computer captivated youth.[1] Here, I will concentrate on the use of Bulletin Boards (BBS), i.e. computer based communication in special interest groups, 'cracking' and the connection of those activities to hacker history. Hacker culture and modernity are intricately connected and this will be made more explicit in a third section, which will begin to explain the culture of the computer captivated in the theoretical terms expounded in my first section. Thus far the analysis will suggest that, for the individual, a command of ICT means positive opportunities to process the social, cultural and psychological aspects of modernity. Fourth and finally, I will raise the issue of what significance their activity has at a societal level. In this case, the point of departure will be theories on sub- and counter-cultures. One conclusion is that the hacker culture has no significant influence on the relationship between 'system' and 'lifeworld', which are central concepts within theories of modernity.

Modernity and Youth

In everyday terms the notion of modern society is associated primarily with technological and industrial developments, capitalism, urbanization, secularization, rationalization and civilization. Here, however, we will concentrate on the social, cultural and psychological aspects of modernity. In all of these areas, modernization is, of course, *in progress*, although at varying speeds. Table 8.1 on page 153 summarizes the different levels of modernity and their relationship to the other areas of social and personal life.

The modern project can be described in various ways, and different authors have emphasized different dimensions. The following account is influenced mainly by Jürgen Habermas's (1984/87) manner of describing and understanding the process of modernity. His notion of 'the modern project' has come to summarize a development which entails (among other things), that the stable structures of previous traditional societies have dissolved and that traditions and religion no longer govern our existence. Mankind's condition is re-created, not only in respect to material conditions but also in terms of cultures, patterns of life and psychologies. Many argue that this process has its origins in the Enlightenment and has been ongoing for several hundred years.

Habermas (1984/87) introduced several different dimensions and scientific disciplines into his complex model of this process of modernization. The principal concepts are the *rationalization of the system*, and the *lifeworld*. The *lifeworld* is the person's everyday life; that is, where we have our social relationships and where we work, have families and friends. The system consists of both state authority and the anonymous and businesslike relationships in the economy.

To understand the relationship between the system and the lifeworld, which Habermas sees as more and more problematic, it is important to understand that the lifeworld formerly comprised a totality; the society and the individual were one and the same. *Rationalization* occurs when the system develops causing a disjuncture between function and consciousness. Both the system *and* the lifeworld have to work (rationalize) to re-integrate this ever expanding gap, as in contrast to the past, the world now almost consists of two parts. In the lifeworld, action is co-ordinated by what Habermas has called 'communicative rationality', an attempt to reach mutual understanding with the help of language. In the system, language is replaced by such forms as power, technology and money.

Subsequently, rationalization has continued both within the system and within the lifeworld. For example, different subsystems are developed in the system such as economics, politics and administration, and the lifeworld is divided into three different structural components – culture (consciousness), society (relationships) and personality (identity). Thus the world appears to the individual as if actually split into different parts, where each component is accompanied by various claims to validity. Every statement and action, for example, can be related to cognitive truth, normative justice or subjective honesty. On the one hand the system is governed by money, power, laws and ordinances, and a goal-oriented rationality develops here. In the lifeworld, on the other hand, the basis is communicative rationality. However, problems arise when instrumental reason, dominant in the system, grows too strong and to a degree forces its way into the lifeworld. Modernity is therefore characterized by the system *colonizing* the lifeworld from which it once originated.

It is important to observe that modernity is an ambivalent process and has both positive and negative aspects. This ambivalence is evident not least with respect to cultural, social and psychological *release* and *expropriation* (Ziehe, 1986a).[2] The first term is inspired by Marx's talk of how early capitalism released the proletariat both from feudal bonds *and* from their own means of production. An old system of oppression with a certain degree of security was dissolved and was replaced by another with both advantages and disadvantages. Cultural release refers to the ways in which previous traditions are changed or dissolved; they erode (Ziehe, 1986a). They do not necessarily disappear, however. What happens rather is that they lose their self-evident character and are open to questioning. Traditions can live on but they are exposed to testing by the individual. At the same time, cultural release puts pressure on the individual to make a number of choices. While the individual's own will, desires and dreams can acquire increased significance, the means of realizing them are still limited. Cultural release is counter-checked by a process of expropriation, which means that institutions and media fill the gap that remains after traditions have atrophied.[3]

Some theorists maintain that the process of modernity – although it is still ongoing – went through a major shift in the 1950s and that we are into a phase of late modernity.[4] Modernity now influences the whole world and touches almost all aspects of life. Global mobility, the broadcasting media, computerization, changed relationships between the sexes and classes, changed norms and conditions of youth are exemplary expressions of this process.

There are two factors that make contemporary youth more obviously affected by modernity than preceding generations. In the first place, there were more areas in the past where traditions and ancient patterns were still functional. Secondly, since the main modernizing shift occurred during the 50s the youth of today are the first to grow up under these circumstances. Their parents, on the other hand, had grown up in a situation where the traditions were still valid (Ziehe, 1986a).

The central implication of this approach for studies of young people is that it provides a model within which the protests, demands and social experiments of many youth cultures and movements can be interpreted as forms of reaction to colonization by the system. In general such cultural activity can be seen as 'efforts to create "free space" where the communicative aspects of the lifeworld may acquire greater vitality – not least for normative and expressive learning processes' (Bjurström and Fornäs, 1988:454).

From this perspective the 'modern condition' results in three tendencies that can be found among youth cultures; *reflexivity*, *makeability* and *individualization* (Ziehe, 1986b and 1989: see Table 8.1). *Reflexivity*, is 'a cultural way of mirroring (individual or collective, subjective, social or cultural) selves or identities through symbolic images in media, verbal language or face-to-face interaction' (Fornäs,1995:45). This socio-cultural reflexivity is not reducible either to intellectual or verbal self-reflection or even narcissism. At the same time as we are more capable of reflecting upon our own individuality, a distance is created within ourselves. Sexuality is an example where knowing seems to be greater than experience today. Young people already 'know' everything beforehand, so in this respect something might be lost. But above all, they can be anxious that they will not be able to live up to the course of events they 'know about' in advance.

Makeability is a demand and a capability to regard more and more things, such as personality and lifestyle, as being open to influence; these are areas where the individual has to make choices rather than simply be the passive result of natural developments or traditions Although this is liberating – it is no longer fate that decides what I am to be – the individual is confronted with the obligation to justify choices made. If the problem in a traditional society was that the individual 'wanted too much' (forbidden actions), now the problem is that he or she 'achieves too little'.

Individualization means that at the same time as the significance of social background decreases, the subjective importance of the inner world increases. Table 8.1 below summarizes what has been said above about the process of modernity.

Level	Objective (external)	Intersubjective (shared)		Subjective (internal)
Aspect of modernisation	Technological Economic Political	Social	Cultural	Psychological
Content	nature matter systems institutions	norms relationships	symbols language styles	identity needs ideals
Effects	technologization rationalization system growth	variety de-normalization	individualization reflexivity makeability	narcissism testing of identity
Tendencies	colonization	social, cultural and psychological release and expropriation		

Table 8.1. The different levels of modernization.[5]

All in all, the overall result of these three tendencies, reflexivity, makeability and individualization is that the *horizons of possibilities* available to the individual increases. Individuals are forced by this apparent expansion in the options available to them to make more choices. This in turn produces a number of different responses or ways of handling these increased horizons of possibilities (Ziehe, 1986b and 1989). Ziehe identifies three types of response, *subjectivizing*, *ontologizing* and *potentiating*. A *subjectivizing* tendency refers to a longing for closeness or physical intimacy in order to avoid being out in the cold. Authenticity and a striving for 'naturalness' are ideals in this case. Hope is directed towards the internal and can be exemplified in practices such as 'speaking out', or body-oriented workshops and dance courses. A current problem for this orientation, however, is that the aura of depth and unfathomability has been lost because of such phenomena as the hippie movement, 'expansion of awareness', group therapy and televised discussion groups. Indeed, Ziehe (1986b: 355) wonders whether the attraction of the internal has already disappeared and quotes a modern proverb: He is just finding himself – I hope he won't be disappointed![6]

Ontologizing (or objectivizing) entails endeavouring to find certainty, seeking a totality, authenticity and naturalness. Re-mystification in new religious groups, astrology and fundamentalism are examples of this. The intellect, rather than emotions, is central here; it is loss of meaning, not coldness, that is to be avoided. Perhaps this should be viewed as a reaction to the belief in constant progress and the over-confidence of others in rational actions. Ontologizing is, to a certain extent, a reinforcement of subjectivization; one is apparently striving toward a pre-modern state.

A *potentiating* tendency means that the individual seeks rather to exceed and radicalize subjectivization in an effort to obtain heightened intensity (to potentiate means to charge something artificially with significance). In this case it is emptiness, dreariness and boredom that are frightening. In this context *potentiation* is an aesthetic category; one can see young people, for example, who deliberately choose to portray reality as artificial. Instead of looking for what is natural, they choose to make it even more artificial:

> The more artificial I make the world and the more artificially I perceive it, the more it is a world created by me, and to that extent my world. The ugly, boring and brutal in this world shall increase aesthetically and skilfully in order to make it ecstatically or ironically accessible (Ziehe, 1989:159, my translation).

Youth cultures as new wave and punk belong here. In general, however, the tendencies to aestheticize are spreading. It is no longer just successful yuppies who are style conscious (evident in clothes, housing and utility goods); many teenagers attach great importance to their exterior. And of course, computer technology offers further means of making things artificial:

> To 'the world's artificiality' can be added the phenomenon of 'the world becoming more and more a question of semiotics'. This expression denotes the upgrading of the world of signs that can be found among wall painters, graffiti philosophers and even with 'computer freaks'. Even for them, their world becomes 'real' as they, in an ironic or naive sense, make themselves semiotic masters of a simulated reality (Ziehe, 1989:159, my translation).

On one level then, computer technology, and interest in it, is a modern phenomenon insofar as it is a new technology. However, we also need to ask what this interest entails for young people at a number of levels; not only are they the first generation to grow up in modernity, but they also devote themselves to a technology that is modern in many respects. To get some answers to these questions we will focus, in the next section, on some aspects of the hacker culture – or the microworld of computer captivated youth.

In Front of the Computer

Computer captivated youth use the computer for many different things but I will focus here upon on two examples, 'cracking' and the use of Bulletin Board Systems, so-called BBS – a kind of forerunner of the Internet[7] The examples are from a study of the Swedish youth hacker culture (Nissen, 1993). During the time of my study, the Internet was around but hardly in the same shape as today and not available to the young. However, as Chris Abbott also discusses in this volume, through private BBS, these young men managed to organize something similar to the Net.

I have already suggested that the common image of computer captivated boys is largely incorrect. In particular, the notion of isolated events taking place between an individual and a machine is fundamentally misplaced. The very fact that computer technology is used for communication is something that militates against social isolation. In order to underline further the many social dimensions of interest in computers I have chosen to describe that which they have in common as a *microworld*. By this, I refer to the computer captivated youths' communication channels, activities, arenas, networks, international background, etc. I choose to use the term, *World* both because it is a world in itself and because the computer-interested are a global phenomenon. The phenomenon exists throughout the world, and each single participant can reach an international arena. *Micro* refers primarily to the fact that the interest in computers is only a part of their life and existence.

Computer-based Communication

Computer technology in itself contains the seed of something completely new: a possibility of communicating through BBSs and large networks of computers (for example, the Internet). At the beginning of the 90s, Swedish BBSs targeted young people who had an existing interest in computers. This was probably a consequence of a lack of modems and because people without this special interest did not know about BBSs, let alone how to get in touch with one. This situation, where BBS is a medium mostly for people sharing an interest in computers, is now changing since modems are becoming cheaper and easier to use at the same time as the Internet has become so famous – even if it is not changing as rapidly as the hype surrounding it would have us believe.

Although the Internet first became well known in the 90s, the possibility of communicating through computers has been used for a long time, and not only by professionals and large organizations. Relatively simple computers can be used for communication with other computers through modems and telephone networks. Bill Landreth (1985) has described how he and some teenage friends spread right across the USA, devoted themselves in the beginning of the 80s to breaking into computers.[8] They were driven mostly by curiosity and by the *challenge* to outwit the security system. Landreth and other young hackers created a moral code whose main tenet was 'look but do not touch'. According to them it was legitimate to break into systems as long as nothing was destroyed. They also informed people responsible for computer security about their experiences in order to help increase the reliability of security systems.

It is these kinds of activities for which hackers are well known, but in reality most of their communication through computers is with each other, as I found out through an in-depth study of one BBS. This was set up by a 21-year-old man in 1988. My study was conducted in 1990 when his BBS had about 150 users (100 of whom were regular users). A BBS offers basically three different services. First, it offers a number of meetings or conferences. A participant makes a written contribution to a meeting, which can be compared with a written conversation with several participants, in which all can read each others' (and previously written) contributions. These meetings have to have a name, like 'Programming', 'Everyday chat', 'Comics' or 'Politics for juvenile delinquency'. Second, the user can send and receive private messages, often in so-called mailboxes. In larger systems this is called electronic mail. Third, the BBS can be used to give or receive computer programs and/or computer files.

Half of the content of these discussions (i.e. 50 per cent of the written texts and contributions) consisted of computer-related discussions; the other half dealt with subjects of varying character. There were discussions on everything from the latest movies to topical political issues. The BBSs, it would seem, serve partly as a forum for discussing computer-related questions, where help, for example with programming problems, can often be obtained from others, and partly as a forum for the discussion of many other topics. By means of these several functions, the BBSs help to keep together the microworld of computer captivated youth.

It should also be noted that the users tend to log on to the BBSs at roughly the times one might expect, and also, that the new communication technology leads to increased communication rather than replacing other forms of communication. The patterns of daily use indicate that BBSs are not some sort of weekend entertainment but that the users, probably just like other young people, have fun together at the weekend. The period 19.00–23.00 reveals the lowest log-in frequency during the nights between Friday and Saturday. Apart from during the night, the frequency is lowest from 19.00 on Fridays, rising subsequently to the highest values during Monday. From then on, the frequency declines steadily until Friday. Long log-ins usually occur during the daytime. Not surprisingly, the highest frequencies were to be found early in the morning, during the afternoons and late evenings or early nights. There is also more activity late at night at the weekends than during other days. A plausible interpretation of this is that on arriving home from a party, users ring up one or more BBSs before going to bed (at this time of the day, the telephone is hardly a suitable means of communication).

Further evidence of this 'normal' use comes from the BBS I studied in detail. There were about 40 different meeting or discussion groups and of the

100 or so regular correspondents 10 young men were easily recognized as heavy users. Together these 10 had written almost a third of the 16 000 available texts on the BBS. The discussions groups can be divided into five different subgroups: messages (to all users); meetings about computer problems; other task-oriented meetings; discussions and meetings with jokes and nonsense. Examples of computer related problems might range from how to solve problems with letters like å (aa) ä (ae) and ö (oe), to how to create a good sound on a certain kind of computer or other programming problem. There were also nine different categories of computer files, mostly filled by Public Domain/Shareware programs and text files.

Those 40 meetings were all open meetings, which means that every accepted user could join them. There were also two other kinds of meetings: closed and secret meetings. A closed meeting is a meeting announced on the list of meetings for the BBS but only open for limited groups. On this BBS there was only one meeting of this kind: the forum for the people who were in charge of this BBS – namely, the founder, and the system operator who in turn used three young men to help him manage the BBS as co-system operators. The existence of secret meetings is hidden from the ordinary user, which, of course, are only open to a select few. In this BBS there were only two meetings of this kind, and with rather few texts. For the record, those meetings did not contain so many secrets: one of them was a discussion meeting for members of a certain computer club, and the other was created 'by people who want to get rid of inexperienced users and to be on their own in that meeting'.

Here we can see that the technology actually results in increased communication rather than leading to fewer social contacts. It is used to discuss different things and exchange messages but also to get help with computer-related problems. This may also be interpreted as a need to communicate in a situation when the conditions of modernity entail that ontologically, one's existence appears less and less evident; and where decisions about one's own future increasingly appear as free choices. Via BBS like-minded individuals are given the opportunity to exchange experiences and thoughts about the future with each other in a way that would not have been possible without the computer. I would also suggest that the tendencies toward cultural, social and psychological release (see above) are met by increased communication, inasmuch we can see not only the erosion of traditional forms of communication but their replacements. This is also qualitatively different from conventional kinds of discussion in that communication takes place in a forum where one is (virtually) anonymous, where so far there are fewer constraints on what can and cannot be said, and where you can 'meet' a large group of people with whom you can share something important.

As has already been mentioned, computer-based communication can also be used to gain illegal access to other computer systems, although I did not find much evidence of this. (Of course, by definition such activity is always going to be difficult to find in the open.) Nevertheless, even though I was attempting to locate and describe the 'normal' state of affairs in this unusual microworld and did not set out especially to find illegal activities, I soon gained the impression that this was not a big issue or at least not an activity that took up much time. Interestingly enough, everybody with a modem had apparently tried some form of illegal entry a couple of times, but I only met two who had succeeded. However, their 'success' did not encourage them to continue. Yet all the young men I met were aware about the reputation of hackers in the mass media, and they were also well informed about groups in other countries who had been successful.

For example, they made jokes about the 'Terrorist handbook'. This is a text file known to be widely available on many BBSs, which contains descriptions of how to make real bombs. At some stage this text was publicized in the mass media and became the focus of a considerable amount of attention. It was posted on the BBS I studied but ironically it could not be downloaded and read since the file was in some way damaged. This was the case in many BBSs although if one tried many different BBSs sooner or later it would be possible to find a file that could be read. This file was described in newspapers as a security risk and raised the spectre of 'underground BBSs'. However, the text is not underground at all. Not only can it be found in open BBSs, the book itself can be borrowed from a public library. Nevertheless, I suspect having it 'visible' on a BBS bestows a 'radical' status on the BBSs' users.

The West German association, Chaos Computer Club, made a manifesto around this issue of proscribed texts, and formulated a coherent political programme in the middle of the 1980s. Viewing themselves as a kind of computer police with political as well as security ambitions, they aimed to point out the flaws in legislation and privacy safeguards in order to make people in general aware of the danger of a fully computerized society. They pointed out the risk of a gap developing between those who can afford to use computer systems and those who cannot (Ammann, 1989; Stoll, 1990; Wieckmann, 1988). One example of their activity consisted of members of the group transferring approximately $50,000 through a home banking system in order to prove the flaws of the system. The money was paid back in accordance with their moral code.

Activities such as these have conferred on computer captivated youth a reputation as skilful computer users – so skilful that they can outwit security systems. Without wishing to belittle the skills of those who are competent in this way, I maintain that this is more a matter of being familiar with the technology than of genius. It is comparable to the pay phone which is out of order and from which one can ring without having to pay. The person who happens to find such a pay phone may be tempted to make a few calls, but that does not make the person in question an expert on telephones. It is roughly the same way with much computer trespassing; seasoned users sometimes find faults or mistakes made by other people which make it easy for those with some experience of computers to gain illegal access to a computer system. In other words, the hacker epithet has to some degree mystified the skills of computer programming, magnifying the fears of the ordinary computer user and endowing these activities with unreasonable prowess.

Despite the degrees of difficulty involved in these kinds of activities, I believe that the desire not only to use computer technology but also to outwit it reflects, on a psychological level, a reaction to the apparent lack of direction in modern society. To the individual, modern society is in many ways difficult to comprehend and uncontrollable. But here is a technology, the most contemporary and salient technology, which has become symbolic, almost representative, of modern society. These youths show both themselves and others that it is possible to get the better of this technology, to overpower it, even if this happens with varying levels of success and with different degrees of difficulty. Of course, many youth cultures can be seen as free zones which are protected from the colonization effects of the system. They are sites which provide space for personal creativity and where the lifeworld's communicative claims to validity and reason can be reinforced. Many other youth cultures set up free zones outside, or parallel to, the system. For the hacker culture, this is achieved by establishing an electronic zone using computer technology as a tool. In it the young not only work with different ways of controlling the technology but also experiment with different values and attitudes towards it.

Cracking

Cracking is an activity which can place great demands on programming skills. It refers to breaking the copy protection of computer games and of other software. (The expression can also be used when someone succeeds in getting past the security designed to protect computer systems from illegal access). In this chapter, however, and often within the hacker culture, the term is used in relation to computer programmes.

In Sweden I found a number of *so-called* cracker groups – or, as we shall see, 'demo' groups. These are informal groups consisting of boys with a shared interest but often with a range of different specialist knowledge. One group, for example, may contain a person who is good at programming, one who is good at cracking, one who knows about sound and another who is responsible for graphics. The members often live in different cities and countries but are able to collaborate effectively with the help of computer-based communication and their own BBS. The use of the computer technology to set up their own strong networks, free zones, with their own moral rules and values is a further example of how they operate within the system.

In particular, contradictory attitudes towards intellectual copyright and piracy exemplify a hybrid morality. For example, according to one boy's view of cracking, it is acceptable to copy software but only within certain limits:

> It is simply incomprehensible, if you are going to . . . just take those programs which I really use, they would cost several tens of thousands

of crowns and to find those programs which I really . . . which I want, which I think are good ones I have to try many different programs and . . . with those it would be several hundreds of thousands of crowns. You just don't have that much money so you don't have much of a choice really . . . My attitude, which I think many . . . purely ethically it is a little bit more okay to make a pirate copy of a program if you use them, if you have them for private use, use them for pleasure so to speak. But if you use, or if you have a company and use the program professionally and make money on it, then you should buy it.

As computer games became more advanced, the practice of cracking developed and involved increasingly complex skills. There are several reasons for this: to be able to make one's own copy of a program (thus saving money); to be able to manipulate the game itself (for example, by getting past several levels through 'cheating' when they could not manage to do it in the game); or simply for gratification and to 'beat' the copy protection. Since it is something of a sport to outwit the copy protection, the *cracker* often wants to show off when he has succeeded. Thus he will leave his signature as a short program at the beginning of the games he has successfully *cracked*: 'This game was cracked by . . .' This type of activity is called creating an *intro*, which can include moving pictures and sounds, etc. However, when this activity is elaborated further, it turns into a form of art and takes on a different function. The products are then called *demos*. It appears that some groups of computer captivated youth got together primarily in order to work on demos as an art form – and to compete with other groups in making the best demos. These groups have in effect given up cracking completely and are gradually transformed into demo groups. In the distance (for both crackers and demo groups), there is the dream, more or less expressed and realistic, of becoming a professional games programmer. This dream is strongly fuelled by a number of computer magazines.

However, although cracking may be an end in itself, or is rationalized in terms of programming skills with vocational aims, the practice of demo making has turned into a culture in its own right. The demos that these groups make are frequently compared with the output of other groups and different international BBSs have made ranking lists on the best cracker/demo groups, much in the same way as rival DJ's 'compete' in clubs or on air. In the case of demo-culture there are also large international gatherings. In the middle of the 80s these events were called *copy-parties* and in Sweden they might involve between 50 or 60 young men getting together for a weekend. For example I followed and observed one group in the late 80s, even participating in their first copy-party 1987. This group – working with *Atari* machines – subsequently arranged their own copy-party in 1989.

Today, known as *conferences*, these parties have developed into big events with more than 1000 participants from several European countries. In Sweden, for example, there were to date, three or four cracker/demo groups all of which had existed for several years with good reputations on the international scene. They had all organized one or two conferences. One of them had three BBSs, one in Sweden, one in another country in Europe and one in USA. A second group I followed used *Commodore* computers. This group participated in their first copy-party in Sweden in 1985, but by the end of the 80s they had arranged two major conferences in Sweden, with up to a couple of hundred participants. They had also participated in a conference in Denmark in late 1988 which included participants from all over Europe. My impression here is that Denmark was one or two years ahead of Sweden concerning copy-parties and conferences. Further examples and information about cracking groups can now be found on homepages on the Web[9]. All of these are examples of how young people use computer technology to form strong social networks. For newcomers it is a challenge to compete with these well-established groups, as well as the opportunity to make a good reputation for oneself. Of course one way of making contact with other skilled people is to make a good demo, and thus gain entry to this level of computer culture.

Like hacking or BBS-ing the activity of cracking also turns out to be an effective free zone. It has evolved in such a way that it is no longer simply a question of outwitting established technological protection, thereby gaining the respect of others and an inner feeling of mastery. What began as breaking copy protection codes in order to make personal copies of computer games has subsequently developed into an art form of its own. What is more, this art form requires very special experience. Of course, this experience is exclusive and can only be gained by someone who has participated in the activity. In order to assess the programming skills required for a demo, you have to know when it was done. You have to know whether those solutions were available then or whether it was the first time someone had done something like this. Technically, for example, it could involve using a large number of colours in combination with a number of objects which move across the screen in a complicated pattern. Both of these effects require a large memory capacity. However, for the demo experts, the nature of the achievement in combining these can only be determined if, for example, you know how great the memory capacity was on the computer that was used when the demo was created in the first place. Thus, participation in free zones must be long-term, and a certain kind of knowledge is required. In addition, special trends in taste are developed within the free zone: it is not merely the technology which determines which music or which types of graphics are deemed to be the *correct* ones.

The technological competence resulting from cracker activity constitutes an important distinction between this youth culture and many others. Control of this technology provides more than an outlet for personal creativity (which is quite central) in the creation of demos. It also creates a reputation for the demo-maker which often goes beyond the free zone. It is not unusual that one can have the reputation of being 'good at computers' even outside the circle of the initiated. This leads to a very favourable situation for what Ziehe calls 'potentiation' (see above). To make a good demo it is necessary to give it a considerable amount of attention, which is almost always combined with long periods of intensive work. We see here how total absorption in something, potentiation, is probably further strengthened by the positive attention given to the results by one's surroundings, both with regard to the demo itself (intra-culturally) and the impression of being good at computers (by closely related adults, among others).

It is also important to understand that the networks of cracker groups within this free zone are often very strong and competent. A clear example of this is that the best groups at least sometimes succeed in developing *products* (demos) which can be measured by the standards of commercially produced computer games, in respect of graphics and programming requirements.

Mastery and Illegal Activities

For both cracking and breaking into computers, command of the technology is crucial. The following account of the history of hacker culture demonstrates that striving for mastery has always been central in this context. This also recurs in research in allied areas; and it leads towards an expanded definition of what hacking might mean.

In the history of hacking, three themes stand out: first, the development of an ethic; second, a tendency toward social and political alternativism; and finally, a trace of illegal activities. It is possible to distinguish three different generations of hackers (Levy, 1985). The first generation were students at MIT (Massachusetts Institute of Technology). In the late 1950s they began to take an interest in computer technology. They quickly established a new, irreverent relationship to it. Up to this point the use of computers was a very closed operation. The users did not have direct access to the machines but the operator was there as an interface. By combining their devotion to computer technology with irreverence, these students came to challenge the established tradition. They developed a completely different culture in which everybody was welcome and people were judged according to their accomplishment with the computer. This gave way to a new phase in the development of computer applications. The students improved techniques, created new operating systems, developed computer graphics, word processing, computer games and the time-sharing system. The activities of this generation, along with the invention of the personal computer (see below) demonstrates that hacker culture has not merely been a reaction to an existing technology but has also contributed to its development.

It was in this environment that the 'hacker ethic' was formed. The content of the ethic was, in short, that computers are fun, access to them should be free, everyone should have the right and the opportunity to use or develop computer technology and programs; skills, and not formal qualifications, were decisive for a person's position within hacker culture.[10]

In accordance with the hacker ethic, these students promulgated a belief in decentralization, as they mistrusted the authorities for trying to limit the use of computers. Indeed IBM, the company almost exclusively connected with computer technology at the time, was demonized as the hackers' principal opponent. Resistance was established against economic superiority in different forms, and the students argued for openness and decentralization. These inclinations against authority in different forms have survived, although with different opponents; they are still apparent in the carefree attitude to copying programs and breaking into computer systems.

The second generation of hackers, which emerged in the 1970s at Berkeley, is perhaps the one that has had the greatest significance for the development of the technology itself. This generation contributed to the development of the first micro-computers, i.e. what are often called home or personal computers. At this time the large computer companies estimated that there was no market for personal computers. Instead they focused on large mainframe computers and effectively left the hackers free to develop the micro-computer. During this period different groupings and meeting-places arose. The Homebrew Computer Club is one of the more famous. Its significance is proven by the fact that some 20 new companies can be traced back to the club. One of these companies is the well-known Apple (Levy, 1985). The company exemplifies a salient feature in hacker history: young virtuosos of computer technology with only a garage to work in, who created a product that would challenge the established computer industry, including IBM. However, Apple was not the only company developed in this milieu. An expansive and prosperous raft of businesses comprising many small companies came into existence in a short time. They were characterized by an easy-going attitude:

> The whole industry was like a club, the easy-going nature of which was visible in the images presented by these small companies: Loving Grace Cybernetics, Kentucky Fried Computers and Intergalactic Digital Research (before it became plain Digital Research). Their very names indicated the fun and humorous side of this community (Haddon, 1988:114).

The second generation further developed the hacker ethic. The distrust of a big brother mentality was explicitly connected with the radical political and cultural climate of the 1970s. This generation was also influenced by ideas about a post-industrial society and the awareness of the increasing importance of communication and information on an ideological level. This alternative view of society can be summarized under three headings: politics of information, convivial technology and the demystifying of the computer. Technical *experiments*, often described as political actions, were carried out, such as placing terminals in public environments to give ordinary people access to computer technology (Athanasiou, 1985; Nelson, 1987). Leslie Haddon concludes:

> In place of this system, these counterculture critics wanted both to gain access to the existing information which was held on computers and to establish an arrangement for creating and distributing new types of information which would be of use to the people. To achieve this, the counterculture critics wanted a decentralised, non-bureaucratic form of computing (1988:108).

It should be noted that these political ambitions were definitely a result of the hackers' own interests and their own positive experiences with computer technology which they wanted to supply to others. This is a very clear example of how those within the hacker culture work with different forms to counteract the system's colonization of the lifeworld. Computer technology is identified as a tool in the hands of the societal apparatus (the system). Having been attracted by the technology, hackers try to turn it into a tool for other purposes.

The third generation of hackers emerged during the early 1980s and is still of vital importance. Levy (1985) describes the emerging computer games companies as the key environment for this third generation. However, this generation of hackers is above all made up of those owning a PC. As the personal computer spread to many homes and individuals, computer games turned into a large commercial business. Today most young people first meet a computer through games. Some of them, however, will do more than play games and some of them appear to grow into hackers.

Even if the third generation is primarily associated with illegal activities, this third tendency in hacker history goes back a long way. The illegal activities go hand in hand with both the hacker ethic (the argument that those who are skilful should also have access to computer technology) and the political alternativism (the idea that information should be freely available, interpreted by some to mean that all programs should be free).

A recurring feature, both in studies of computer captivated people and in their own accounts, is a desire and an endeavour to control and outwit the technology. 'Mastery is of the essence everywhere within hacker culture' writes Sherry Turkle (1984:234, see also Shotton, 1989). As a Swedish boy says: 'It is a sort of technical problem, and then you don't see anything around you. This problem is all that exists; it's an enormous challenge to solve this and it's a great kick to succeed, an ego-trip.'

Thus, an ambition to master computer technology permeates hacker culture – but as this is one of modern society's most charged symbols, it is, on another level, I suggest, an attempt to master modernity.

Mastering Modernity

It has previously been argued that many youth cultures can be explained as zones which are free from the system's colonization of the lifeworld; zones where space is given to other values than the goal-rationality of the system. In this respect, the computer captivated youth have chosen another route. Instead of creating free zones *outside* the system, they have chosen to devote themselves to one of the most important aspects *of* the system; the technology. At a time when the development of society seems to be going faster and faster, when we have entered into a late modern phase and technology appears more and more problematic, they endeavour to master a technology that has been presented as being of major importance for the future.

Essentially I am suggesting that instead of merely establishing free zones, computer captivated youth come to grips with the problems entailed in the colonization of the lifeworld in a radically different manner. Instead of strengthening the lifeworld's own conditions through isolation, they try to master colonization by breaking into and vanquishing one of the most important components of the system, that is technology. It is not difficult to visualize this as an individual response to the process of modernity. In many ways, this would appear to be an effective strategy, at least for the individual. However, for society something different may be at stake and I shall return to this perspective below.

Entirely independent of whether individual mastery of ICT is a good way of responding to the colonization of the lifeworld by the system, the effects are often very positive for the individual in question. The feeling of mastering this new, complex information and communication technology can be set against a common tendency in the past decade to describe the world as chaotic and unwieldy as a result, among other things, of the dissolution of traditions and the increased *horizons of possibilities*. A young man's feelings of insecurity and powerlessness can be compensated by a feeling of control over something – in this case a specific technology. Moreover, this compensation is reinforced by the great symbolic value of the computer. The very fact that the adult world describes this tool as important while at the same time many adults themselves do not control it, presumably strengthens the satisfaction of mastering the technology. Computer technology can hereby be described as a tool for young boys to cultivate and master their existence and, at least symbolically, the pressures of modernity.

It is not only a question of symbolic mastery. The labour market of today is a clear example of how youth are exposed both to *inclusion* and *exclusion* (Ziehe, 1989). Inclusion (which means that the dividing line between the generations is vanishing) can be illustrated by the young hackers who are often more skilled than many people in the older generation. However, the broader pattern is for exclusion (sustaining the dividing line between the generations), and this is maintained since today it is almost normal for young people to have difficulties in gaining access to the labour market. Young people with knowledge of computer technology differ in this respect from many of their peers, because at least for some of them, there is a demand in the labour market.

Thus, no matter whether individual mastery of computer technology *per se* is an impossible means of responding to colonization of the lifeworld, it still gives computer captivated youth greater opportunities to take advantage of the growing *horizons of possibilities*. It is also clear that this interest falls within the bounds of the potentiating and ontologizing responses to this increased horizons of possibilities. The high valuation of computer technology in society leads, for example, to the fact that computer interest stands out as a perfect activity for *potentiating*. Not only do the boys experience strong intensity (for example, during the very long programming stints at the computer), but they also learn something in an area where knowledge is coveted. It is a form of double sanction!

Here we should also consider what Ziehe calls the new conservative counter-offer against culturally oriented efforts. He argues that more dynamic life planning works to contradict intensification. Emptiness, avoided by intensification, is fulfilled instead by competition, the desire to perform and the joy of innovation (Ziehe, 1986b). That which begins with intense emotional experiences can later be replaced in this way, not least when the interest is transferred to a profession.

There is also a flavour of *ontologizing*. The wisdom that can be found in controlling computer technology can also be seen as a form of search for completeness. It does not contain 'complete answers', as a doctrine of faith can do, but it contains a confidence in *one* method to find solutions to 'all' problems. In many of the discussions about different subjects in BBSs, it is evident that many participants think in terms of finding the optimal solution.

Handling computer technology (or ICT) appears to be the perfect tool for mastering modernity. What starts as an attempt to master (alone or along with others) a technology – that is, something that exists within the system – results in appropriate and liberating reactions on other levels. On the surface, hacking looks like an attack on one of the most important aspects of the system (by illegally spreading programs and illegal access to computers), but simultaneously, an important way of processing modernity is taking place on social, cultural and psychological levels.

The fact that endeavouring to master the computer also works as a successful tool for mastering modernity evokes the question of what influence the existence of hackers, or computer captivated youth, have upon society itself. In order to get close to an answer I will conclude by referring to theories about sub- and counter-cultures.

Changing the System from Within

The theories of countercultures developed by the Centre for Contemporary Cultural Studies (CCCS) can be used as an model to analyze the effects of the computer captivated youth on the system. In particular I want to question whether their microworld can be described as a counter-culture. In their studies of youth, Hall and Jefferson (1976) developed a subculture perspective. Researchers in this area have mostly been interested in youth cultures resisting the dominant culture, but they have also developed theories about the ways in which the culture of middle-class young people has dissented from the parent culture. They have called the latter 'countercultures'. A subculture, according to them, is part of a larger culture, but it is also a subordinate, and often suppressed, culture. Subcultures are characterized by deviation from dominant norms. In this perspective the theory of subculture is a theory about suppressed groups in society, for example, youth, their strategies for 'solving' their societal vulnerability and their protests against it by means of clearly outspoken deviance.

Countercultures, on the other hand, primarily mark a break within the dominant culture. Since a counterculture can only develop *in opposition to* the dominant culture, it represents an 'internal opposition in the whole society', and therefore a 'crisis in the dominating class itself' (Fornäs, Lindberg and Sernhede, 1989:40). In subsequent discussion countercultures have been given a double function: partly to contribute to the *adjustment* of the dominant culture to new circumstances, and/or partly to unmask this culture and *develop new alternatives* (Fornäs *et al.*, 1989). It is argued that subcultures are leisure cultures, while countercultures are more likely to be found in central institutions in society. From this perspective the hacker culture must be seen as a counterculture.

The first two generations of hackers contributed, as we have seen, to the development of computer technology (for example, computer games and the PC). They also helped bring about a changed attitude toward computers in general. All this was accompanied by political and ideological expressions in an accepted counter-cultural manner. As I have suggested above, the making of the PC as a tool to counteract the colonization of the lifeworld can be interpreted in terms of the dominant culture treating the problems that computerization has caused; and this was the contribution of the second generation of hackers. But is this a process of adjustment or the development of new alternatives? It is obvious that the second generation endeavoured to find new alternatives. In reality, however, there was a halt at adjustment. Bryan Pfaffenberger's (1988) view is clear from the title of his article: 'The social meaning of the personal computer: or, why the personal computer revolution was no revolution'. He claims that the second generation of hackers did not reach their alternative goals. He mentions decentralization as an example: microcomputers indeed spread to many homes but they were mostly used for pleasure. At places of work, the PC originally replaced terminals connected to central computers. Today the computer industry attaches great importance to internal networks, which again open the way for a centrally regulated use of computers. The counter-cultural feature of the second hacker generation seems above all to yield adjustment and not renewal.

Can the activities of the third generation of hackers be regarded in a similar way? The question can be directed toward their illegal misuse of computer information and copying and spreading of software. Do they bring about important changes in society, or do they mainly articulate a rhetoric to defend illegal actions of their own? From a theoretical perspective, it need not matter whether separate individuals really adopt a code of morals or only hide behind it; the important thing is the effects of their actions at a cultural level. The mere existence of hackers, for instance, makes the holder of a computer file aware of the knowledge that the files are accessible. The existence of illegal misuse of computer information in itself, committed out of curiosity or for idealistic reasons, contributes to the fact that large computer systems cannot be built secretly. In this way the hackers have contributed to the dominating culture by moderating the tension between the need for co-ordination through central organs and freedom from strong central control. The real effects can, however, be questioned. The computer virus affecting about 6,000 computers in the USA in 1988, which was attributed to the efforts of hackers, did not involve damage or costs of any great size. On the contrary, it meant an advance for companies in the business of computer security, as well as demands for more severe legislation against the illegal misuse of computer information and police interventions against computer captivated youth (Ross, 1991).

The hackers have actively acknowledged technical developments and at the same time formed a counterculture. Furthermore, they have contributed to the public upgrading of the significance of computer technology and to a confidence in technological solutions, according to the formula: technology *per se* is never to blame, only the use and the users. They have contributed to the development of problems they said they were combating. This apparent contradiction is probably not unique to hackers. In fact, similar discrepancies are also unravelled in writings on countercultures.

As I have already suggested, counterculture is said to have a double function. The function of unmasking the dominating culture and developing alternatives is difficult to achieve and because of that the counterculture acquires an affirmative character. To a great extent, this situation arises because countercultures exist within the dominating culture. But the problem probably becomes clearer when the basis of the culture in question is a modern and generic technology and not a social institution. It is chiefly countercultures of the latter type which have been made the subject of research. In a modern society, technology – not least the new information – and communication technology tend to be arranged in a systemic manner. It is very difficult to bring about changes that challenge the conditions formed by the system itself. Therefore, it is not surprising that computer captivated youth, or hackers, who have an affirmative attitude to the computer technology, will contribute to the survival both of the computer technology as a large technological system and of the societal system for which this technology is a means to an ongoing process of rationalization.

Notes

I would like to thank Mauiice Devenny for help with the translation of this chapter and Julian Sefton-Green for comments that helped me improve my arguments.

1 I am using empirical data from the late 1980s and early 1990s, which focuses on computer captivated youth in Sweden. The main data of the study is provided by a series of observations and interviews. Twenty young men, between the ages of 15 and 20, were interviewed several times. These interviews were conducted as unstructured but focused conversations. Initially, as expected, there were difficulties in getting in touch with the field. The entrance found was a computer club which had several minicomputers in its possession. For a short period I participated in the activities of the club. All the interviews were made with boys or young men. This is not surprising since hacking is known to attract mostly males. My awareness of differences between the sexes was high throughout the project, but although I made some efforts to find female hackers, I was not successful. The only girls I encountered took part in activities of some BBSs. However, the numbers were small. Examples from Swedish youngsters emanate from Nissen (1993).

2 A principal theme in Ziehe's previous works was that just as we can see social and cultural changes in association with the growth of modern society, changes have also occurred on the mental level. This is most evident in the theories of a 'new type of socialization'. The concept was the subject of much discussion after the publication of Ziehe's doctoral dissertation in 1975. The new type of socialization refers to increased narcissistic tendencies, which others have also mentioned, for example, by psychoanalysts such as Kohut (1971), and Lasch (1979) among others. Keniston's (1960) 'alienated youths' is one of several examples of similar models. Ziehe's interest later shifted from mental/subjective to cultural dimensions. In his later works, he takes his point of departure from Habermas's theories on modernity.

3 Ziehe, (1986a, p.30, *et passim*) Ziehe often emphasizes the ambivalent character of the concepts, but where expropriation is concerned, he tends to stress its locking function. However, as Fornäs (1995:44) points out, expropriation also contains positive traits, 'opening communicative means for formerly tabooed or non-communicable experience'.

4 The concept of *late* modernity was launched by Fornäs (1995) but is in line with Habermas and Ziehe, for example.

5 The figure is one of many different ways of dividing up modernity in its constituent parts. This figure is a combination of two figures in Fornäs (1990) which in turn are inspired by models in Habermas (1984/87). I have chosen to use Fornäs' models as they include a further development of Habermas's work, which, on the intersubjective level, does not distinguish between the social and cultural aspects. Habermas connects different societal institutions to the different levels: objective – science, social – law, subjective – art. As Fornäs (1990), states, however, art is very intersubjective, thus he proposes instead: objective – science, social – law, cultural – art, and subjective – intimate sphere/psychology.

6 Ziehe, 1986b:355.

7 *CBBS* (Computerised Bulletin Board System) would be a more correct term but BBS is the one normally used).

8 Landreth wrote his book after he had been arrested by the FBI, prosecuted and sentenced.

9 See for example http://www.df.lth.se/~triad/triad/. Further Web based information about hacking/crackers may be found at: http://www.flashback.se/hack/.
10 Strictly speaking this is not really an ethic, but rather a moral code.

References

Ammann, T. (1989) *Hacker für Moskau* Hamburg: Rowohlt Verlag GmbH.

Athanasiou, T. (1985) High-tech alternativism: The case of the community memory project, Radical Science Collective (Eds) *Making Waves: The Politics of Communication*, London: Free Association Books.

Bjurström, U. and Fornäs, J. (1988) Ungdomskultur i Sverige, in Himmelstrand, U. and Svensson, G (red.) *Sverige – Vardag och Struktur*, Stockholm: Norstedt.

Fornäs, J., Lindberg, U. and Sernhede, O. (1989) (Eds) *Ungdomskulturer: Identitet och Motstånd*, Stockholm: Symposion.

Fornäs, J. (1990) Senmoderna tider, in Fornäs, J. and Boethius, U. *Ungdom och Kulturell Modernisering*, Stockholm: Symposion.

Fornäs, J. (1995) *Cultural Theory and Late Modernity*, London: Sage.

Habermas, J. (1984) *The Theory of Communicative Action, Vol. 1 Reason and the Rationalisation*, Cambridge: Polity Press.

Habermas, J. (1987) *The Theory of Communicative Action, Vol. 2 Lifeworld and System*, Cambridge: Polity Press.

Haddon, L.(1988) 'The roots and early history of the British home computer market: origins of the masculine micro' unpublished PhD dissertation, London: University of London.

Hall, S. and Jefferson, T. (1976) (Eds) *Resistance through Rituals*, London: Hutchinson.

Keniston, K. (1960) *The Uncommitted: Alienated Youth in American Society*, New York: Harcourt, Brace & World.

Kohut, H. (1971) *The Analysis of the Self: A Systematic Approach to the Psychoanalytic Treatment of Narcissistic Personality Disorders*, New York: International Universities.

Landreth, B. (1985) *Out of the Inner Circle*, Bellevue, WA: Microsoft.

Lasch, C. (1979) *The Culture of Narcissism: American Life in an Age of Diminishing Expectations*, New York: Warner.

Levy, S. (1985) *Hackers: The Heroes of the Computer Revolution*, New York: Dell.

Nelson, T. (1987) *Computer Lib: 'You Can and Must Understand Computers NOW'*, Washington, DC: Tempus Books.

Nissen, J. (1993) *Pojkarna vid datorn: Unga entusiaster i datateknikens värld*, Linköping Studies in Arts and Science No 89, Stockholm/Stehag: Symposion Graduale.

Pfaffenberger, B. (1988) The social meaning of the personal computer: or, why the personal computer revolution was no revolution, *Anthropological Quarterly* **61**(1), 39–47.

Ross, A. (1991) Hacking away at the counterculture in technoculture, in Penley, C. and Ross, A. (Eds) *Technoculture*, Minneapolis, MN: University of Minnesota Press.

Shotton, M. (1989) *Computer Addiction: A Study of Computer Dependency*, London: Taylor & Francis.

Stoll, C. (1990) *The Cuckoo's Egg: Tracking a Spy through a Maze of Computer Espionage*, London: Bodley Head.

Turkle, S. (1984) *The Second Self: Computers and the Human Spirit*, London: Granada.

Weizenbaum, J. (1976) *Computer Power and Human Reason: from Judgement to Calculations*, San Francisco, CA: W. H. Freeman.

Wieckmann, J. (1988) (Ed.) *Das Chaos Computer Buch: Hacking made in Germany*, Hamburg: Rowohlt GmbH.

Ziehe, T. (1986a) *Ny Ungdom*: Om Ovanliga Läroprocesser (Plädoyer für ungewöhnliches Lernen, Ziehe & Stubenrauch. H, Reinbek: Rowolht) Stockholm: Norstedts.

Ziehe, T. (1986b) Inför avmystifieringen av världen: ungdom och kulturell modernisering in Löfgren, M. and Molander, A. (Eds) *Postmoderna Tider?*, Stockholm: Norstedts.

Ziehe, T. (1989) *Kulturanalyser*, Stockholm: Symposion.

Notes on Contributors

Chris Abbott is a Visiting Research Fellow at the School of Education, King's College, London. He teaches on the PGCE and Masters courses at King's and specializes in the area of IT and literacy. He was previously Director of the Inner London Educational Computing Centre. He has written widely on aspects of information technology for the Times Educational Supplement and other publications.

David Buckingham is a Reader in education at the Institute of Education, University of London, UK. He has directed several major research studies of media education and children's relationship with the media. His extensive publications include the edited collections *Watching Media Learning* (Falmer Press, 1990) and *In front of the Children* (British Film Institute 1995). He is also the author of *Children Talking Television* (Falmer Press, 1993), and *Moving Images* (Manchester University Press, 1996).

Helen Cunningham is a Lecturer in media and cultural studies at Middlesex University, UK, where she specializes in teaching about youth culture, media audiences and new media technologies. She contributed to *In Front of the Children* (British Film Institute, 1995).

Jörgen Nissen PhD, is an Assistant Professor in technology and social change, Linköping University, Sweden. His unpublished Swedish doctoral thesis (1993) was titled 'The boys at the computer'. Previously he has worked on several evaluations of computer use in schools and is now involved in the research programme 'Man, information technology, society' (the MITS-group).

Helen Nixon is a Senior Lecturer in the School of Communication and Information Studies at the University of South Australia. She has worked as a teacher of secondary school English, a tertiary English lecturer and a teacher educator. Her current research interests are media constructions of literacy education, including computer literacy, and discourses about young people and the new technologies in contemporary media cultures.

Julian Sefton-Green is Lecturer in media education at the Central School of Speech and Drama, London. He is a course leader on initial and continuing teacher education degrees and teaches cultural studies, arts education and media production at undergraduate and postgraduate level. He has co-directed research into young people's creative use of new technologies in the home and written widely on aspects of media education. He is co-author with

David Buckingham of *Cultural Studies goes to School* (Taylor & Francis, 1994) and *Making Media* (English and Media Centre, 1995).

Joseph Tobin is a Professor in the Department of Teacher Education and Curriculum Studies at the University of Hawaii, where he works in a field-based teacher preparation program and teaches classes in multicultural education and qualitative research methods. He has a written several papers and books on Japanese culture, society, and education including *Preschool in Three Cultures: Japan, China, and the United States* (Yale University Press, 1989) and *Remade in Japan: Consumer Tastes and Everyday Life in a Changing Society* (Yale University Press, 1993).

Karen Orr Vered is a PhD candidate in critical studies, University of Southern California, School of Cinema-Television. She also holds an MA in cultural anthropology with an emphasis in visual anthropology from Temple University (1991). She is also an educational specialist for multimedia software at University of Southern California's Annenberg Centre for Communication.

Index